ONE LITTLE SPARROW

Life's a test, do your best.

Judith A. Wallis

ONE LITTLE SPARROW
First published 2018

Copyright © Judith A. Wallis 2018

All rights reserved. Without limiting rights under copyright reserved above, no part of this publication may be reproduced, stored in or introduced into a database and retrieval system or transmitted in any form or any means (electronic, mechanical, photocopying, recording or otherwise) without the prior written permission of the author.

ISBN: 978-0-6482828-8-4

Published with the assistance of: *www.loveofbooks.com.au*

To my dear family

*You will recognise yourselves I'm sure.
This story has been written around remembered events in my
life — a life in which some of you shared. Times, places and the
sequence of events have been altered and embellished to create
a fictional story based on real events.*

One

All I have to do is cross the room. A trio of crones in black hats glower over their teacups as ignoring censorious stares I weave my way between sombrely dressed relatives. Fingers touch mine. My cousin David offers empathy until his sister hisses in his ear and he, like a dog brought to heel, withdraws his hand. I send him a grateful glance, slip into the hallway and close the door behind me. There I remove my stilettos and tread barefoot up the passage to my mother's bedroom.

Late afternoon light filters in through rain splattered glass. So little has changed in this room I feel my absence might be numbered in minutes rather than years. Only the large wire-wove bed my parents shared is missing, replaced by a single ensemble. I open a dresser drawer and the well-remembered fragrance scents the air. Mother's reading glasses and coin purse lie alongside an organza bag filled with lavender from her garden. Quickly, as though fearful of being caught, I search through the miscellany of scarves, gloves and handkerchiefs, bypassing pretty pieces of inexpensive jewellery, a box of loose face-powder and her lipsticks. Deep in the drawer's recess, tucked beneath a cake of scented soap, I find the photograph and withdrawing it from its hiding place I again study the face of the unknown man.

As a child I pestered my mother forever asking, "Who is this man? Is it Dad when he was young?" Always she evaded my questions and taking the photograph replaced it out of sight at the back of the drawer, deepening the mystery and heightening my curiosity. Now the identity of my mystery man seems destined to remain an enigma. Unless . . . surely there must be someone who knows his name?

Mother's burial service — held only three hours ago and attended by friends and relatives who gathered graveside beneath a canopy of black umbrellas—is strangely distant. Yet the night I fled this house and its matriarch ruler remains clear in my mind. By running away I became an outcast; an audacious and unworthy daughter. For years I have borne the disapproving looks and held a civil tongue. Today I am seen as the wayward daughter who has returned to attend her mother's funeral wearing a cherry red coat and no hat! I want to stand on a chair and shout in retaliation: *Don't you understand? Not everyone has more than one coat and as I attend neither church nor racecourse, I've no need of a hat.*

Doug's face appears at the door. "So this is where you're hiding. Are you okay?" he asks. At twenty-four and soon to marry Celia, my kid brother is no longer a kid. The four year age gap between us, at first nothing at all, became an abyss in our juvenile years. Were we now bridging that divide? I hoped so, for I have always loved my red-headed freckle-faced brother.

"Everyone's gone. Mrs. Stuart has stayed to help Aunt Libby with the dishes. You remember Lily Stuart from across the road? She hasn't changed a bit; big as ever." Doug yawns and as he stretches his arms above his head, I realize how tall he has grown. "I'm about to drive Celia and her parents out to the farm. Do you want to come? We'll be back by seven."

"No thanks, Doug. I'll stay here and put a meal together if you like."

His long handsome face splits in a well-remembered grin. "That'd be great. It's good to have you back, Ana. He pats my knees with brotherly affection then pushes up from the bed, his lanky frame unfolding like a road map until his hair catches in the beaded fringe of the rosy-pink lampshade above. He ducks, aims a finger-gun and through gritted teeth warns, "Your days are numbered, Pinkie."

"Doug, we're leaving," Aunt Libby calls.

"I'd better go. There's clean linen in the cupboard. Choose any bed. Sleep here if you like. Bye, Sis. See you soon."

Doug seems the same as always, relaxed and humorous. I pluck at the quilt. Does he see me as the playmate and confidant of our younger years or as the selfish sister who fled without warning leaving a thirteen year old boy to care for a widowed mother? Ten years ago, no one could have guessed how ill she would become.

Moments later I hear the murmur of farewells. Footsteps clatter down the steps to the street. Alone in the quiet house I ease back onto the pillows. Outside the rain has slowed to a musical pitter-pat. A sliver of sun creeps in borrows colour from the rose-pink curtains and spreads it over the adjacent wall. Dust particles dance on slender beams of gold, the suffused light creating an ephemeral capsule in which I rest, lulled and near to sleep.

Day drifts into dusk and as the air chills I hear from the darkness sounds I once knew by heart, the slow creak of contracting roof and walls. The house, so familiar and sheltering by day, has become the playground of phantoms that skitter and slide in the shadows. These forgotten images eddy about the bed. They remind me of past actions and goad me to regret. Among them is the ghost of my mother. She points an accusing finger. 'Ungrateful child, feel unloved do you? Unloved. Unwanted.' The jeering words reverberate in my head. Desperate to shut them out, I clasp my hands over my ears.

"Ana. What is it? Are you having a bad dream?" Doug's tall frame looms in the light that streams from the passageway.

"Yes. Sorry, I must have fallen asleep. I haven't prepared dinner."

"Don't worry. Celia came back with me. She's cooking us a meal. Come and join us when you're ready."

Cold water drips from my face as I lean toward the bathroom mirror and search my eyes for clues. *Who are you? What is your role now you are no longer a daughter?* My mother thought the word daughter synonymous with dutiful, while I foolishly assumed mother meant magnanimous. We each failed the expectation of the other. My mirror image morphs and I am nine years old, reliving the day Doug and I rushed laughing and jostling into the kitchen. Hot and thirsty after running races with friends on the street we came indoors for a drink but before the tap could be turned, our mother called. We stood before her; the harsh prickly surface of the coir mat scratching our bare feet as eager to be off, back outdoors to play, we twisted about waiting for her to speak.

Her shoulders straight, her hands folded beneath her apron, she looked down at us. "I have to tell you," she began, her voice devoid of emotion. "Your father is ill. You may not have him for very long."

Shock snatched my breath away. Fear churned in my stomach and tears coursed my cheeks. I wanted her to say something, anything that would give hope to an inconceivable future. I stepped forward, my arms open ready to share a comforting hug. But Mum's hands remained beneath her apron. In a silence as big as the sky, she turned her back. Then taking a wooden spoon, she returned to stirring the jam cooking on the stove. The pain of her rejection struck like a knife to the heart.

I pulled Doug's arm and turned him toward the door. Thirst forgotten we returned to the street.

"Hurry up, we're waiting for you," our friends called.

"It's okay to go." I told Doug as hunched against the gate post, I pressed my forehead to my knees.

With a rueful smile and a shrug of my shoulders I push melancholy aside and hurry to join Doug and his fiancée. The kitchen is warm with domestic bliss. Doug, his long legs stretched beneath the table, is reading the local newspaper as Celia, a frilly half-apron tied about her slim waist and huge oven mitts on her hands, lifts a delicious smelling casserole from the oven. A pot bubbles merrily on the stovetop. The Beach Boys croon from the radio.

"Ana, come and sit down." Doug folds the paper then leaning over, gives Celia a caress as she places the steaming dish on the table. I sit with my back to the wall watching as Celia moves between the stove and table with bowls of green vegetables and baby carrots. Seated beside Doug, she says grace, quietly offering thanks for the food and for the support of family and friends in a time of sorrow.

"Great food, love. You're my best girl ever, the one that can cook." Doug's grin is appreciative and Celia's response quick.

"The best, but certainly not the first!" she quips. "Did you know, Ana, your brother enjoyed his reputation as a Casanova?"

Doug's freckled face is turning pink and delighted to see he still blushes I give myself a little hug. Years ago I would have teased him without mercy, pointing out his fairness which is unique in our dark haired family. Father used to ruffle Doug's ginger mop and declared him a foundling, left on the doorstep by pixies.

His eyes on his plate, Doug thumps the bottom of the sauce bottle. "I saw you talking to Ray this morning," he says changing the subject. "It's funny having a brother I don't know. Fifteen years is a big age gap."

True, I thought. Our dad's two older children, Ray and Fran, left home when Doug was a year old. We seldom saw them after that. In my early years my half-sister Fran and I shared a room. She looked out for me. Bathed my scraped knees and taught me words to the songs on the wireless.

My half-brother Ray was different; a teaser and always in trouble. This morning, before leaving for the funeral service, I had joined him on the back porch. Unwilling at first to face me, he turned aside, his cigarette diminishing an inch with each drawback. We had both neglected our mother and returning home after so long away was no doubt as hard for him as it was for me. Had we been able to converse, our guilt might have been eased. Still, he'd given me a half smile when I laid my hand on his arm as we parted.

"Ray told me he worked at a service station. Some little place up north. He seemed in a hurry to get back," I say, hoping Doug has more information about our older brother.

"His step daughter is expecting a baby any day."

"Step daughter?" I echo.

"Ray remarried, to a fiery lady who keeps him in line, by all accounts."

We know Ray has led a hapless life and not wishing to talk about my own recent unhappiness, I shy away from this area of conversation. As I search for a neutral topic, Celia, unable to open a bottle of preserved peaches, asks Doug for help. With a show of strength Doug assists, proclaiming he is as strong as an ox and has never had a day's illness in his life.

"Not true. What about the night you almost died?" I say wondering if he remembers.

"Please, tell me more." Celia looks to me, her eyes wide.

"His nibs here," I begin, "was confined to bed with a fever and mother sat on his bed reading Peter Pan to us. The part about the crocodile coming tick-tick-tick for Captain Hook, when all of a sudden she cried out and dropping the book, gathered Doug into her arms. His head fell back and his limbs were all floppy. He looked like my Raggedy-Ann—and he had no eyes, they had gone white.

"Terrified, I ran down the dark passage shouting for Dad. He came at once, gave mother a comforting hug and lifting me up, piggy-backed me across the road to the Stuarts' house. There weren't many phones in our street and Stuart's was the nearest. When Dad returned home, I was left with Mrs Stuart.

"We were still at war," I continue. "Blackout paper covered the windows and no lights shone. In the sitting room, Mrs Stuart cuddled me on her knee. A fire crackled in the grate. Fascinated by the oddly shaped shadows flickering over the walls I was almost asleep when a white horse reared up from within the flames. I pulled back in fright. Sparks exploded into the room and in the scramble to toss the burning embers back into the fire before the carpet burned, the horse vanished. No one else saw the horse and by the time the commotion settled and Mrs Stuart lifted me back onto her lap, I felt better, as if a crisis had passed.

"And it had. For when I returned home next morning, Doug was sitting up like Jacky amongst the pillows with mother beside him, spoon feeding him like a baby—" I pull back as Doug grabs a cushion and threatens to biff me.

"I'm glad you survived." Celia murmurs, whipping away the cushion and dropping a kiss on the top of Doug's head.

"I told you my sister was a weird kid. White horses indeed!"

Our help with the dishes declined, Doug and I move to the living room to await coffee. While he drops into what is obviously his favourite armchair, I wiggled about on the hard couch tucking cushions behind me. The room is bland, devoid of character and as if sensing my thoughts, Doug scribes a gesture that takes in the entire room.

"I have plans for this," he tells me. "If I knock that wall out and combine your old room with this one the sun will get through, create a bit of light and warmth in here. It's always so bloomin' cold on this side of the house."

While I ponder the logistics of such a big undertaking, the phone rings in the hall. Doug is at the door in two long strides. He returns looking puzzled. "That was Mum's solicitor. He's asked us to his office on Monday. The will . . . Can you stay an extra day, Ana?"

"Not really. I've two small children, remember. They're staying with my friend, Marie, but she has to work on Monday. It's too late to phone now. I could ring in the morning."

"Good. Well, I can tell you, it seems mother managed to squirrel away more money than I imagined. I always had the impression she lived week to week but from what MacLeish tells me, I was wrong."

Embarrassment brings a flush to my cheeks. This is business that belongs with Doug and mumbling about seeing if Celia needs a hand, I hurry to the kitchen.

"Perfect timing, Ana, will you please bring the cake?" Celia smiles her thanks, lifts the tray and carrying it to the coffee table, sweeps aside a pile of condolence cards sending them sliding to the floor. I gather them up.

Fran and I had read the cards earlier. She suggested we take half each and write our thanks to the senders. I'd looked at the pile of letters and cards; thought of the numerous phone calls noted on the wall pad alongside the phone and shuddered. The idea of having to contact these people, most of whom would have a fixed small-town impression of me, brought a flutter of panic.

"Wouldn't it be better to have cards printed? I'd be happy to help address them."

"Good idea, Ana. I'll talk to Doug. He's sure to know someone here who can do the printing." Fran excelled at organizing. "And one of us will have to collect the cards from the wreaths at the cemetery."

Astonished by the number of graveside wreaths, I wondered about the change in my mother. Something or someone must have drawn her from the hermit-like existence that followed our father's death; a new interest perhaps or the return of an old friend? An image of the sepia coloured photograph in her dresser drawer came to mind.

"Sugar, Ana?" Celia's question pulls me back to the present. She passes the cups and there is a lull, a soft sadness as we sip in silence.

"Did you make the cake?" I ask Celia.

"No. My mum. She's the whiz at cake making. She is going to make our wedding cake."

"Wonderful. Have you set a date yet?"

"Early June," Doug mumbles. His head down, he picks cake crumbs from his jersey.

"Late June," Celia's voice is firm. "Late June," she repeats pleasantly, "because of the cows."

"What do you mean? What do cows have to do with weddings?"

Celia laughs. "Surely you remember? Cows rule this part of the world and the only time of the year they don't have to be milked is mid-winter. Late June is the only time my parents will be free. They want to give me a wonderful wedding."

"And I," Doug gives his chest a final brush, "have arranged to go skiing. First snows down south. It would make a perfect honeymoon. Just think of it, Celi. The cabins there are not really cabins but luxury units with under-floor heating and huge open fires. Imagine bearskin rugs and sleigh beds piled with down-filled covers and pillows. Think how snug we shall be." Doug leans across and poking Celia lightly with his elbow asks, "what do you say, my love, my dearest?"

They seem so young, Doug and Celia. Was I ever so starry eyed? A momentary wave of self-pity brings a tear to my eye. Keeping truth hidden, not with lies but by constantly remaining alert and by clever twists of conversation managing to avoid talk of myself and thereby keeping an illusion of happiness—that required constant effort. And it all began because I could not bear to hear my mother say, 'I told you so.'

To cover my feelings, I stack the cups on the tray. "Well, kids, it's my bedtime."

"Kids!" Doug's pretended indignation is lost in his smile. Offering Celia a hand, he pulls her up from her chair. "Come on, kid. I'll drive you home."

"Thank you." She drops a light kiss on his cheek before enfolding me in a loving hug. "Goodnight. Sleep well," she whispers.

I am rinsing the cups, hot water gushing into the sink, when I hear Doug's feet pounding up the steps and back around the house. He stops in the pool of light beneath the window and calls, "I meant to say I'll probably be late back. I have a key. Don't wait up. See you."

To show I understand, I wave and he is off again, running back to his patiently waiting Celia. My little brother is a lucky man.

The water gurgles from the sink and I give the wrung-out dishmop an extra shake before hanging it on its hook. My mother is gone but a strong sense of her presence remains in the house and I take care to leave things clean and tidy as she would have done.

From within the linen cupboard, I select sheets and towels. The room at the bottom of the passage, the one I used to call mine, has been redecorated in pale lemon and white. Without my teenage clutter the small room appears larger. I run my hand over the dresser feeling the silky smoothness of the white painted surface. Images from the past flash by and I am swept along with them, through tears and laughter, love and loss. I make up the bed; my body following remembered moves, tucking corners, plumping the pillows.

It is late but I am not sleepy and wearing my red coat over my nightgown I kneel on the window seat. Twenty years ago I had climbed from my bed to sit here as I am now, my wakefulness stemming from a dream in which a white bird and Cyril had glided in ever ascending circles. White horses, white birds, their source unknown, they had appeared throughout my life as messengers of love and happiness and sometimes, to forewarn of misfortune and death.

When I was young, our mother's cousin, Cyril, came from England to visit us. Delightful, sometimes loud, often funny and always so kind to us, he had joined us on a walk into town. At Dicker's bookshop we stood aside allowing Mum to enter first. Well drilled in manners, Doug and I behaved as taught, respecting our elders—most of the time.

Inside the shop, our leather soled shoes pattered on the oiled floor boards. While Mum collected our weekly magazines and comics, Cyril wandered to the rear of the shop and I followed. He selected books one at a time, lifted them down, read a little then replaced them on the shelves. I found a series of Biggles books and called Doug to come and look. I liked the Biggles stories and read a lot of books meant for boys. After a quiet word with our mum, Cyril asked Doug and me to choose a book each. I immediately reached for the newest Biggles book but Mum shook her head. I knew what that meant. I was a girl. I should select a book suitable for a girl. Wearing my disappointment like a cloak I mooned along the children's section until Cyril handed me a book with a black cat on the cover, *Jennie* by Paul Gallico.

"Or perhaps this one?" he offered Noel Streatfields' *Ballet Shoes*. How did he guess I wondered? How did he know I longed to dance and that I loved cats, sometimes even more than people? I remembered the way Cyril had smiled down at me; his eyes fill of concern, wanting me to be happy.

Cousin Cyril stayed for six wonderful weeks. He and Mum were the best of friends. They talked a lot, especially in the last weeks of his stay. Dad, I think was a bit sceptical, unsure of what to make of Cyril's flamboyant ways. Doug adored him. I loved him.

Two

By morning the rain is gone. A breeze from the open window gives life to the lace curtains and large squares of sunlight pattern the carpet. A puzzling rhythmic sound draws me from my bed. Outside on the street a boy, his lips pursed in a soundless whistle, zigzags his bicycle, the rear wheel squeaking as he lobs rolled newspapers onto the front porches of neighbouring houses.

Minutes later, dressed in warm slacks and a jersey, I take an apple from the bowl on the kitchen dresser and slip outdoors. The surrounding garden seems so much smaller than when I raced along this path on skinny girl legs, past tall hollyhocks and sweet-william, past the leaky downpipe and its flaky paint, to leap, near flying, down the steps to the gate. Today I cover the distance at a leisurely pace and from the top step search the gully below for familiar landmarks.

As a child I loved the gully. On either side of the stream, beneath vine entwined willow and karaka trees, nature provided an ever changing kaleidoscope. Fast growing saplings, a diversity of ferns and patches of bright green sphagnum moss awaited discovery. As the only girl in the street, I was often excluded by the boys. Alone, in the quiet of the gully, I happily absorbed all that was new and wonderful; the green haze surrounding bare willow branches in spring, the brick-red roots that spread spider-like from the reeds and occasionally, an intricately woven bird's nest blown from a tree.

In high summer all the children in the street joined in the rough and tumble games of cowboys and Indians. We crawled through long grass armed with wooden guns and bamboo bows and arrows, rode imaginary horses up the hills and lit campfires on the sandy strip at the bend of the stream. There we toasted pieces of bread on sticks. Hunkered down in a circle eyeing each other from beneath the lowered brims of our straw sunhats, or in my case, a headband stuck with chook feathers, we gripped the sticks, our hands black, and with our teeth tore off chunks of smoky bread. It never really became toast, but we all declared it the best of food.

These games often ended with me being tied to a tree and forgotten as the boys galloped off to desperate shootouts from behind the water trough or the hen house. Meanwhile I sat watching grasshoppers, awaiting my rescue. As time passed the air become cooler, the shadows longer and mothers called from distant doorsteps. Anxious, and not wanting to be late for tea, or worse alone in the dark, I shouted to the boys. "Come back. Come and untie me." Usually Doug came and together we trotted home to tea.

Before being allowed to play, there were tasks to be done. For a shilling a week Doug and I mowed lawns with a hand mower and trimmed the edges, crawling along using a pair of shears as long as our arms. We kept the kitchen coal bucket full and kindling box replenished and under Mum's eagle eye I learnt to tidy, dust and mop. Saturday mornings I filled a bucket with hot soapy water and tucking my dress into my knickers, crawled about scrubbing the back porch.

Six days a week either Doug or I collected fresh bread from the bake-house a block from home. With a clean flour bag and sixpence pushed into my pocket, I'd chant aloud *Tread on a crack, marry a rat* as I ran, leaping over the moss filled cracks that snaked across the broad pavement. Sometimes, seduced by the smell of warm bread, I'd tear a wee piece and eat it on the way home. Once, when he was quite small, Doug arrived home with only the crust of a loaf, having eaten the entire soft centre. His sheepish grin as he handed the bag to mother won the day and she forgave him.

A piercing whistle interrupts my thoughts and as I turn, I see a red setter bound effortlessly up the hill to a man silhouetted against the sun. Could he be one of the boys I grew up with? I cannot tell and with a brief wave he is gone, the red dog gambolling alongside. I glance at my watch. Fran will be here soon to sort through our mother's things.

"Ana, you're up early. Couldn't you sleep?" Doug is leaning out of his window, his hair tousled, flannelette pyjamas crumpled. His early morning vulnerability fills me with a sudden rush of affection—but when I see his PJ's are patterned with brown teddy bears I almost choke trying to smother my laughter.

He pokes out his tongue, grins and shutting the window calls, "Breakfast in half an hour."

We fall easily back into a comfortable childhood habit of eating breakfast on the back steps, spooning crunchy cereal and sipping steaming tea from large cups, each of us lost in our own thoughts.

"A penny for them," I say to Doug.

He is gazing at the giant marcrocarpa tree that towers over the gully. It grew, as it had for as long as I could remember, with all branches lopped from its fifteen metre trunk leaving a solitary, flat green spread at the top.

"I was thinking how you were the only one able to climb that tree and how peeved the boys were to be outwitted by a girl. We all tried you know, but there was nothing to hold on to, nothing to take our weight. Only twigs."

Deep inside my chest I feel a warm blip and a tiny smirk makes my lips twitch. There had been a lot of boys in our street and their remarks about the inferiority of girls, especially those who wore glasses, had been difficult to bear. "I loved being up there," I tell Doug. "I imagined myself in a boat on the sea or floating in the sky."

"I always thought you were a weird kid."

"And you weren't? Do you remember the day you jumped off the roof?"

"Me?" Doug wipes a hand over his face as if erasing the idea of anything so foolish.

"Yes, you, up on the roof, your friends calling from below, 'Come on Superman. Show us how you can fly.' I can't believe you weren't scared, Doug. I was. And you were only seven, maybe eight years old."

"I reckon my guardian angel worked a lot of overtime."

"I'd agree with that." At the sound of Fran's voice we both look up. She is twelve years older than me and of a steadier nature. Chalk and cheese sisters, we share the same father but have different mothers. There is comfort in her hug and I have to blink away a tear.

"Well, do I get a cup of tea?" Fran asks as we step apart.

"Of course, come on in." Doug leads the way into the kitchen where the three of us sit with fresh cups of tea. We keep the conversation general, smiling, laughing a little, careful not to intrude too deeply into each another's personal life.

Finally Doug speaks directly. "We need to sort out the furniture and bigger items. I know you only have a couple of days, so perhaps if we do it now? Fran and I agree. "Good. Once that's done I'll leave you to go through the rest of Mum's things. Take what you want. But please, leave me my bed, the frypan and the coffee!"

We begin, moving from room to room. By lunchtime our choices are made and Doug drives to his business in town leaving Fran and I to sort through cupboards and drawers. We work steadily through a multitude of items, rediscovering long forgotten objects. Some, like the funny metal hair curlers with rubber grips and the butterfly clips that had crimped our hair into waves, trigger laughter. We are amazed our mother has kept such antiquated items. But the framed photographs of our father, so young and handsome in his military uniform, make us acutely aware of a part of our lives that is gone forever.

"I still miss him you know," Fran speaks quietly.

"Me too. He was never too busy to talk and knew so many things other fathers didn't; the names of trees and grasses and clouds. Even the weeds that dared to grow in his immaculate vegetable garden."

"He taught me the beauty of different timbers. Showed me how a smear of oil would enhance their grain and colour. He was seldom angry. I trusted him."

"So did I," and I sniff a little as I slip several photographs into Fran's box of selected items.

"I think we need another cup of tea." Fran's hand is warm on my shoulder. "Would you like a slice of Celia's cake?"

I nod yes. I had loved my father. We all relied on him. He could repair anything from teapots to tractors and was always willing to lend his larger hand to our smaller ones.

One dark frosty morning he shook me awake and helped me to dress in layers of warm clothing. So many layers I had walked stiff-legged with my arms outstretched and been unable to climb the stile to the cow paddock. Instead, he lifted me over, his strong arms swinging me high in the air. My hand in his, we trudged over the frosted grass to the byre where the milk-cow and her new calf lay in an aura of warmth. There we squatted in the hay and Dad placed my fingers in the calf's mouth. Surprised by the suction, I'd tried to pull free. I remember Dad laughing, tousling my woolly hat and knocking it down over my eyes.

The rising sun soon warmed us and with the top layers of my clothing slung about Dad's shoulders, I'd been free to run. A startled rabbit leapt from the hedgerow and a skylark whirred to the heavens where it had hovered, pouring its song onto our upturned faces as we stood hand-in-hand in that glittering frost-covered field, my father and me.

Fran calls from the kitchen. "Tea's ready, Ana."

"How lovely, this is like English high tea."

"I thought we'd have one last tea party for Mum." Fran sets the teapot on its stand.

"I remember her embroidering this." I lift the edge of the starched, rose-embroidered cloth, the deep crocheted border heavy in my hand.

"Do you? It must have taken years. She began working this when I was at primary school."

"She put it aside while waitressing in the teashop. I guess she had enough to do, making our clothes, knitting, looking after Dad."

"She was always busy. Everything had to be just right. Her greatest concern was "What will the neighbours think?" What will they say?" Fran is mimicking — making fun, but I feel on edge, unable to laugh, for my mother had demanded I too conform to the expectations of others. When very young I was given both freedom and considerable encouragement to express my independent nature. But we all changed when Dad became ill; our mother most of all. And after that, no matter how hard I tried, I could never please her. She was always saying: 'No, Ana.' 'Don't be silly, Ana' or 'That is out of the question.' To argue was useless. Over time I had imbued her fear of small-town censure and would no doubt carry the scars of its constraint for the rest of my life.

And what might the neighbours say if they knew of the errors I'd made? Nowadays there would be a quick flurry of gossip over the back fence and the whole thing soon forgotten. I stir my tea and hope I am right.

"Well, what do you think?" Fran is lining up the apostle tea spoons on the cloth. "These are quite valuable now. Shall we have six each?"

I pick up Peter, turning him over in my hand. He is the only one I recognize although I once knew them all. "It would be a shame to break the set. You have them, Fran."

"Are you sure?"

"Yes."

"Is there something special you'd like?"

"I hoped there might be something of Grandma's. I know Mum kept a lot of her things. Books, the lovely crystal bud vase. Her cross stitch of course and—" I stop, afraid I am presuming too much but Fran laughs.

"You're welcome to them. I've no time for pretty these days. I pour my milk from the bottle and scoop jam from a jar."

"How liberating."

"And I often leave dishes in the sink."

Now I am laughing, delighted to hear Fran has outgrown the benchmark and skittled the standards that had supposedly set our place in society. "I throw away old dishcloths. I don't boil them anymore," I tell her, "and I refuse to steam-press bedsheets." Helpless with laughter, we rock, our arms tight across our tummies. Calm at last we again sip tea and I pass Fran another slice of cake.

"At Grandma's house," I say, smiling at the memory, "the frost made snowflake patterns on the windows and out on the frosted lawn, a million fairy lights flashed in the sun. I thought it a magical place."

"Not me. The house was so quiet. And I was always being told to be a lady; to walk, not run, to sit up straight and keep my elbows in. I couldn't wait to get home."

"Really? I loved the steady tick-tock of the big clock, and Granddad chatting to me, encouraging me to tell imaginary tales. 'What if Cinderella did not get home before midnight and her coach was gone, poof! How would she get home?' he would ask me, his hands spread wide. I loved how his blue eyes crinkled with laughter as I told him my stories."

"So you didn't mind Gran coming here to live when Granddad died?" Fran waits for my answer as I hesitate.

"No, I liked her. She didn't say much but I think she understood me. She was kind." *And certainly easier to approach than my mother.* An increasing tightness in my jaw together with a need to move pushes me to my feet. I clear the table and rinse the dishes. In a moment my tension will ease and the underlying anger cool. It will. It always does.

As I wipe down the bench Fran gives me a nudge. "Come on. Let's do a bit more sorting."

By five o'clock we have reached Mum's room and as Fran lifts the blinds, the setting sun tints the grey room pink. Unlocking the wardrobe I pull open the doors and together we gaze at the accumulation of garments, hats and handbags. Fran is first to speak.

"Would you like anything from here?"

"No. But Aunt May might like the fur coat. She always admired it."

"Good idea. Shall we ask the aunts to choose a few things?"

"They're coming for lunch tomorrow. We can ask them then." As I close the wardrobe and pass her the key, I feel Fran's appraisal.

"Shall we call it a day? You look tired, Ana. Are you well?" Concern shows in her face and I hear it in her voice.

"Yes. No. Yes." I'm faltering, my voice breaking. I long to explain the deep rooted pride that has kept me isolated from friends and family for so long. Years ago, before my children were born Fran suggested a life without my husband. Had she seen the heartache that lay ahead? Could she have known I would stubbornly cling to the notion that love conquers all only to be disillusioned time after time? Mum did her best to warn me and I ignored her. Now it is too late to make amends.

I sit on the bed fumbling for a handkerchief and finding my pockets empty reach across and take one from mother's drawer. We sit close, Fran and I, her arm about my waist, the lavender scent from the handkerchief mingling with our thoughts, our memories, all too personal or too precious to share. After a long moment I pat her hand and whisper my thanks.

From within the drawer I take the photograph and passing it to her ask, "Do you know who this man is?"

"No, sorry, I don't." Fran is looking at her watch. "Ana, love, I should go. The children will be back from the movies. You don't mind being here on your own?"

I reassure her and accompany her to the gate carrying a bag of books and other relics of her childhood. A brief girlhood that was over before I even knew her. "See you tomorrow," I call as we wave goodbye.

The powerfully emotive objects Fran and I pulled from storage have drawn me into an emotional whirlpool. Things like the old enamel plates used to set toffee and fudge and the plain glass vase that for years stood at the centre of the kitchen table. Filled with seasonal flowers it had been the focal point of the room and once, during a big earthquake, Fran had reached out and held it safe until the shaking stopped. At the back of the linen cupboard I discovered my first ever sewing effort; a sacking oven cloth blanket stitched with red wool. Mum had kept it all these years. Perhaps she cared more than I knew.

Returning to Mum's room I lift the photo from her drawer and holding it close, lie propped against the pillows. The slow steady beat of my heart gently propels me to think ahead, to re-establish both peace and happiness in my life; the purpose of which, like the man in the photograph, remains an elusive mystery.

All through my childhood I concocted fanciful stories about the roles this handsome man might have played in my mother's life. The arrival of a new vicar's assistant raised my hopes of discovery. Mum and Mr Haycock went to school together. He'd put a frog in her lunchbox and once, lifted her onto a wagon when, with a group of friends, they set off on a hayride. In the evening, after the dance and lulled by the steady clip-clop of the horse's hooves, they journeyed home beneath a harvest moon. When telling me this, my mum's eyes looked dreamy and I felt all tingly thinking this man from her past, might be my mystery man.

The vicar and Mr Haycock were invited to afternoon tea; the snow white cloths for the tea trolley starched and ironed to perfection, the best china washed and the silverware polished.

By two o'clock everything was ready. Doug and I, dressed in clean clothes and with our hair neatly brushed, were under a solemn promise to stay that way. Unable to sit still, I darted back and forth between the sitting room and the front door. I so wanted our visitor be the man in the photograph.

The sharp rat-tat-tat of the door knocker sent me hurrying into the passage where I hid behind the velvet curtains. Mum ushered in the vicar and shook his hand. Hardly daring to breathe I peered through the curtain fringe. Mr Haycock appeared and I drooped with disappointment. No way could this rotund and effusive little man be my mother's secret love.

Mum caught me lingering and called me forward. His chubby fingers caressing mine Mr Haycock leaned forward, "Dear child, how like your mother you are," he said. He screwed his round red face into a smile and for a horrid moment I thought he was going to kiss me. As politely as possible I had released my hand and led the way to the sitting room.

Enough of the memories, I tell myself. Life's disappointments are best forgotten. Pass or fail, life goes on and each day brings new opportunity.

Thinking ahead to the evening meal and the family lunch tomorrow I go check the food in the refrigerator. The shelves are full. Celia's parents had brought cold meats and fresh scones and cakes, someone else a large bacon and egg pie. There is no need to go to the shops. I make a fresh pot of tea and sip, both hands cupped about the mug as I lean back against the sink. Finding the mug was a surprise. There are only two. Mum had always served pale tea in china teacups. It was the proper thing to do.

The 'proper thing' ruled so much of my dull lower middle class life. I had wanted more. Why did we not own a car?

Everyone else owned a motor vehicle. Even a new bike would have helped but I was twelve before mine arrived and Mum chose it, not me. I hoped for a shiny sports model. Instead I received an upright roadster. "Because it is stronger and will last longer," she'd said. That was true. The bike was still in the shed. I'd seen it today.

As a child I did not see myself as ungrateful. I found delight in simple things; a flower bud, a silver snail trail, green moss, blue sky or pink wool. I'd been happy making things from cardboard, paint and glue — but was never indoors if I could be out. When young, I presumed all things possible and that setbacks rarely lasted long.

When I was ten I fancied owning a brightly coloured beach ball. I'd seen magazine pictures of happy sun-tanned families playing at the seaside and somehow convinced myself a striped beach ball represented the height of wealth and happiness. I pictured myself at the centre of a group of friends playing on the beach, the huge red white and blue ball being tossed high in the air and bouncing on the golden sand. That was imagination at its best. Our local beaches were black iron sands. I'd never seen real white or yellow sand.

The same year I discovered beneath the Christmas tree a parcel that felt and smelt like rubber. Sure as eggs were eggs, it contained a beach ball. Christmas day finally arrived and when it was time to unwrap our gifts, I put *that* parcel aside, savouring the anticipation. At last I slid off the string and unfolded the paper to reveal — a dull green bathing cap.

Swamped with disappointment, I burst into tears and blubbed something about the cap being the wrong size rather than admit how foolish I had been.

I learned at a young age it was better not to show need if one's needs were unlikely to be met. Doug and I used to play the tickling game. With fingers, feathers or grass stems we tickled each other, the soles of our feet, our ribs, the backs of our necks. Whoever kept a straight face for the longest time was the winner. These games did not last long as I quickly learned to control the instinctive need to pull away or laugh.

As I grew older my progression in what began as a game, became a means of protection, an outward appearance of coping, of being calm. I believed this person to be me and was unaware that inside this pious persona the real me was fermenting; brewing into a catastrophic emergence.

At dusk Doug arrives home for a hurried meal, changes his clothes and again telling me not to wait up for him, rushes off out. I decide to have a hot bath before going to bed and finding some bath salts, lavender of course, I add them to the steaming bath water. My need to be still, to file away the disturbing emotions exposed earlier as Fran and I pulled forgotten objects from storage, is upmost in my mind.

The large cast-iron bath allows me to stretch full length and I lie back, close my eyes and relax. *Phssst.* My eyes fly open at the sound and as I look up the overhead light glows orange, flickers, and dies. I am in the dark.

No longer relaxed, I stare into the darkness. An orb of street light glimmers faintly through the frosted window and I concentrate on its glow. You are safe, I tell myself. The doors are locked. You are no longer a child. But on this night reason fails to calm my turbulent thoughts and I pull the plug, dress ready for bed and return to the kitchen.

A quick hunt in the cupboards provides drinking chocolate and crème biscuits. While the milk heats on the stove I set a tray then carry my supper to the living area. The light from the standard lamp does little to cheer the room and as I attempt to tuck my legs beneath me in the comfiest armchair, I find myself reflecting on my childhood fear of the dark.

It is a winter's night and we are all gathered in the kitchen. Dad has opened the little door on the fire box. The heat from the coals warm me as lying on my tummy on the floor with my colouring book, I carefully colour Minnie Mouse's dress bright red. Mum is watching, encouraging me to stay within the lines. She sits in her wicker chair, her slippered feet on the step before the open oven, her knitting in her lap. It's so cosy here. The clock on the mantle ticks steadily on.

"Time for bed, Ana."

I hate those words and stall, wanting to stay in the warmth and the light.

"Now, Ana!" Mum gives me a poke with her knitting needle. "Fetch your pyjamas. You can change here by the fire."

I turn to Fran. "Come with me, please?"

"No. You're a big girl now. Off you go."

My room is at the top of the passage and the only light switch on the far side of the spooky hall curtains; velvet drapes big enough to conceal a bogey man or two. More, if they hide in the doorways that line the dark passage.

Full of dread, I drag a chair across to the passage door. "There goes lightning bug," Dad comments as I climb up and turn the handle. The others moan as the door opens and icy air from the top of the house sweeps into the room.

"Quick. Shut the door," they say.

Shutting the door means I am in the dark, alone. I am on full alert; every nerve stretched, ears strained, eyes searching. The passage grows in length. Unspeakable horror lurks behind every door. Ghosts, Germans and the three huge dogs with eyes as big as dustbin lids from the tinderbox story, they are all here, waiting to get me.

The speed of my sprint to the light switch at the far end of the passage should be in the Guinness Book of Records. What a relief to turn on the light. With my pyjamas clutched to my chest, I brace for the run back. Draw a big breath, turn out the light—and run like the dickens to where that wonderful glimmer of light shines through beneath the passage door.

"Open the door," I call pounding with my fist. "Open the door."

"Say please." A voice answers.

"Please," I beg.

Often they argue over who will get up from their seat and while they argue, I wait, huddled against the door in the dark. Finally it opens and I tumble through to a barrage of,

"Shut the door."

"It's freezing."

"Ana, hurry up. Shut that door."

My fear of the darkness lasted many years and I was often teased by my siblings and cousins. The only person to understand my terror when in the dark was my cousin David.

Three

In the summer of the year I turned eleven, our cousins came into town for the annual Agricultural show. Doug and I cycled to the showgrounds to meet them. We arrived out of breath, pushed our bikes into the hedge lining the road to the main gates, paid our entrance fee and ran to where twelve-year-old Dell waited for us. Heather, my age, and seven-year-old Neil joined us. David had gone off alone.

We walked, looking at everything; the chairoplane, merry-go-round, dodgem cars and the ghost train. At the tunnel of love we stopped to watch couples alight. One girl kept hitting a bloke with her handbag and we cheered her on. We passed signs inviting people to see a fat lady, a bearded lady and a strong man. Near the end of the alley, strange music drew us to where ladies wearing flimsy clothes and with veils over their faces danced on a stage outside a large tent. A dark skinned man with a loud hailer strode about urging people to step inside. He bent over Neil and Doug. "Come on lads. Come and see the wonders inside." He winked.

"How much?" Neil asked, jiggling coins in his pocket.

"Half price for you, two and sixpence."

Heather gasped. "No, Neil," she said and taking her brother by the arm, pulled him away. "Come on. I'll get candy floss and we'll all share it."

We finally spent our money in side show alley in the hope of scoring prizes impossible to win. Empty handed, hot and thirsty, we returned to my aunt's car for lunch. Aunt May insisted we all rest for an hour and we sprawled on rugs beside the car eating popcorn and swapping stories until David returned laden with prizes.

"Make my bed for a week and you can have this." He held out a Kewpie doll to Heather. Fixed to a crook the Kewpie wore a stiff net skirt and a glittery headband with a gold star. I would have made his bed for ever for a doll like that. David offered us sweets. "Take a handful," he said, and our eyes popped as he passed round an enormous bag of toffees.

Seated on the rug with his back against the car door, David shared his bottle of soft drink with us. In his long trousers and checked sports jacket, he looked quite grown up. Leaving David in charge, Aunt May returned to the trades' hall and as my cousins related tales of daring escapades and hilarious pranks, I came to see my life in town as boring. Nothing that exciting ever happened to me. When I was little, young enough to use the chamber pot beneath the bed and not run outside to the dunny, I had spent a night or two at each of my aunt's. They had been fun times away from home without Mum and Dad.

I once asked my mum why, when her two sisters were married to dairy farmers and lived in the country, she had married a townie. She shuddered, "All those mucky clothes, cow poo and smelly gumboots at the back door? No thank you, I would not like that one bit!"

"But it is so nice in the country," I wheedled, thinking my cousins' life far more exciting than my own. Resolute, Mum lifted her chin.

"Each to their own," she'd said.

Imagine my delight when in the summer break that same year, Mum announced a two week holiday on Uncle Harry's farm.

We caught the early morning goods train and because there were no carriages, rode in the guard's van along with an assortment of boxes, caged hens and mail bags. The heavy sliding doors remained open allowing the hot summer smell of newly cut hay to flow into the van. As we neared the farm our excitement grew and Doug and I were constantly warned to sit still. How great to be a dog, I thought. To stick my head out the door and let the breeze blow my hair.

The Matapu station looked nothing like the large station at home. There was no platform, signals, or lights. Not even a water tank. Just a tin shed beside a cart track in a paddock. Not that it mattered as Uncle Harry, his arms folded across his broad chest, stood waiting beside his battered truck.

We piled aboard, Mum in the front with our uncle. Doug, me and Dad on the tray at the back, our backs against the cab, our bottoms bouncing over every rut as the truck rattled along the gravel road. At the river boundary, our cousins waved their hats and hollered a welcome before leaping from the fence to chase after the truck. David and Heather led the way but Dell, who was quite plump, slowed to walk as the others ran all the way up the last big hill to the farm house.

Our cousins had no fears. They rode horses, explored great tracts of bush and hung over the fence talking to a massive jersey bull while scratching its back with a stick. None of them were afraid of the dark. They loved the dark and after sunset, in that strange half-light when the sky turns indigo and the farm-buildings, fields and fences lose colour, they coaxed us out to play chase. Only fourteen-year-old David realized I kept looking back, making sure the house lights remained in sight.

Last thing before bed, Aunt May insisted each child go to the lavatory. The dunny, as they called it, was at the bottom of the yard, a long way from the house. A narrow track led through grass seldom mowed, past the feed sheds, the lemon tree and a high boxthorn hedge whose spikey branches rasped against a corrugated fence. Heard in the dark this sound, like ghosts dragging chains, scared me near to death.

Finding my way along this track at night was not my only terror, as hens that missed the sundown curfew to their roost, sheltered in the dunny. My arrival at the door would set them off like squawking firecrackers, the explosion of feathers and noise as they flew over my head and into the night more frightening than anything I could have imagined. After two or three nights of me begging the others to walk with me, David loaned me his torch and sometimes walked with me as far as the lemon tree. Not wanting to be called a scaredy-cat, I forced myself to walk the last few yards and soon my pretended bravery became real.

Several neighbouring families came to help turn and stack hay. My dad's eldest sister and her large family of grown-up sons came. All the men had long beards and I heard Aunt May tell Mum the women did not cut their hair or wear make-up. Nor did they have a radio or read newspapers. How odd. But they were nice people, just different.

While the men worked in the fields, several mothers took a bunch of kids to swim in the river. Excited and twittering we split into separate groups to change, girls one side of the bushes, boys on the other. My cousins dived in at once, striking out for the far side where a steep, fern covered cliff rose high above the dark water.

As I approached the water, Mum called to me. "Ana. Leave your glasses here. Don't go in the water with them on."

Without my glasses, the world about me changed. Solid objects became misty blobs of colour that ran into one another. It was quite pretty and I didn't mind. Besides, in places I knew, I remembered where things were and seldom had a problem. Here, everything was new. The distance between rocks and bushes or even which was which as yet unknown. I waded into the water and stood alone, one step out from where the toddlers played. In the deep area beneath the cliff, the older children dived and swam sleek as seals. At last they came from the river, laughing, shaking their heads, water flying from their hair. Amid much giggling and splashing, big sisters captured the younger children, wrapped them in towels and helped them to dress. I collected my glasses and went to get dressed. There was no need to towel my hair. It was dry.

At lunch time Aunt May summoned the men from the field by banging a pot with a large spoon. They went first to the river to cup water over their faces and then dried themselves with their shirts before sprawling relaxed beside the rugs spread with baskets, boxes and cake tins. They talked in that slow comfortable way farmers do, their fingers stripping seeds from dry grass as they discussed the price of poddy calves, the weather and the possibility of buying a tractor to replace the horses. The amount of food reached banquet proportion as the women served hot pies and pastries. And the raspberry cordial, poured from a cream can left to cool in a shady area of the river, was so cold it hurt my throat.

The men did not linger. After eating they rose, slapped their hats against their thighs and nodding thanks to the women, started back up the hill. I saw my mum run after Dad and as they talked, he held her shoulders, but she did not smile. Not even when he blew her a kiss as he followed the others back up the field. The boys ran off together. Aunt May packed the remaining lunch into the truck and taking Dell with her, returned to the house leaving Mum and the other wives chatting quietly in the shade.

From where I lay on the rug, the thick rounded shapes of the blossoming hawthorn hedge looked like scoops of ice-cream plopped from a giant's spoon. Furry black and yellow bumble bees with pollen spilling from their bulging knee sacks clambered in and out of the purple foxgloves that grew at the water's edge. A myriad of small insects sang and flies with brilliant green wings hovered over me.

I must have fallen asleep for when I opened my eyes, the line of men turning the hay had reached the top of the hill. The younger men had removed their shirts and slipped their braces from their shoulders letting them dangle. I could see my father, his collarless shirt open at the front, sleeves rolled above his elbows; his body working in a slow steady rhythm as he lifted and turned the hay.

Heather dropped down on the rug beside me. "Doug is cross because my dad made him put his shirt and hat back on, told him he'd look like a beetroot if he didn't," she said.

"Where did the boys go?"

"To the old railway hut. Looking for adventure they said. I didn't want to go. It's a long way to walk back."

"Yeah, why don't we make our own adventure, something secret no one knows about?" I asked and when Heather did not reply, I knew I would have to think of something. "What about a midnight feast?" The best schoolgirl stories described midnight feasts; secret candle-lit affairs held in out of bounds places. All we needed was somewhere to go and some especially nice food. Aunt May's pantry overflowed with food. Surely a small amount would not be missed.

Heather agreed to get a candle and I the matches as Dad smoked and kept a flap of wax matches in his jacket pocket. And I had David's torch. Nothing would get me to that lavatory after dark without a torch.

"We should decide where to have our feast then we'll know what to take," Heather said.

"Why not here? We could light a fire on the sand, make a Maori oven." I knew how, I told her. We'd done it at school. Besides, I had a Girls' Brigade camping badge. My marks had been the best.

"It's a long way from the house," Heather looked doubtful.

The white painted house with its red roof sat neatly at the top of the second hill, the afternoon sun glinting on the windows. It did not look far away.

"Well, where else?"

Heather stood gazing around, her brow furrowed as she plucked flowers from the hedge and let them fall, crumpled, from her fingers. She spun about, "I know, the cowshed."

"What! That mucky place."

"Is not. You haven't seen it without cows, when it's all washed out. It's nice. Anyway, I can't come way down here at night. Mum would have a fit." I was about to say her mum would not know but realized I'd be wasting my breath. Heather continued. "How about we take my roller skates and skate around the concrete yard?"

The cowshed might not be so bad. I'd not tried roller skating.

A long cooee from where the haymakers toiled on the hillside made us look up. Dad waved his hat then beckoned.

"Dad wants me. Come on." We ran, but slowed to a walk as we climbed the last of the long hill.

"Look, see what I've found." Heather and I crouched beside him as Dad parted the stubble to reveal three baby rabbits. I lifted one into the palm of my hand and stroked it gently with a finger. The tiny creature shivered; ears flat, eyes closed. Its energy so fragile I might have been holding a dandelion seed-head. Ed and David came to see what we were looking at.

"What are you going to do with them?" David asked.

"Kill them," said Ed. "They're a pest."

Horrified, I hugged the baby to my chest. "I shall keep it for a pet. All of them."

"Ana love, they are wild rabbits. They are not strong." Dad got to his feet and rested a hand on David's shoulder. "Perhaps their mother is looking for them?"

"I'll look after them." I reached down, picked up the other bunny and putting both into my skirt, gathered its hem to make a carry-bag.

"Hold on." David removed his hat and holding it out indicated to Heather she should put her rabbit in. "Your's too," he said to me. I reluctantly placed the babies in the hat. "Come on. I have to go home to milk. I'll show you where the old hutch is and you can fix them up." Carrying the hat David strode off down the hill with Heather and me close behind. At the house gate we met Aunt May taking afternoon tea to the men. She stopped to look at the rabbits.

"They're sweet. Don't let Peter see them. You two girls can help Dell peel the vegetables for dinner. I must go. Bye."

"What did she mean, don't let Peter see them?" I knew Peter was the black farm cat.

"He'll eat them," said Heather.

The sooner the rabbits were safely in the hutch the better and I held David's hat and the wee rabbits close as he clambered over old fence palings and sheets of iron behind the feed shed before finally dragging the hutch out onto the grass. Without waiting for thanks he pulled on his gumboots and crossed the house paddock calling to the dogs to bring in the cows. Heather and I put clean straw in the hutch and settled the rabbits, giving them a carrot and some clover to eat. We also hung a sack over the back so the farm cat could not see them should they venture out of their nest.

Later, as we peeled vegetables in the kitchen, we planned our midnight feast. We would take the food now, while no one was home and hide it in our room along with the roller skates, candle and matches.

"What are you two whispering about?" Dell stood in the kitchen doorway, her hands on her hips. Dell was a big girl. Tall, and well, big — and bossy. She was only a year older than me but she acted like she was fourteen.

"Come on. Out with it. What are you up to?"

"We're going to have a midnight feast."

"Tonight? Just the two of you?"

We nodded, still uncertain of her response.

"Can I join in?"

This was unexpected. Heather and I exchanged a quick glance. "Yes. But don't tell anyone. It's a secret."

The vegetables had never been so speedily prepared. As Dell put the last pot on the stove, Heather and I collected school lunch boxes to put our food in. Dell helped her mother in the kitchen every day and knew which things we must not touch. As we wrapped the last sandwich in wax paper, we heard the truck return. Our tins full and the lids snapped shut, I hurried to the bedroom and hid them beneath my bed.

The boys and my parents arrived back with Aunt May and we all went to see the baby rabbits before settling indoors to await the evening meal. Exasperated with Doug for getting sun burnt, Mum sent me to the washhouse to fetch calamine and cotton wool. When I offered them to her she flicked her hand at me.

"You do it," she said rubbing her fingers over her forehead. Mum often got migraines and we kids had learnt to be quiet. Doug came when I called and taking off his shirt allowed me to gently dab his sunburnt skin with the calamine.

"Thanks, that feels better," he said.

Aunt May met me as I carried the bottle back to the washhouse that served as both bathroom and laundry. "Call everyone in for dinner, please Ana. Get them to hurry up."

I searched and rounded up both children and adults but couldn't find my dad anywhere. I tapped Mum's arm. "I can't find Dad. Has he gone to the milking shed?"

Mum smacked my hand away. "I don't know. Have you looked in the sitting room?"

Aunty's sitting room, like our own, was seldom used. The blinds remained at half-mast; the room filled with an atmosphere of brooding, an unwillingness to be disturbed. The door was ajar and as I eased it open, tiny shivers skimmed from my neck to my knees.

My father lay on the couch, his hands folded on his chest. I stepped closer. His head had slipped from the cushion and his mouth hung open a little. In the evening light his face was somehow different. Thinking he was asleep, I moved quietly across the room.

"Dad, it's dinner time." I laid a tentative hand on his. He was cold. Something was wrong. But he was breathing. I could hear the shallow sound. Swiftly I turned and left the room. I had a strange feeling of being two people. One walking fast to get help and the other saying, "Keep calm."

I found Mum at the table and remembering the smack I'd received earlier, stood back. "Mum, I think Dad is sick. He looks different." Along the table forks froze and eyes stared. Mum pushed me aside.

"I knew he had done too much. He will not listen. Not to me, the doctor or anyone." With angry tears in her eyes, she hurried to the sitting room with Aunt May close behind.

Holding back my own tears, I stared down at the crisp pastry covering the steak and kidney on my plate. It had smelt delicious when Dell lifted it from the oven but now offered less appeal than a rotten apple. I felt Doug looking at me, questioning. When I glanced across, he lowered his gaze. To hide his fear, I thought. Was our father going to die? Here? *Now*?

I could hear my sandal kicking the chair leg. We were forbidden to kick the furniture but I was unable to stop.

Aunt May reappeared and beckoning Neil out from behind the table told him, "Run over to the shed and get your dad. Tell him Uncle Jack is ill. David can finish up at the shed. Go, quickly now," and turning him about by the shoulders, she sent him out the back door. "Dell, you see the others eat their tea and get ready for bed." She came then and stood behind my chair. Her hands gripped my shoulders, holding them firmly till the kicking stopped.

"Eat your dinner, Ana. Your father will be all right." Her voice was kind, but also sad. I knew people tried to be nice, to be kind but sometimes the things they said were not quite true.

While I pushed potatoes and peas around my plate the others moved onto dessert. We heard the car pull up at the front door but no one spoke. Mum came in wearing her coat, her handbag beneath her arm. "Uncle Harry will drive us to the hospital," she said. I thought she meant all of us and slid from my chair. She held up her hand. "You stay there," she said her finger pointing at me, her face stern. Then, with a nod to Doug she hurried from the room.

The car doors banged. The engine sparked into life. At the road gate there was a pause before the car drove through carrying my father away. Gone — without so much as a goodbye hug.

My eyes brimmed with tears. Worried about my father and resentful at being left behind, I went outside to the rabbit hutch. It was almost dark. My fingers searched the straw for the soft furry feel of the baby rabbits. Were they hiding? Lifting the flap, I looked inside. The hutch was empty. A short distance away, scattered beneath the lemon tree, were little tufts of pale grey fur; all that was left of three baby rabbits.

Black Peter sat washing his paws at the entrance to the feed shed. At the sight of him, sitting there, placid and uncaring, my anguish rose in a choking tide to vent itself at the cat.

"Murderer!" I yelled. "Bastard!" Ripping lemons from the tree I hurled them at the cat. My aim was not good. Lemons splattered over the path and on the walls. Still I kept throwing. "Bastard!"

"Ana. Stop." David grasped my arms and holding me, made me sit on the washhouse step. "What's all this about?"

Between sobs I told him about father going to hospital and of the missing rabbits. David listened and when I was calm, sent me to wash my face with cold water.

"Off you go now. I won't tell," he said gathering up the last of the smashed lemons and throwing them over the fence. I hesitated, wanting to say something, even hug him. But David was not the sort of boy you hugged.

"Thanks," was all I could manage.

Indoors, while Heather and the boys played snakes and ladders, I curled in a corner of the couch and read comics until bedtime. As I climbed into bed, my toes kicked the hidden lunchboxes. Hearing the sound of the tin hitting the roller skates, Heather murmured "We forgot our feast."

"Never mind."

"Goodnight, Ana."

In the last moments before sleeping I prayed for my father, begging God to make him well. My dreams were peaceful.

Beautiful white horses, their coats flecked with gold, grazed in a sunlit forest glade and at dawn, when the crowing of the farmyard rooster roused me, I struggled to hold the image.

Fully awake and without disturbing Heather, I slipped from my bed and padded barefoot down the hall to Mum and Dad's room. The bed had not been slept in. In my aunt's bedroom Uncle Harry's good clothes hung over a chair, the blankets tossed back as if left in a hurry. David's room was also empty; the blind raised, the window open. On the dresser, two bright goldfish swam through wavy green grass in a glass bowl; the shiny orb a beacon in the small untidy room.

The door to the boy's room creaked disturbing Doug and Neil who bounded out of bed full of beans.

"Is Dad back?" Doug whispered when Neil went to wash.

"I don't think so. But Uncle Harry is. We can ask him."

Heather appeared beside me fully dressed, her long hair in neat braids. "Come on sleepyhead. Time you were dressed," she said.

By the time the milkers returned Dell had organised her band of workers into preparing breakfast while she packed lunch for the hay-makers. Today the dried hay would be carted and stacked. Heather and I met Uncle Harry on his return from the shed.

"Morning girls. I think you aunt would like to talk to you, Ana. You talk to her," he said disappearing into the dark recess of the washhouse.

Why do adults so often leave children fearing the worst? Do they think only grownups are capable of serious thought? Mum had told us our father was going to die. Doug and I lived with that minute by minute. It was the reason we seldom played away from home when he was there. Why we left our toys to follow him to the tool shed or out to the garden and why I practised running as fast as I could. Ready for the day when mother would say 'Run, Ana. Run. Phone for the doctor.' I planned to run like the wind to a neighbour with a telephone. I knew who would be home and when. There was no point in going to Mrs Stuart on a Monday because she'd be at the church, cleaning postage stamps for the mission. I was doing what I could to be helpful. To fob us off with half-truths was not fair. I hoped Aunt May would tell us the truth. We found her in the kitchen ladling out porridge.

"Good morning, Ana, Doug." Aunt May put down the pot and sat on a nearby chair. "Your father is recovering. He's resting at the hospital and will be home in a few days. Your mother will remain in town but you and Doug can stay here with us until the end of the week. Would you like that?"

Doug nodded happily but I turned away to hide my tears and heard my aunt sigh. Lost in thought I sat silent as the others chattered over breakfast, making plans for the day ahead. While staring down at the creamy milk covering the porridge in my plate, I remembered the white horses from my dream — and the fiery horse that had appeared when Doug was so ill. He had recovered. Dad was going to get well. I knew it. I just *knew* it. And picking up my spoon, ate every scrap of porridge on my plate.

With our morning chores out of the way, we children ran down to the hayfields. From a distance the action at the stack appeared in slow motion. Lines of men swung pitchforks full of hay high onto the carts where it was evenly spread by Ed and his brother. Enormous brown and white cart horses, their great shaggy feet big as dinner plates, ferried the hay to the stack where the activity continued.

A huge grabber with claw-like tines unloaded the cart lifting the hay high onto the stack where expert stackers switched it back and forth weaving it firmly into place. All the children took a turn to guide Ben, the quiet old draught horse as he plodded patiently back and forth pulling the rope attached to the grabber. When it was my turn I climbed first onto David's shoulders then hoisted myself over onto Ben's back, a back so broad, my legs stuck out sideways. Leaning forward I patted Ben's neck urging him to 'Walk up' so the grabber would swing up and over the stack. When the stackers shouted Hoi! I commanded him to turn and the hay was lowered to the stack. I felt important sitting so high and pretending to control the enormous horse. In truth, Ben knew it all and turned when the stackers shouted. He did not need my commands.

By the time Aunt May called the workers to lunch half the field had been cleared and clouds loomed on the horizon. The men studied the growing cumulonimbus, talked of a shift in the wind and rain before nightfall.

They returned quickly to work. The sun disappeared and an ever increasing black cloud took over the sky. The men worked in silence, their faces grim. But when Bloss wearily pulled the last cart-load of hay to the stack, a shout went up and pitchforks flew as grabber after grabber load swung aloft. Another shout and men slid from the stack leaving old Walter to weave his waterproofing magic. Tools were collected, the grabber dismantled and loaded onto a cart; the younger lads sent trudging over the fields to bring the cows in. Lightning flashed and as the first big drops of rain fell, we threw a cover over stuff in the back of the truck and tied it down.

"Quick. Get in." Aunt May held the truck door open and we scrambled over one another, piling up on the bench seat to leave enough room for her.

Thankfully the really heavy rain did not come until after dinner when the day's work was done. I asked Uncle Harry if the stack would be all right. Everyone had worked so hard.

"Aye," he said and returned to reading his newspaper. Uncle was so accepting. He did what he could, what he knew he should, and then let it go before turning his attention to the next job in hand.

On the last night of our holiday a halo of rainbow colours surrounded the moon. Dad once told me this meant a change in the weather. Tomorrow the sun would shine again.

Aunt May drove us to the train. Squashed together on the back of the truck with our cousins, Doug and I bounced, laughed and shouted as the old Chevy bucketed round the bends. Still laughing we descended at the station. A moment later the engine appeared in the distance and we ran up the ramp to the little platform where we waved and shouted for the engine driver to stop. At first we thought he had missed us but then the train slowed and finally ground to a standstill. In single file we trudged over rough stones alongside the track, past the long line of goods wagons to a single carriage behind the engine. Extending his hand, the guard pulled Doug and me up the high carriage steps. Aunt May handed in our bag and a small paper parcel. Dell passed me a rolled up comic.

"From David," she called waving madly.

The whistle blew. Clouds of grey smoke billowed past the windows and our cousins stepped back as the train began to move. For a short time the truck kept pace alongside the carriage, its occupants grinning and waving, until finally it slipped back and disappeared from sight. Doug opened the paper package to reveal two pieces of chocolate cake and some almond cookies. I unrolled the comic from David. He had sent a brand new Mary Marvel. We ate, holding the comic between us and nibbling around the almonds in small bites. Twenty minutes later the train pulled into our station. Mum was on the platform. She waved to us and kneeling on the seat, I waved back, happy to be home.

Four

On Sunday mornings my mother used to pack me off to the Methodist Sunday School. Four years old and dressed in my Sunday best I rode my tricycle, pushing up hill for two blocks then along a narrow track across a vacant lot. In autumn I lingered there feasting on wild blackberries and in summer, to pick wild flowers. Ahead was the church but first I had to cross the broad, river-stone parking area at the Farmers' garage. This required effort and pushing hard on the pedals, I bumped my way over the stones.

In church I sang, joining in the choruses while pretending to read the words in my hymn book. Through word and music I absorbed the requisites of humility kindness and forbearance. The prayers inspired me with hope and I developed a child's trust in a heavenly father who listened to my prayers and if I was good, would willingly fulfil my every need.

On my first day of school in 1944, Fran walked beside me on the mile long stretch of main road to the infant school where she left me in the care of a large lady wearing a long dress. The infant mistress, Miss Sibble, kept strict control over her flock of five-year-olds. Any child who swore had their mouth washed out with carbolic soap and the smallest misdemeanour resulted in a sharp smack, as I discovered when I took my nice new drawing book and pastels outside at playtime. On my return to class, I proudly showed Miss Sibble my picture. Never had I been subjected to such a tirade and when I backed away, she had caught my arm, gripped me firmly and slapped my legs.

I sobbed out my woe to Dad. "Sorry, pet," he said ruffling my hair. "You have to go back. Everyone has to go to school."

A short time later, Miss Sibble retired. The students were relieved, and I suspect the teachers, also a lot of parents — several of whom had been to the school to complain about the way she treated their children.

Doug celebrated his first birthday that year. Both Fran and Ray left home and I catapulted from being the adored baby of the family to the eldest child. One moment I was playing dress-up and fairies, the next swamped with responsibilities.

Now, seven years on and with father so ill, my chores increased. I helped with the weekly wash, prepared vegetables and ran messages as well as gardening and cleaning. Some of these chores I took upon myself but soon resented. Afraid of being seen as uncaring, I grumblingly did as my mother expected. Rarely did I go to the gully, or to play with friends.

Two weeks after our return from the farm, Dad came home from hospital looking thin and tired. Mum began part-time work at a cafeteria and Grandma took over the preparation of our evening meals.

A new school year began and Doug and I raced off, eager to see our classmates again. My new teacher, Miss Webber, arranged her students in order of talent and I sat smugly amongst the brightest students in the first row of desks. What did it matter if I could not spell?

At playtime I searched the playground for my best friend, Ming. Her real name was Margaret Olive but I called her Ming. For years we had run to and from school together, racing along the clay path beside the main road or in summer, through the grass where hare-bells bloomed and clouds of tiny blue butterflies rose to surround us. Ming was a year younger than me but that did not matter because we always found things to talk about. We rode our big sister's bicycles to the library, the swimming baths, and to Girls' Brigade meetings. We collected Weet-bix cards, swapped stamps and practiced our gymnastic skills swinging upside-down from the branches of the cherry tree in Ming's front yard.

Unable to find Ming in the playground that day, I called at her house on my way home from school. Her mother led me to where Ming lay listless in her bed.

"Ming?" She looked so different, my eyes went misty, my tongue thick. At last I managed, "I missed you today."

"Hello, Ana." Ming turned to face me, her brown eyes sad. "I missed you too. Who's your new teacher?"

I explained the class seating arrangements and Miss Webber's threats of dire punishment for those who did not work hard. Soon Ming's cheeks were rosy and between sips of orange cordial, she told me how her big sister had won a radio in a raffle. "I love listening to the stories and the music. Even the football and the races," she confided with a smile.

When I left, Mrs Thomas walked with me to the gate. "Come again soon," she said.

Ming's time at school was irregular. Whenever she had to stay in bed I changed her library books, took her flowers from Mum's garden and delivered the homework set by her teacher. She was my best friend. In the good times, when she was strong, we cycled to the Presbyterian hall in the High Street to attend Girl's Brigade. When she was ill I went alone and on the way home, lingered in the summer sunset to window-shop the deserted main street. On dark winter nights I peddled home as fast as I could. Occasionally, the compulsory carbide cycle lamp clipped to the handlebars would fail. Unable to ride on the road without a light, I instead scooted at great speed along the pavement until I reached the bakehouse corner. In the street ahead tall hedges and trees created cavernous shadows along the footpath. To avoid confrontation with any fearsome creature, real or imaginary, that might hide there; I wheeled my bicycle down the middle of the road. I marched along, singing loudly and with great fervour.

God will take care of you,
for all the way, through every day.
He will take care of you
God will take care of you.

And perhaps He did, for I always returned safely home.

One morning Miss Webber took our entire class to King Edward Park where a large stork, blown off its migratory course, had taken up residence at the fishpond. None of us had seen a live stork and apart from their reputation as a delivery service for newborn babies, knew nothing about them. We walked in a crocodile line to the park entrance where all talk ceased. At a signal from Miss Webber we tiptoed forward.

The stork stood at the pond's centre, its image reflected in the smooth water. Awed by the sight, the children in front stalled and were bumped forward by those in the rear. By the time we righted ourselves the stork, taller than any of us, was moving slowly away, each delicate step creating multiple circles on the surface of the water. At the far end it paused, still as a statue.

Behind the stork, on a branch of an elm, a girl sat swinging her legs. I thought it odd the bird did not react to her presence and puzzled, I stared hard at the girl.

"It's Ming," I said out loud.

"Where?"

"Over there, in the tree."

"I don't see anyone." My classmate whispered afraid the teacher would hear us. "There's no one there, Ana."

"On your feet, everyone," Miss Webber spoke softly. "Move back the way we came in. Quietly now."

Still watching the girl I thought was Ming I joined the line and when she gave me a cheery wave, I raised an uncertain hand in response. When I looked again the stork was out of sight, the tree empty.

At the end of class I ran all the way to Ming's house to ask if she'd been to the park. I found her sitting on a box in the back yard, reading. "Wasn't the stork huge?" I asked.

"What stork?"

I was wrong. Yet the girl looked so like Ming. How odd.

"Your teacher asked me to bring your homework." I pulled the papers from my bag to show her when a sudden gust of wind sent them flying across the grass. Laughing, I chased after them.

"Let them go. I don't want them." Ming's happy cry was followed by a strange sound and I turned to see her bend forward, blood dripping from her nose.

"Put your head back. Here, have this." I offered my handkerchief then watched in horror as her blood flowed down my school bag and pooled at her feet.

"No. Get, Mum," she pleaded. I was already running toward the house.

Mrs Thomas came with a large bath towel that turned red before our eyes when held beneath Ming's chin. "Ana. Run to the corner and get Doctor Richard. Now, please," she added as I hesitated, still looking at Ming trying to catch the blood soaking through the towel. Dark lines ran down her thin arms and dribbled from her elbows. "Ana! Go!"

I ran and pushing open the surgery door, gasped my message to the lady behind the desk. The doctor left at once, pulling on his overcoat and leaving instructions as he hurried out the door. My mind awhirl I returned to Ming's place, knocked at the door and waited. Like us, Ming's family did not have a phone and the houses on this stretch of road were few. Perhaps Mrs Thomas did not know the people next-door.

The door opened. The doctor came out carrying Ming wrapped in a blanket. She looked so small as he eased her gently onto the back seat of his car. "I'll drop by in an hour. Let you know how things are," he said.

Mrs Thomas wiped her tears with the corner of her apron. I searched my pockets for a handkerchief then remembered leaving it in the back garden. As I squatted at the outside tap, washing the blood from my bag, Mrs Thomas called me indoors. She had made tea for us both and added extra sugar. On a happier occasion the sweet drink would have been a treat. I sat opposite her, stirring my tea, not knowing what to say.

"You and my Margaret have been friends for a long time. Good friends. I don't think you've ever had an argument. Thank you for fetching the doctor, Ana."

"I've been practicing running for my father. We don't have a phone either. He's ill and Mum says he cannot get well."

"I'm sorry," Mrs Thomas held my hand. "We may both lose someone we love. Margaret has leukaemia."

That evening, as Mum and I cleared the table and stacked dirty dinner dishes in the sink, I asked her what leukaemia was.

"A disease of the blood," she said.

"Do people with leukaemia get well again?"

"Rarely. Why do you ask?"

"Ming has leukaemia. Her mother told me today. Ming had a terrible nose bleed and Mrs Thomas asked me to get the doctor. When Ming went to hospital her mum cried. So did I."

"Is this true?" Mum turned to look at me, a bundle of cutlery in her hands. I thought her concern meant she was sorry for Ming and perhaps for me. I nodded yes. A snort escaped my mother's nose as she dropped the knives and forks into the sink. "I always thought the child looked consumptive. Why you chose her for a friend I'll never know. I don't want you going to the Thomas house, Ana. Do you understand?"

Head down, I busied myself drying dishes, hiding my hurt. I did not understand. I was allowed to visit other houses. Why not Ming's? Was it because her father was a gardener? I dared not ask.

On Saturday, I was out of bed before the sparrows put their boots on. I planned to secretly visit Ming after church the next day. If I hurried through my chores this morning, I could go to the library and choose books for us both.

I carried the tools down the clinker path to the vegetable garden. Before Dad became ill, I had loved helping him, sowing seeds and watering them; rushing to tell him when the tiny green shoots appeared. Now the hours of finicky hand weeding, hoeing and raking on my own had become hard work. I'd given up Saturday basketball to help at home. Even so, there was less time and more work.

Nor were things going well at school. I'd been downgraded twice, my seat in class now two rows away from my clever friends. Imagine my dread when Miss Webber asked me to remain behind after the final bell. When we were alone, she leant back against her desk, her eyes searching my face.

"Well, Ana, I am concerned at your recent lack of diligence. Can you tell me why your work has changed for the worse?"

"No, Miss Webber." I hung my head and longing to be out of the room, dug the toe of my shoe into a crack in the floor boards.

"I think I should come to your house and have a talk with your parents."

My head snapped up, my eyes on her face. Miss Webber had soft skin and fine frizzy hair that curled in tight little ringlets about her ears. "Please don't do that, Miss Webber," and through copious tears I blurted out about Dad being ill and Mum working. I told her about Ming and of Grandma moving in to our house and how there was no time to do all the things people expected me to do. Miss Webber listened, her head to one side, her hands clasped loosely in her lap. When at last my sobs faded, she took my hands in hers.

"Ana, look at me. I am sorry. Now, I think you and I need to work together to improve your schoolwork. You are a bright intelligent child." She looked directly into my eyes. "Will you let me help you?" I nodded. "Very well, we will say no more today." She released my hands and I gathered up my things. At the door I looked back. Miss Webber was smiling.

I crossed the empty playground and lost in thought meandered slowly homeward. Startled by the sudden whinny of a horse I halted and finding myself alongside the horse paddock, clicked my tongue to call the ponies. Ming and I loved them. When called they would amble to the fence and push their soft noses into our hands in search of treats.

The horse that startled me was new; silver grey, fine boned and fidgety, very different from the familiar, and solid brown ponies. The silver horse nuzzled my hair, which made me feel shivery all over, but when I put out a hand to pat her, she tossed her head out of reach. Unsure, I waited to see what she would do. Again she pushed her soft warm nose into my hair and blew little snuffles that spread strands across my face. I laughed aloud, pleasure dispelling my despondent mood. Gently, ever so gently, the horse bunted my shoulder before trotting off to join the other ponies.

For a week or more, whenever I passed the paddock I stopped, hoping to see the pale horse but the only occupants were the three brown ponies. I sought out the owner of one of the ponies and asked her who owned the silver horse.

She shrugged. "I don't know. I've never seen a silver horse."

Could I have imagined such a thing? The horse looked real — but so had the girl in the tree. This silver horse was different from either the fiery horse that came when Doug nearly died or the beautiful dream horses, so vividly remembered from when Dad collapsed after haymaking. Nevertheless, I was convinced all brought the same message. Things were about to get better.

Shortly after my talk with Miss Webber I was summoned by the school nurse, stripped to my vest and those awful navy-blue school knickers we all hated and given a thorough health check. Sticks in my mouth, instruments with lights in my ears and eyes; I even had to cough on demand when my back was tapped.

"Good, nothing to worry about." The nurse's brisk comment was a relief.

The note sent home to my parents suggested I be given malt with halibut oil to build my strength. I also needed new glasses. Mum was upset.

"How can I be responsible for the health of child who refuses to eat her greens and who would rather go hungry than eat milk puddings? And with your father off work so often, where is the money for new glasses supposed to come from, the tooth fairy?"

Grandma calmly stitched her embroidery, waiting for my mum to stop finding problems. Gran was my mother's mum but they were so different. People said I looked like my mum. Yet she and I . . . well, sometimes I wondered if I had been swapped at birth!

"Rose," Gran said when Mum stopped fussing, "I would like to buy Ana's new glasses."

With the help of my new spectacles I threaded the fine needles Gran used for her embroidery. Gran, unlike Mum, was never upset. She stood tall, moved with an easy grace and never left the house without first putting on her corset; even if only going as far as the letter-box. Doug and I fizzled into sniggers whenever we caught sight of the heavy, peach coloured garment—which was not often as whenever she washed it, our gran hid her corset between two bath towels, pinning it securely in place with large safety pins. Neck to knees we called those old corsets, all bones and laces and rows of hooks and eyes. Well, I supposed, when armour and chain mail went out of fashion, they had to give the workers something else to make.

Gran tried to turn me into a lady. "Walk. Slowly, Ana, slowly," she instructed, often with despair in her voice as the book balanced on my head slid to the floor and I collapsed in a fit of giggles. About the house, under her watchful eye, I did my best to please her but the moment I went out to play I tugged off my shoes and hat, pushed them into the front hedge out of sight and ran off to join the boys. Ever hopeful of being invited to share in their games, I followed them to the rubbish dump where they shot rats with BB guns. I even offered to help collect the empty bottles they sold to the bottle man — anything to be a part of their gang.

Miss Webber kept her promise to help me with my schoolwork and introduced me to Maisie, who, with exemplary patience, showed me how to sort the letters that became mixed on the page. She said I had mild dyslexia and between us we would fix it. Maisie was the kindest person ever and when I finally found the courage to tell her of the white horses and the kotuku, she gave me a hug, saying I'd been given a special gift and must never be frightened by it. Slowly, week-by-week, my marks in class improved.

Dad went to see a natural healer and returned home all smiles. Because the aluminium pots we used were now thought to poison our bodies and weaken our brains, he replaced them with new enamel saucepans. A man delivered a brand new motor mower and for a while, until the novelty wore off, Doug and I fought over which of us would mow the lawns. Our dad seemed so much better. He smiled more, helped us with our schoolwork and sent us to play with our friends.

I had almost finished the weeding when Dad appeared at the end of the veggie patch carrying a large cardboard box. He grinned a greeting then stooping, worked his way toward me, filling the box with the pulled weeds.

"Come on, up you come," he held out his hand. Smiling and shaking my head I stood without help. Dad pulled a face. "You are right. Better we don't both end up in the dirt."

We stood looking at each other. My dad was so thin. His old gardening jacket hung in loose folds, while his trousers bunched about his waist and his belt, newly punched with additional holes, was wrapped almost double. Even his shoes gaped around his feet. As he looked at me an expression of gentle wonderment smoothed his face and I felt his love flow over me.

"Ah, Ana you're growing up fast." He drew me close and I was surprised to find my forehead pressed to his shoulder, my nostrils filled with the smoky smell of his jacket. I had indeed grown tall as my last remembered hug was at third shirt button level. For a long, tender moment we held each other. Finally we stepped back and looking into father's eyes I saw and understood acceptance. Acceptance of how things are and of doing the best we can with current circumstances. I resolved there and then to give more, to be willing to do all that needed doing — for father, Ming, and for mother too.

"Thank you pet, you've done a grand job here. Off you go now. Go do something nice."

Dear father. He always understood.

The following afternoon I set off for the hospital freewheeling along the main road with my gifts for Ming hidden in a brown paper bag in the basket on my bike. At the entrance to the ward I waited with a growing group of visitors until a nurse lifted the brass bolts on the doors allowing us in. Embarrassed by the clatter of my leather-soled shoes I tip-toed the length of the ward. Unable to find my friend, I asked a nurse.

"Miss Thomas is in a single room. Are you her sister?"

"No, we are friends."

"I'm sorry. Only family may visit her." I did not have to ask. I knew how ill Ming was. Swallowing hard to keep back my tears I held out the book, the bunch of flowers resting on top. "Please give her these," I said and thrusting them into her hands I hurried out, down the verandah steps and across the lawn.

Ominous clouds darkened the sky. Wanting to be home before the storm broke I pushed my bike hard against the strong southerly wind. Someone called from behind me and as I wobbled to a stop, Ming's older brother Ian halted alongside. "Hello, Ana. I thought I recognized you leaving the hospital. Were you visiting your father?"

"No. I went to see Ming but was not allowed in. Family only, the nurse said. How is she?"

Ian looked down at his shoes. I looked too. His feet were huge. He was tall and thin, like a stick insect and though not handsome, his face was clear skinned, not pimply like other sixteen-year-olds I knew. He had the same brown eyes and straight dark hair as his sister. As we stood, holding our bicycles, the first sting of sleet struck us from behind.

"Quick, into the church porch," Ian said and pushing our bikes we ran. There was just enough room for us to squeeze into the alcove with our bikes. Side-by-side we watched horizontal rain fly past the entrance. Without the coat Mum had told me to bring — she thought I was going to play table tennis at Peter's place — I was freezing. I tugged my jumper sleeves down over my hands. Ian unclipped a rolled-up raincoat from the carrier of his bike and shook it out. "Here, take this," he said. He was wearing his school shorts, his bare legs covered with goose bumps and turning blue.

"Let's share." I sat down, my back against the door and making room for him, spread the coat over our legs. There was a small pause then we both spoke at once. "Are you going to leave school this year?" I repeated when Ian indicated I should speak first.

"If I get a scholarship I will. I'm aiming for a diploma of horticulture. What do you want to do, Ana? What course will you take when you move to High School next year?"

"I'm not sure. I want to be a veterinarian but Maisie told me I would have to train in England. It costs a lot of money and with Dad being so ill . . . Maybe I could be a librarian? My Aunt Libby works in the library. And Ming and I talked about opening a florist shop together. That would have been nice." Realizing I had admitted to a future without Ming, I stopped talking. "Sorry," I mumbled.

Ian pleated the sleeve of his raincoat into a neat tight pack. "It's all right. I've accepted Margaret may only have a year or perhaps two . . ." He pulled the sleeve open and let it fall, his hands raised in a gesture of submission. "I like to think we are born for a purpose and when that purpose is completed, we can go home to where we came from."

"You mean going to heaven is like going home?"

"Yes. There's a part of us lives for ever, elsewhere, while the physical part of us, born here on earth, is here to learn."

"Like taking a test or an exam?" I asked intrigued and wanting to understand.

"Mmm, yeah. Things that make us better, stronger."

"But Ming is only eleven and others are old. Does that mean some people are slow to learn or for some reason have to do more?"

"Perhaps. Maybe some come not to learn but to be an example, to teach others. Our Margaret is sweet and kind. She never complains. I've learnt from her." Ian's fingers pleated the coat sleeve a second time.

I stared out at the rain, thinking of my father and all the things he'd taught his children; the way he provided for us and showed us how much we were loved. Mother too. Though often impatient, she fed and clothed us exceptionally well. Something in what Ian said made me see the difficulties in my life as blessings rather than disasters. If I could hold onto that idea instead of feeling angry or disappointed when things did not go as I hoped, I could say to myself, 'This is a test. Do your best.' That was easy to remember. 'This is a test. Do your best.'

"Pardon?" Ian stood at the entrance looking back at me. "Come on, Ana. The rain has eased. We'd better go before the next big shower."

I passed him his raincoat and watched as he pushed his gangly arms into the sleeves. "Thank you. I'm glad you called to me." I felt embarrassed and my cheeks were hot.

"Yeah. See you." With a brief salute he swung his leg across his bicycle and rode out onto the road, his body bent double against the weather.

My disappointment at seeing him ride away was acute. What had I hoped for? That he might cycle home with me? Ian was leaving school and probably had a girlfriend. He'd have no interest in a pre-teen with an unruly mop of curls and fisheye glasses. Rather than follow him, I rode home through the back streets where the industrial buildings provided shelter from the wind and rain.

"This is a test. Do your best," I shouted at the cloud filled sky, my words echoing back off brick and tin as I sped along the pavement of the deserted street. "This is a test. Do your best!"

By final term Ming had been absent for weeks. Mother remained adamant. I must not visit Ming at home. For a while I left notes and little surprises in her letter box. But without replies, my goodwill faded and I found a new friend. Lynn often invited me to her home where cheery greetings of, "Hello, Ana. How are you today?" were decidedly different from my mother's tight-lipped demands to know if I'd completed my chores and homework. What had I done to make my mother so distant? I yearned for the kind of warm friendly relationship Lynn shared with her mum.

The day Ming arrived back at school and ran to find me, Lynn and I were holding hands and laughing. At the sight of Ming standing nearby, her pale face a pinched expression of hurt, I froze. In that moment I didn't want to be her friend, I wanted to be *me*.

"What do you want? I'm busy," I snapped and turned away from her.

My stupid selfish act escalated into a playground war. We each gathered supporters and refused to speak to each other or the opposing girls. Whenever we met, we thumbed our noses at each other and once a group of Ming's supporters passed me holding their noses and complaining of a bad smell. The whole affair was deplorable as a dozen or more juveniles searched for power in the worst possible way: that of hurting others. Our feud raged on and when the term ended, Ming and I parted without saying goodbye. Bristling with hurt pride, we ignored each other throughout the summer holidays.

Preparations for my transfer from primary to secondary school were complete. IQ tests and vocational guidance interviews finally over. Stacks of text books rested on the floor at the foot of my bed, a new uniform hung in my wardrobe and Fran wrote promising me a watch for Christmas.

When Mum told me of a new bicycle waiting for me at the bike shop, I begged to go immediately to fetch it. A vision of Lynn's new sports cycle; a gleaming dream of shiny blue and white, with gears, hand brakes, a broad padded seat and a dynamo light filled my mind. I couldn't wait to show her my twin model.

But Mum had chosen an up-right roadster. It was the most expensive gift I was ever likely to receive and I hated it.

At twelve, my diplomacy was not strong. I tried logic, anger and pleading but mother refused to exchange that green monster of a bike for a sports model. It was sturdier, she said, and would last longer. As usual, mother's word was law.

Christmas arrived to the sound of brass bands playing carols beneath strings of coloured lights in the streets. High Street was closed to traffic on Christmas Eve. Crowds of people walked on the road calling out greetings and throwing confetti and paper streamers over one another while small boys armed with water pistols terrorized anyone in their path.

When the new school year began I rode the new bike because I had to. Walking two miles carrying heavy text books would have been foolish. We do what we have to do. Besides, of all the bikes crammed into the school bike sheds, mine was not the worst, and by mid-term I'd saved enough pocket money to replace the narrow leather seat with a broad cushioned one. My disappointment in the bike was miniscule compared to the worry of fitting in at a new school.

Students from a large number of primary schools attended the local High School. Of the four courses available to girls, the top was a literature course, nicknamed the Brains Trust. To our surprise Lynn and I found ourselves on this course and there struggled with the complexities of French verbs, trigonometry, algebra and science. For the whole of our third form year we moaned our way through long hours of homework and studied for numerous tests in subjects we had not previously heard of and were certain we would never, ever use.

Most pupils in our class had holiday jobs and steadily growing bank accounts. Those who planned a professional life talked of working part-time while attending university. I was sure I could do the same. But each time I raised the idea with Mum, she changed the subject. Lost, with neither goal nor plan I plodded on.

Five

Mid-way through my second year at high school, the Principal announced a new uniform, a change from the heavy serge gymslip, blazer and tie worn through the hot summer months. Instead we were to have a navy linen pinafore and a short sleeved blouse. Overjoyed with the news, I rushed home to tell Grandma.

Most days I arrived home to find a trail of discarded clothing; my kid brother's school bag, shoes, socks and jersey left in the living room. On this day I peered into empty rooms. There was no one about. Rather than disturb the silence, I removed my own shoes and walked back down the passage in stockinged feet. My cat wound herself about my legs. "Just you and me, puss," I told her, scooping her into my arms.

A note from Dad stood propped against a biscuit tin on the kitchen bench. Uncle Harry, he explained, had been gored by a bull and was in hospital. He and Mum had borrowed Lily Stuart's car and taken Gran to the farm to keep an eye on our cousins. Doug was with his friend Dudley and I was to spend the night with our neighbour, Mrs Stuart. There was a kiss and a P.S. *We will be back at lunchtime tomorrow.*

The thought of Uncle Harry being gored made me shudder. The old bull we kids had scratched and talked to while on the farm had no horns. It would be the young bull. His horns were not large, but big enough make a nasty hole, or holes . . . poor Uncle Harry. Tomorrow I would make him a get-well card. Meantime, my own news would have to wait and pushing disappointment aside, I turned to practical things. Puss, her grey tail stretched long and flat, crouched beside her bowl waiting to be fed. The tinned food she ate smelt terrible, like fish guts left in the sun. I hurriedly filled her dish, gave her a pat and went outdoors.

Overhead the sky stretched pale and clear, the air still, a sure sign of frost. My arms full of bundled sacks and scrim I toured the garden covering anything likely to be damaged by frost; the lemon trees, mother's favourite purple Lasiandra and the delicate pink Luculia already in bud. On my way back to the house I paused in the twilight stillness. A small night bird, its pinions dark against the bleached sky, swooped low over the house and out to the paddocks beyond. Hunched against the cold, my hands deep in my pockets, I watched it fly out of sight. Previous sightings of unusual birds brought sadness into my life. I hoped this was not another presage.

"Hurry up, Ana. Dinner's nearly ready." Fergusson Stuart's voice carried clearly across the deserted street where lighted windows glowed orange and in the still frosty air, columns of grey smoke rose like spears from nearby chimneys.

"Shan't be long," I called back.

Mum sometimes let me borrow her red scarf. I found it in her drawer and taking advantage of their absence, lingered in my parent's room. It never changed. I felt for the photograph tucked in its usual place as were all the other items in mother's drawer: in all her bedroom drawers, in the linen and kitchen cupboards, and in the boot cupboard in the washhouse — everything neat and exact. In our house, you could open any cupboard in pitch darkness and guided by memory alone, be certain of finding what you wanted. It would always be there. My bedroom was the exception. Often messy and undusted, the state of my room was, my mother said, an abomination.

"Hello, Mystery Man," I addressed the photograph. "Would you like to tell me your name? No? Very well, you may go back in the drawer." How childish I thought, smiling at my silliness. Sometimes my need to let off steam came out in inappropriate ways. Ordinarily I kept a tight rein on my behaviour and did my best to fulfil the expectations of my parents and teachers.

Would there ever be a time when I could be *me*? Who was I anyway? Just a long list of what other people thought I ought to be.

Over dinner I asked Mrs Stuart if I might attend the church youth group as usual.

"Yes, dear, your mother told me. Are you sure you don't mind walking alone?"

"No. It's Friday, late night shopping. There'll be people about. We usually go to the Black Cat Café afterwards, but I'll be home by ten."

I stood before the hall mirror buttoning my coat over Mum's red scarf. Dark curls bulged over my ears. My head resembled a blimp. I'd never be beautiful. Not even pretty and tapping my reflection on the nose with my knuckle, I offered consolation. "Don't worry kid. You can run faster, climb higher and think quicker than most. You'll be all right," then calling goodbye, I set off at a brisk pace for the church hall.

After two hours of exhaustive youth club activities my friends and I glowed with warmth and wellbeing. Amid a friendly cross fire of light hearted banter, we stepped out into the night. In two and threes, some wheeling bicycles, all talking and laughing, we made our way through the late night shoppers in the High Street. The café was a block beyond the main shops. We all trouped in and while the boys went to the jukebox, the girls squeezed up to fit eight around a table. A moment later, the Everley Brothers belted out *Wake Up, Little Suzie*, setting us off, singing along with the chorus.

"Can I buy you a milkshake, Ana?" Peter's request surprised me. His family recently moved into a house near the bakery and we sometimes cycled to church together.

"Yes. Strawberry. Please. Thank you." My words came in little hops and I hung my head to hide my embarrassment. Helen gave me a nudge.

"I think he's sweet on you."

"Don't be silly," I nudged back, "I hardly know him."

Half an hour later the carefree conversation and laughter flowed with us from the cafe to the street and as we separated into smaller groups, Helen glanced nervously down the now dark and empty street. "I hate walking home alone. You all go south while I go north," she said pulling her woolly hat down over her ears.

Helen. Wait." Peter looked at me. "We could walk with Helen. Then I'll double you home on my bike."

"Fine, but I mustn't be late. Mrs Stuart is expecting me by ten."

"Marvellous." Helen linked an appreciative arm to mine and we set off with Peter riding slowly beside us. Ten minutes later as Helen called good night from her gate, I settled on the bar of Peter's bike ready for the ride home. A short distance down the road we heard an ominous flapping sound, wobbled a few yards then stopped. Peter pushed the bike under a street light and squatted down.

"Sorry, Ana, we'll have to walk. Look, the nail is right through the tube." While we did not dawdle, we did not hurry either and by the time we reached Stuart's front gate it was after ten thirty.

I found Mrs Stuart by the open fire in the sitting room, her embroidery in her lap. My apologies tumbled out followed by an account of Helen's fear of walking alone, Peter's kindness and the flat tyre.

"I don't know what to think, Ana. I've been very worried. And I saw the boy at the gate."

Saw the boy? Did she think I'd been out on a secret date? Indignant and defensive I pushed my point describing Peter as a considerate young man who went out of his way to escort two young girls home. Surely she could see that.

"There, there. I'm not accusing you. It's late. I think we should both go to bed. Off you go. I've put a hot water bottle in your bed." With a sigh Mrs Stuart gathered up her sewing, placed the guard before the fire and left the room. I followed, guided by the soft glow of a night light in the guest room.

The lamplight fell across the bed, its covers turned back over an invitingly fat patchwork eiderdown. A book of short stories lay beside two plump pillows and on the bedside table, chocolate biscuits and a glass of milk. Her kindness made me feel guilty; ungrateful. Tiptoeing back down the passage to her door I tapped gently. "Mrs Stuart, the room is lovely. Thank you." There was no reply.

Tucked snugly in the big bed I drifted into sleep thinking how nice it was to have Peter single me out.

A sharp rat-a-tat-tat woke me and as I reached for my glasses, Ferguson's mop of springy curls appeared around the edge of the door. "Morning, Ana. Mum said to tell you she is making breakfast."

At the breakfast table, Ferguson, his eyes twinkling with cheekiness, gave me the thumbs up sign behind his mother's back. What, I wondered, did that mean? Then, as I opened my mouth to make amends for the previous night, Mrs Stuart placed her plump hand over mine.

"Hush, Ana. I'm sorry I doubted you. Let us say no more."

My offer to wash the breakfast dishes refused, I repeated my thanks and ran home, leaping up the steps to where my cat waited in the morning sunshine. With the windows opened, the scent of early jonquils filled the house and humming happily, I checked the cupboards for something nice for my parents' lunch. I found a can chicken soup and with basil, garlic chives and oregano from the garden, I could make herb bread.

Midday came and went; my parents still not home. I flipped an organza throw over the lunch table and went to the gully to look for pussy willow buds. Far above me a faint green haze tipped the bare lacework of willow branches. An intense aroma of humus rose from the nearby bog and near the boxthorn, where last year a fantail had built a tiny cobweb-lined nest, I found a few silver-grey buds tinged with red. I climbed up then stretched to pull the branch down. As it sprung back, I heard the sound of the awaited car turning the bake-house corner.

Back along the track I sprinted, clambering up the slope to the road as Lily's Vauxhall turned onto the grass in front of her house. Mum stepped out. Happy to have my parents back home I called and waved, but without looking my way, Mum ran up the steps and into Stuart's house. Dad remained in the driver's seat, his head bowed, looking for something on the floor I thought. When I reached the car, my smile faded.

"Dad?" Fear weakened my voice. It came out in a squeak. I tried again. "Dad, are you all right?"

"Yes, pet. I just need to rest a while."

"Out of the way, Ana." Mum's fingers grasped my upper arm and turned me aside. "John, slide over on the seat. Lily will drive you home from here."

With my father safely in the passenger seat, Lily squeezed her bulk behind the wheel, eased the car onto the road and across to our front gate. Mum and I followed. Ferguson ran ahead to open the front door. Between us we helped Dad inside and onto his bed. Mum lifted his feet and slipped off his shoes. Lily went to fill hot water bottles.

Dad lay back against the pillows breathing heavily. Frightened and with tears about to fall I reached for his hand.

"You may go, Ana." Mum pointed to the door.

I left, dragging my feet and misery from the room. Hidden behind the garden shed, I took a stick and stabbed the soil. Hurt, angry and sniffing loudly, I mentally defended my right to be with my father. Again and again I jabbed until the stick broke and I threw it away.

Puss came and curled herself into my lap. Her soft grey fur reminded me of the pussy willow and I returned indoors to fuss over an arrangement of silver buds and yellow primroses. I carried the vase to the bedroom door and having received a nod from Mum, placed it on the dresser beside the bed. Wanting to be of help, I offered to make a cup of tea.

"When the doctor has been, he should be here soon."

Mrs Stuart followed me out, puffing quietly along behind me. "Will you help me bring your mother's things in from the car?" she asked.

Glad to have something to do, I carried in boxes of apples, turnips, fresh eggs, meat and bacon brought from the farm. Mrs Stuart called Fergusson from the couch where he'd been reading Superman comics. Together we walked to the street. Fergusson brushed against me. "Sorry about your Dad, Ana," he whispered.

An unusual stillness pervaded our house, the quiet broken only by Dad's breathing and the tick of the mantle clock. I even heard the tiny clicks of Mum's rings as she twisted her fingers together, clasping and unclasping her hands. Hoping to remain in her good books by doing something useful, I cleared a space on the lunch table and began my homework. In the atmosphere of waiting that filled the house, even the scratch of my fountain pen nib on the page seemed intrusive.

For an hour we waited, separate, but united in our listening for the doctor's arrival. He came at last, climbing the steps to the open front door with a firm steady tread.

Beyond the swagged curtains in the hall the inaudible voices murmured on. The clock ticked steadily into the afternoon. What was taking so long? At last I heard the squeak of mother's bedroom door and the doctor's voice.

"Well it's your decision, John. I wish I could persuade you otherwise. I'll see you again on Tuesday." Mum and the doctor moved out onto the front verandah where he said, "If you come to the surgery at four o'clock I'll have some medication ready for him."

I heard her agree, say thank you and goodbye. The silence was no longer oppressive. Mum moved about in her room opening and closing drawers, no doubt unpacking after the night away.

Now was the time for tea. I plugged in the electric jug and as I returned from emptying the teapot, Mum entered the kitchen ahead of me. Her brow creased in a frown, she rubbed her forehead with her fingertips. She looked both tired and worried. "Ana. Have you seen my red scarf?"

"I wore it last night. I hope you don't mind. I'll get it." I stopped. The scarf had not been among the things I unpacked earlier. My mind flew over the events of the previous evening. I remembered hanging it beneath my coat at the church hall. What then? I'd not worn it home. I must have left it in the cloakroom. "I'm sorry. I must have left your scarf at the hall. I know I didn't have it at the café or Helen's place."

"Helen's place! What were you doing at Helen's place?" Mum glared at me. Behind her, the jug boiled. Soon it would bubble over but I dared not move to turn it off. Rushing my words as I watched Mum's mounting anger and the now bouncing jug, I explained Helen's fear of the dark, Peter's offer of help, the flat tyre and having to walk home.

"How could you? I leave you for one night. *One* night! Whatever will Lily think of us?"

I then did a very stupid thing. I told her Mrs Stuart had seen Peter at the gate. But when I tried to explain my account of events had been accepted, Mum's agitation increased. She called me bad hurtful names. Then whack! She slapped me. We stared at each other. Mum, red faced and shaking, me holding my cheek, stunned, unable to believe such a thing could happen.

I recovered enough to push past her and turn off the jug. Water covered the bench. Hearing a sound I turned. Dad stood hunched between us, one hand gripping the doorframe, the other pushed against his stomach.

"What is happening? Rose, my dear, I had no idea you were so upset. I'll have the operation if you think it's best." Grey faced, he crumpled to the floor.

Our spat forgotten, we knelt beside him. Mum patted his cheeks then wrapping her arms about him, rocked him like a baby. After a moment his eyes opened and he looked at us as if he had forgotten who we were. My mum kept repeating his name and smoothing his hair.

"Now, Rose, don't fuss so. Help me up," he said. Between us we managed to seat him on a chair and a short time later, one either side of him, we walked him along the passage back to his bed. I left them there and went to make tea. Tears stung my eyes and my hands shook. Bent over the sink, I splashed cold water onto my face. Here I was, at home with my parents, my family. Yet never in my life had I felt so alone.

Mum declined my offer to cycle to the surgery saying she wanted to talk with the doctor. Hoping for a comforting word, I helped her into her coat but her brusque farewell cut deep, adding to my feeling of rejection.

From across the hall I watched my father sleeping. Then closing my bedroom door, pressed my face to the pillow and sobbed.

I woke next morning to an overcast day, the sullen grey sky reflecting my mood. Without Doug's noisy nine-year-old chatter and music from the radio, the brooding atmosphere within the house felt charged for change.

Rice bubbles snapped, crackled and popped as I poured milk into the bowl. Mum passed the kitchen door carrying her chamber pot (discretely covered with a cloth) and went outdoors to water the pansies. Her pansies grew bigger and better than any others. Their scent however, was questionable. Water swished and sloshed as she scrubbed the chamber pot in the washhouse and I rinsed my breakfast dishes at the kitchen sink. I wanted to ask questions about Dad and Uncle Harry. Nervous after yesterday's incident, I needed to choose the right moment. The arrival of Doug and his friend Dudley interrupted my thoughts. A mini assault team of two, their sandals slapping the concrete path, they ran shouting around the house to the back door. By the time I put down the plates and moved to the back step, Mum had already grasped the two lads firmly by the collar.

"Quiet. It is Sunday," she said.

"Sorry." Doug shook himself as Mum released her grip. "I came to ask Dad to fix the kite. It broke." He held out a tangle of cord, paper and wood. "Dudley's mum said I can stay another night or two. Can I, please?"

Mother looked at Dudley who nodded.

"My Da saw the doc's car at your place. An' it was in the paper about Doug's uncle being gored in the backside by a bull. Said he had broken ribs an' all. So mum said if it helps, Doug can stay with us." Dudley looked expectantly up at my mother who faltered a moment under his direct gaze.

"Well, yes. Please thank your mother for me. Shush!" She shook a finger at Doug. His excited yipping stopped. "Now, wipe your feet and come indoors. Get the little case, Douglas. You will need clean clothes for tomorrow. And please, be quiet. Your father is sleeping."

I returned to the kitchen. Mum came to stand beside me. "Ana, wrap half a dozen eggs and put some of those apples into a bag for Dudley to take home."

"Mum?"

She turned to face me, resignation in her expression and without speaking, waited. I wanted to ask about Dad's operation and whether it would make him well again, but my courage failed and instead I asked would she mind if I went to church.

"You may go. Don't forget to bring my scarf home."

While I polished shoes on the back porch, the boys buzzed back and forth collecting things to take to Dudley's house. Throughout this activity the brooding stillness remained. It hung over me as if waiting for the right moment to reveal itself.

Dressed for church, hat in hand, I fronted the mirror in my room and heard Ferguson greet the boys at the gate.

"I've a note, a phone message for your mum,"

"I'll take it to her." Doug raced off round the house leaving Dudley and Ferguson discussing the frangible nature of kites while Mum, who'd also heard the boys, went to collect the note.

From my room across the passage I could see Dad packed about with pillows. He wore baggy striped pyjamas. With hurried steps Mum returned to the bedroom, pulled her coat from the wardrobe and bending to kiss Dad on the forehead told him the doctor had telephoned. "I'm going across to Lily's to ring him back. I shan't be long."

I waited until the boys left and my mother out the gate before tiptoeing across to Dad. Kneeling down I took his hand in mine and held it against my cheek. He opened his eyes.

"Ah, little lightning-bug." He called me that because when I was small I ran everywhere instead of walking. "All dressed up I see. Where are you going?"

"I'm going to church."

"Church?" He sounded puzzled. "Is it Sunday?"

"Yes. I'm going to talk to Reverend Warrender about becoming a local preacher. My friend Muriel, Lester Pierce and me; we plan to do the eighteen month course together. I am a bit young but the Reverend promised to consider my application and let me know today."

"Have you mentioned this before?"

"No. I wanted to be sure I was accepted first."

"Well, well." Dad's eyes closed again. Still holding his hand between my own, I leaned closer.

"Dad? Will the operation make you well again?" I felt his fingers squeeze tightly about my hand and for a long moment he said nothing.

"No, Ana. I don't think anything can give me back the health I once had. We must face facts. Death is part of life, as hallowed and as beautiful as birth."

"But I want you here. I need you."

"Listen to me, pet," Dad pulled me closer; tucked my head beneath his chin and wrapping his thin arms about me continued. "Of course you will miss me as I will miss you. Miss all of my family. The house, the garden, even Smoke, wicked old cat that he is. I am but one person in your life. You have a family who love you. Love them back. You don't have to be strong or brave, just caring and kind. And be honest — with yourself and others. My dear, Ana." Dad rocked me ever so gently in his arms. Finally he kissed the top of my head and held me to one side to look at me. "You're a good girl Ana. I'm proud of you. Remember that."

I leaned over to kiss his cheek. "I will. I promise," and as his fingers slid from my hand we exchanged small smiles.

"Ana."

"Yes?" Paused beside the bed, I could hear Mum's footsteps approaching the gate.

"Ana, your mother's life has changed too; in ways she never imagined. You are young and more adaptable to change. Just think things through and do your best."

I hugged him once more. To my surprise there were no tears. What he said was true. While bemoaning my own losses I'd not considered Mum's situation. I had expected her to remain the same.

"I promise," and with a last touch of my hand on his shoulder I slipped quietly back across the passage.

Mum paused at my bedroom door.

"You still here, Ana? You'd better hurry. You'll be late for the service."

"Just going. I'll bring your scarf home. Goodbye. Bye Dad."

"Thought I'd missed you, I was about to ride on." Peter said when I met him at the corner.

We rode in single file, bumping along the narrow grass track through the shortcut. At Princess Street we paused for a solitary car then crossed into the gravelled yard of the Ford garage. The rough roadway potted with oily rainbow-coloured puddles led directly to the church. As we approached, the sun broke through. The tall porch pillars gleamed. I steered my bike around the water thinking this scene was like life itself.

Once past the hard and rough areas, there was recompense. The church represented that reward.

With five minutes to spare, we parked our bicycles and entered the Sunday school hall. Gym equipment left out from the day before filled one end. Small boys hung from the parallel bars, their ties askew and shirt-tails out, their hair neatly in place, thanks to a generous dab of their dad's Brylcreem.

All except Lester, whose fine dark hair fell forward and hid his eyes. He sat on a form near the door, his focus on a spinning yo-yo that rose and fell with hypnotic rhythm. A handsome youth renowned for his quick wit and devil may care attitude, Lester, already out of school, worked at the Post Office.

"Hello, Les. Can you walk the dog?" Peter asked. The yo-yo kept its steady rise and fall. I felt Lester's gaze from beneath that stock of hair. It gave me an odd feeling of being excited and unsure at the same time. Lester Pierce went out with talented girls; dancers, musicians or top basketball players. Pretty, clever girls, none of them like me. Turning to the younger children, I clapped my hands for attention.

"Time for church. Come along, please." Peter and I helped the lads tidy their clothing; tucking in shirt tails and tying shoe laces before sending them, single file into the church. My class, a group of seven-year-old girls sat on either side of me. Peter, Lester and some other boys settled in the pew behind us. During the silent prayer I heard the faint whine of the yo-yo travelling its string. Further down the pew someone sneezed, the most almighty sneeze imaginable and when we left the church for classes in the adjoining hall, I heard Lester say, "Watch your step, lads. You might slip."

My little group of students called me Miss Dockery which made me feel like a grown-up. The lessons, simple stories, were read from a prepared syllabus but the children's questions challenged my limited knowledge. The syllabus was basic. I wanted to know more, to better understand my place in the great scheme of life. The girls also wanted answers and I found myself turning their questions back to them, asking what they thought. This brought about lively discussions and sometimes arguments. I discovered that if I paused and closed my eyes for a moment, the right answer would come. My own words often surprised me for they described probabilities, things I had not previously thought of. At first startled, I came to trust the words that came from within me; simple satisfactory answers that kept everyone happy.

Later, as the girls helped me tidy the room after class, Lester appeared in the doorway. When the children left he came in. He held Mum's red scarf and ran it back and forth through his hands.

"This yours?" he teased, whipping the scarf behind his back as I moved to take it.

"My mother's actually."

"You'd better have it then. I found it Friday night, on the steps outside the hall."

"Thank you."

"Er. Er. Um."

"I have a name you know," I teased back thinking he might have forgotten who I was.

"Yeah, I know, Ana-banana." Lester shrugged and grinned. Then with a flick of his head that shook the hair from his eyes, he looked directly at me. To my surprise his eyes were a startling clear grey. "The seniors are having a dance in three weeks, the twenty-first. You want to come?"

The curtain of hair resettled. I blinked. "Yes, thank you. I'll have to ask my mother . . ."

"The scarf lady. Ok. I'll see you. By the way, we start the local preacher's course Wednesday week, 7:30 at the parsonage. See you there if not before." Hands in pockets, he sauntered off to join a group of people on the church steps leaving me surprised and excited. I'm sure my mouth hung open.

"It is unusual to find such dedication in one so young," the Reverend murmured shaking my hand as he confirmed my place on the course.

I sped home, shoved my bike into the shed and pulling the scarf from my bag, flew indoors to share the news. For the second time in a week I found the house strangely quiet. My steps hesitant, I followed the passage to my parent's room and looked in. The bed had been made, the quilt tucked neatly over the pillows, the rose satin eiderdown folded at the foot. The room so hushed, so deprived of life; the incidents occurring here in the past twenty-four hours could have been imaginary. I retraced my steps through the empty house and found a note on the kitchen table.

Ana, I have taken your father to the hospital.
If I am not home by 5 o'clock, peel some potatoes for tea.
There is cold meat in the safe.
Mum. P.S. Feed the cats.

The last of my happy anticipation dissipated. A strong feeling of injustice took its place. For years I'd seen myself as the hero in Dad's life-saving rush to the hospital. At night, in bed, I imagined how I'd run to the nearest phone and call for an ambulance. I'd raced to and from primary school, preparing for the day I'd prove myself useful. 'Run quickly Ana. Get help,' they'd say and I'd run like the wind.

It was so unfair. Almost as bad as my mother seeing me as a peeler of potatoes and feeder of cats. Would I ever have an opportunity do something important? My emotions hurtled from desperation to anger and back again — until I remembered the things father said earlier in the day and my indignation turned to searing shame, quickly followed by a flood of hot tears.

The young are adaptable, he'd said. True. My bout of tears over, I immediately felt hungry and while eating a sandwich lunch, decided to help Mum by polishing the floor.

Armed with a tin of wax and polishing cloths I got down on my hands and knees, buffing over and over until the linoleum shone. By the time I finished, my disgruntled feelings had vanished.

Afternoon became night. I lit the living room fire, placed Mum's slippers on the hearth to warm and turned on the lights making the place cosy and bright. She came at last and wearily closing the door behind her, looked about.

"This is very nice. Thank you, Ana." She took off her coat and sat at the table while I busied about fetching her slippers and making tea. As I put the tea tray on the table, Mum made a little choking sound and began to weep. For a moment I hesitated, then standing behind her, put my arms about her shoulders and laid my cheek against her hair.

"Sorry, I am so sorry," she sobbed. "I'm lost without John and feel too old to be working. I don't know how I will manage without him."

"We'll help you, Doug and Gran and me. We'll manage, you'll see," I smoothed her hair, and saw it was already speckled with silvery strands that glittered like frost in the morning sun.

Mum reached up and for a precious brief moment, caressed my arm before reaching for her cup. Over tea I learned Dad was to have his operation next morning and I offered to walk to school for the week leaving my bike for Mum to ride to the hospital. It was the last week of middle term. I'd not have much to carry. While dishing up the vegetables, I shared with her my plan to become a local preacher and asked if I might attend classes at Reverend Warrender's house on Wednesday evenings. Then, keeping my tone casual, I told her of Lester's invitation to the dance. I carried our plates to the table praying she would say yes.

"Very well, Ana. You may go."

She must have known I wanted to hug her, but such emotion was too new, too sudden. Besides, I'm sure my pleasure showed as I voiced my grateful thanks.

Later that night my prayers were thankful too. My faith in the doctors' ability to ease Dad's pain was absolute. And with my place in the study group assured, I'd see Lester on Wednesday evenings. His invitation to the dance meant . . . what? That he was interested in me? Fizzy with excitement, I snuggled deeper in my bed and closing my eyes, drifted into peaceful slumber.

Six

At recess next day Lynn and I spread our raincoats on the damp grass and sitting cross-legged, opened our school lunch boxes. Behind us an imposing three-storied block of classrooms provided shelter from the wind. Out beyond the quad, pewter clouds filled a leaden sky that merged with unpainted asbestos prefabs, the dullness reflected in puddles along the broad concrete path that led to the music hall. Used for gym on wet days, the hall accommodated end-of-term dances and of course, music. Today the choir was practising, *D'ye ken John Peel,* their voices rising above the chatter and laughter of a thousand students.

In between bites of a peanut butter sandwich, I chronicled the weekend's events, Uncle Harry's accident, my dad's collapse and his operation earlier in the day. Then skipping the bit about Mum slapping me, I shared my excitement of studying to become a local preacher and lastly, Lester's invitation to the dance.

"Golly. Nothing like that ever happens to me. Fancy you having a real date with Lester Pierce." Lynn's voice was loud.

"Who has a real date?" asked one of a group of girls next to us.

"Ana has."

"Really? Who with?"

"Where are you going?"

"What will you wear?"

The conversation shifted from clothes to make-up and even hairdressers. Mum cut my hair. I'd never been to a hairdresser, but I let the girls think otherwise and basked in their attention until the bell sent us scattering.

"Bye, Ana. See you tomorrow," they called as if we had known each other for years rather than minutes.

After school Lynn walked with me, wheeling her lovely sports cycle along the pavement as far as the shops. "Ana, I hope there will be good news about your father."

Sobered by the thought of Dad's operation and wondering what news awaited me at home, I gave her brief hug then calling goodbye, waved as she rode away. I hurried then, dodging between shoppers in the main street my bag thumping hard against my back. At the top of our street I paused for breath. Before me the road dipped down to the green sprawl of the creek then up, to where our house nestled into the side of the hill.

Two bicycles rested against the front wall, the sacking bags Doug used to carry newspapers hanging empty from the bar. Suddenly fearful I raced down the hill, leapt the steps two at a time and pitched in through the open kitchen door. Two lads looked up startled, each holding a fat cheese sandwich, their mouths round black holes.

"Heck, you gave us a fright. I thought it might be Mum," Doug said.

A loaf of bread, butter, cheese and the amount of spilt cocoa and sugar on the bench told me why. "Well, you should clean up before you sit down to eat. Why aren't you out delivering your papers?"

"All done. We did it together. Dud's good at chucking."

Dudley grinned at the praise. "Don't worry. We'll clean up," he said.

"Good. Make it quick. I'm going to change." I knew I was acting the big sister. The age gap between Doug and I had inexplicably widened over recent months. We seldom spent time together. "Mum's coming," I called, as through the window I saw her turn the corner and cycle down the hill.

Sounds of rushed activity came from the kitchen, scuffling and clipped conversation; a thump, then laughter. "Man, that floor is slippery." Dudley rose rubbing his backside as I returned and quick thinking Doug hastily set cups and saucers on the bench.

"Hello Mum. I'm making tea for you," he said as she appeared at the door.

"That's nice." Mum teetered on the polished floor and reaching out I took her arm. She had not mentioned the shiny floors and now my effort to please seemed to be causing a problem.

'Is Dad all right? Is the operation over?" Doug took Mum's coat and hung it over the back of a chair.

"Yes, it is over. He is doing well." Mum drew us close and gave us both a squeeze. 'Now, about that cup of tea, Doug?" she asked, bending to kiss the top of his head.

"Can we see Dad tomorrow?"

"Not tomorrow. Wait until the weekend. He will be stronger then."

Doug and I accepted this without question. Mum had hugged me. That was enough. The idea she might be fulfilling her own need for love and support never occurred to me.

The last days of the school week flew by. Flattered by the attention from girls I hardly knew, I pushed aside the possibility of being untruthful. Not in what was said, but in the unspoken as I became adept at evasive conversation.

On Friday after school I dallied alone in the High Street gazing wistfully at the window displays. In Mackie's shoe store I spotted a pair of red wedge sandals and slipped inside for a peak at the price tag. They were lovely but costly. While considering what I might do to earn the shoes, I saw my bicycle outside the butcher's and knowing Mum would be close by, searched for her. I found her in the bookshop where years before Cousin Cyril had bought Doug and me beautiful books.

"Mum, I've seen the most gorgeous pair of red sandals. Will you come and have a look? Please?" I asked, my fingers crossed behind my back. We stood side by side admiring the shoes and though Mum agreed they were nice I guessed her attention was on the price tag. "May I have them? Please, for the dance."

"I will have to think about it, Ana."

Not the answer I'd hoped for but better than an outright refusal. The dance was still two weeks away. If I kept my fingers crossed all the way home — mother might buy the shoes.

Grandma returned from the farm the following morning and as I helped put away her things she handed me a flat parcel. Opened, it revealed a length of silky white fabric that fell into soft folds when gathered. Mum sewed beautifully and made all our clothes. I immediately sorted through her collection of dress patterns and found the perfect style. Confident of making myself a dress for the dance if Mum or Gran guided me through the more tricky seams, I soon had their approval.

The first time we visited Dad after his operation, Mum warned us not to chatter as Dad was still weak and needed rest. No words could have prepared me for the change in him. He had somehow shrunk. Become so much older. His thin body now hardly a bump beneath the bedclothes. Holding back tears I laid my cheek against his chest. I loved him so much I wanted to stay there but feared my weight might hurt him.

Doug had hesitated by the door and I drew him to a chair beside the bed where he sat, puppet like, waiting for someone to pull the strings. "Doug's been staying at Dudley's place. They did the paper run together, did it in half the time." I squeezed Doug's shoulder as I spoke.

"Hello," Doug's voice came out high pitched and funny.

Dad's green eyes flickered then steadied. "Hello son. Tell me what you've been doing." With growing enthusiasm Doug described his time at Dudley's house and as he listened, Dad's face softened and a smile hovered at the corner of his mouth. When Doug finally paused for breath, Mum tapped his arm. He looked up, his face colouring. "Sorry."

Mum took Doug's place beside the bed, then catching my eye, and with a barely perceptible inclination of her head, indicated Doug and I should leave. We said our goodbyes and were at the door when Dad spoke, "Ana, the study class?"

I turned, smiling, thrilled he had remembered. "Yes. I've been accepted. The classes start on Wednesday. And Lester Pierce has asked me to the seniors' dance. I'm making a new dress."

My parents exchanged one of their secret looks and smiled. Watching them I felt the tight bubble of apprehension within me burst. My tentative moves toward independence were finally being accepted. Father was safe here in the hospital and Mum, well; we were getting along just fine.

Doug walked silently beside me through the dim corridors. I guessed he found the changes in our father's appearance hard to accept. When we emerged and stood together blinking in the bright sunlight, I wondered about Ming. Was she here? Dare I sneak in to see her? Better not, best not to upset Mum.

"Dad will be well cared for here. It's the best thing, Doug." I walked ahead between the freshly turned flowerbeds to the cycle rack near the gate. There I swung my leg over Dad's old roadster and rode slowly along the edge of the tar-seal waiting for Doug to catch up. I'd learned to ride on this bike and being too small to sit on the seat, rode under-bar with Dad holding the carrier. Round and round I went in big wobbly circles, his hand keeping me steady until I learned to steer straight.

"Race you," Doug yelled in my ear as he came alongside. Head down he sped off toward the main road. Tossing dignity aside, I followed. Out of breath and laughing we met up at the corner. "I won. You buy the ice-creams," he crowed pointing to the ice-cream sign outside the park store.

For a moment we looked at each other and then shaking a finger to emphasize the words, recited: *We do not buy ice-creams on Sunday! Oh no! Whatever next!* We then doubled up with laughter because one Sunday, while out with Grandma, we had asked her for an ice-cream; our innocent request refused.

Long before Grandma came to live with us, she and Grandpa sometimes visited us on a Sunday. They were terrible days, dreaded by us all. Fran and Ray usually disappeared. One time, Grandma discovered Doug and me playing Snap. With a single smooth movement, she scooped our cards from the table and put them in a high cupboard before lecturing us on the evils of card games. Sent to my room in disgrace, I quietly stitched new clothes for my doll. Gran found me there and again read the riot act, this time stressing Sunday as a day of rest, not work. Petulant, I pursed my lip and asked, politely, what she thought I might do. 'Read your bible, child. That is what Sunday is for.' Thankfully, by the time Gran moved in with us, her attitudes had softened.

The August school holidays arrived and I rose early, keen to begin sewing. Everything was ready. The old treadle machine dusted and oiled; pins, scissors and sewing instructions organized, but first I had to wash the breakfast dishes. Through the window I could see Doug on the clinker path that bordered the kitchen garden. He pushed a piece of paper beneath a stone then strode across the dirt, his lips moving.

"What are you doing, Doug?"

"Measuring." He returned to the porch and lifting a book from the step, waved it at me. "I borrowed this from the school library. It's all about vegetable gardening. I thought I'd do the planting for Dad. It's the right time, isn't it?"

"Yes. It is."

"Good. I'll start today." Opening the book he read aloud. "First prepare the ground to a fine tilth. What's a tilth?"

"You have to hoe the soil until it's fine and crumbly. Then rake it smooth."

"I can do that." He unfolded his skinny schoolboy body and disappeared into the shed, reappearing a moment later with tools slung over his shoulder. I stared after him, torn between wanting to share his enthusiasm and help with the garden or doing my sewing. The sewing won. Two days of rain midweek halted the garden preparations but I sewed on, pinning, tacking and machining, unpicking, pinning and sewing again until my dress was a perfect fit. By Friday my eyes were tired and my head ached from four days of prolonged concentration. When Gran suggested a day outdoors would clear my head, I went to see how Doug was progressing with the vegetable garden.

A large area of ground awaited planting, the fine even soil dark after the rain. The sound of Doug's happy whistling led me to the shed where I found him going through the numerous tobacco tins used to store a variety of plant seeds.

"Hey, Ana, what are these?" He thrust a tin of tiny papery seeds at me.

"Parsnips maybe. Or Queen Ann's Lace. I'm not sure."

"Don't worry. I'll ask Dad on Sunday." He put the tin to one side. "These I know. Want to help plant them?"

The morning passed quickly. My headache disappeared and by the time Mum called us for lunch, we'd planted half the garden, the neat wooden labels standing erect at the top and bottom of each row.

Later in the day Mum returned from the hospital all smiles. Our dad was stronger. We no longer needed Mum with us when visiting him. On Sunday afternoon, we hurried to Dad's room where Doug immediately produced the tobacco tins from inside his shirt.

"What are these seeds? We're spring planting for you," he said. By the time the visitors' bell rang at three o'clock we had all the information needed to complete the garden project. This time there was no reluctance or concern as we hugged Dad goodbye. Without conscious thought we had delegated our previous care of him to the nursing staff and were now free to do what young people do best. Be ourselves.

What I lacked in patience I made up for with determination as I attended to the tedious task of hand stitching ten buttonholes. At last the sewing was done, my dress ironed and ready to wear. Mum bought the red sandals and left them on my bed for me to find. Grandma remembered a necklace of red and gold china beads from long ago. Together we hunted through boxes of stored items and found them. They were a perfect match to the wide, shiny-red plastic belt.

On the evening of the dance, the last rays of the setting sun created a golden glow in Mum's room. Allowed to wear makeup for the first time I lifted her lipstick from its place beside the neatly ironed handkerchiefs in her dresser drawer. The gold cover popped apart, the cherry red within complimenting the line of shilling sized buttons that fastened my silky white dress. I applied the colour with great care, rolling my lips together as I had seen my mum do, then stepping back, admired the effect. My eyes seemed brighter, my hair darker, shinier and when I tilted my head, my curls brushed my shoulders. I saw myself as Deanna Durbin, confident and pretty, a long swag of dark hair flowing down my back. Smiling, I held out my dress and with a graceful twirl, curtsied to the beautiful girl in the mirror.

I returned the lipstick to the drawer, my fingers instinctively searching the back corner for the photograph. Finding it, I held it up to the fading light. The man was slim, his tanned skin dark against the whiteness of a shirt worn half buttoned and the sleeves rolled back from his wrists. Who was he and what part had he played in my mother's life? For as long as I could remember my questions had gone unanswered. Mum's response, if any, gave me nothing.

"What do you think, Grandma?" I waited, framed in the doorway of her room, my newly acquired femininity on display.

"Come in child. Put on the light. Let me look at you." Gran stood, her hands clasped at her waist, a gentle expression on her face. "You look lovely, Rose," she called. "Come and see your daughter."

Confident of approval, I held out my arms and turned before their admiring gaze. For a moment, Mum looked down, one finger resting on her lips. Then, as my grandmother slid a comforting arm about her waist, she smiled. "Your dress is very nice, Ana. Now run along and enjoy the dance. Please don't be late home."

Half-way down the passage I turned to look back. Arms linked they stood in the doorway; their heads touching, light spilling out around them, watching as I walked away. A line had been crossed. The barriers that held our separate positions, lowered. Each of us felt the shift in our relationship and I was happy to leave them holding the child I had been.

I avoided the shortcut on the way to the hall, walking instead past the library and picture theatre in the High Street. I left my coat unbuttoned to show my dress and when strangers smiled and said hello, I felt so happy, I could have danced down the street.

"Ticket please." The young man at a card table in the foyer held out his hand.

Ticket? I had no ticket. My confidence vanished. Had I somehow misunderstood? Lester had been no more than polite when we met on Wednesday nights and had not once mentioned the dance.

"Les, Lester Pierce invited me," my words stumbled out. "Is he here?"

The young man pulled open the heavy swing door to the main hall. "Lester!" he bawled, "you're wanted. Out here," he added with a jerk of his thumb.

Lester jumped from the stage and weaving between the couples on the dance floor, made his way toward me. Stepping into the foyer he let the door swing shut behind him. That simple action, the closing of the door, changed the atmosphere. The people around us, all the sounds; music, voices and laughter faded mysteriously away as we stood, looking at each other. Lester wore a dark suit and a bow tie, his debonair appearance heightened by the curtain of fine hair that fell across his brow. With a now familiar toss of his head, the hair flicked back and his eyes twinkled.

"Put away your coat, Ana-banana and come in." His voice gave me a feeling of welcome, but before I could answer, he turned and disappeared back into the hall.

Alone and puzzled by his behaviour, I lingered in the ladies' cloakroom until the crush became too much. Forced out, I trailed a group of older girls into the main hall and found Muriel. She smiled up at me from her seat at the end of the hall. "Ana. Come and sit with us."

Muriel introduced me to her friends and as we chattered, Lester passed us with a pretty blonde girl who gazed adoringly up at him as they glided across the floor. Seeing them turned my dreams to dust. Near to tears I bit my lip. Time to buck up, I told myself and turning to the shy young man beside me, I coaxed him to talk. A moment later Peter's elder brother, Eric, asked me to dance. With practiced ease, he twirled me across the hall to meet his friends. For the rest the evening, the boys, all lively country lads, made sure no girl was left sitting alone.

I was having such a good time I forgot to look for Lester and was surprised when he confronted me as a new partner in a lively Gay Gordons. He grinned and gripping me about the waist spun me so quickly I became giddy and would have fallen had he not held me. Still grinning, he passed me to my next partner and whirled away in the opposite direction. Everyone was singing along to the music, tunes from the war years and I could hear Lester's voice above the others. When we met up again, the band was playing *Abe, be my Boy*. Lester changed the words to 'Annie be my Girl' and guided me into the centre of the ring where couples who preferred not to change partners, danced at a more leisurely pace.

He complimented me on my dress and admired the necklace. Out of all the girls in the hall, Lester Pierce was talking and singing to *me*. I was totally smitten by his attentions. The music changed to *Cock o' the North* and Lester's strong voice again took the lead as he bellowed 'Auntie Mary had a canary up the leg of her drawers.' Laughing hopping and skipping he whirled me back into the circle and with a final cheeky grin, was gone.

When the supper waltz was announced and Eric's pals made a beeline across the floor, I hung back hoping Lester might ask me to dance. When he did not appear, I danced with the butcher's apprentice, his hands a patchwork of sticking plasters, his steps hesitant as he guided me through a stately slow waltz.

After my brief taste of Lester's undivided attention, I craved more but pretended indifference as I watched him incline his head and flash charming smiles toward half a dozen other girls. When the ladies' excuse-me was announced, Muriel gave me a hard nudge. "Go on, ask him. I know you want to," she said.

Perhaps Muriel had not heard the adage; 'It's polite to wait till you're asked'. I had, a thousand times. It was part of the precept of pride mothers passed to their daughters. Be it foolish or protective, the lesson was clear. Never show your emotions.

So I waited with a friendly face and a hopeful heart. I danced with other boys but when the lights dimmed for the last waltz and my new friends were swept away, their heads filled with notions of romantic dalliance, I sat alone. My disappointment was intense and rather than accept pity for the wallflower I had become, I slipped into a dark alcove beside the stage until the lights came on and we gathered to sing *God Save the Queen*. Not wanting the girls to know I would be walking home alone, I waited until almost everyone had gone. Outside on the driveway I gazed up at the sky, awed by the clarity and splendour of the Milky Way.

"Ana."

I turned at the sound of my name. Beneath the street lamp Lester drew on a cigarette then flicked the butt before stepping forward.

"I thought you were never coming. Come on. I'll walk you home."

For a fleeting moment I wondered what had happened to the courteous requests I'd been taught to expect. Words like 'May

I?' or 'Would you like me to?' It was a brief thought however, quickly replaced with a realistic 'You Tarzan, me Jane'.

At first we walked briskly for the night was cold but our pace slowed when the conversation turned to our theological studies. We had both read well ahead and considered several alternative responses to the theories offered in our textbook. Soon our banter became a more serious exchange and when we stopped for the third time to argue our point of view, Lester laughed.

"Who would have thought quiet little Ana would have so much to say. Where did you learn all these ideas?"

"When I was very small my grandfather and I used to make up stories. He asked questions that made me think."

"You're still very small," he teased and tucking my shoulder beneath his encircling arm, held me close as we walked on. At the corner of my street he stopped and gently turned me so we stood face to face. But Lester was looking up at the stars so I looked too. "Do you think we might continue our walk around the block?" he asked. "You would be home in less than fifteen minutes." Still gazing up at the night sky, he waited for my reply. I felt safe in Lester's company and thought what mother didn't know, couldn't hurt her—and I was not going to tell.

"That would be nice," I said and daringly looped my arm lightly across the back of his jacket as his arm again encircled my waist. On the clay track where the road dipped to the creek, we paused beneath the shiny leafed Karaka trees that overhung a sagging five-wire fence. The fetid smell of stagnant water mixed with the earthy aroma of fallen leaves rose from the gully floor. Yet this was, without doubt, the most romantic place in the world as I received my first kiss. It was brief, tender and alone. A single kiss.

For a short time we walked in silence before slipping comfortably back into conversation. At the front gate I tilted my chin, just a little, hoping there might be another kiss. Instead Lester ruffled my hair and in a rather gruff voice said he would see me at church in the morning. With a brief nod he strode across the street and up the hill. Halfway up he turned and walking backwards, waved goodnight.

Later, as I lay in my bed reliving the evening, I pushed aside a vague feeling of concern, a feeling that Lester was somehow different from other boys. I concentrated instead on the blissful and exciting moments, building them into romantic fantasies of lasting happiness.

Seven

In the weeks following the dance, Lester often walked me home after the Sunday evening services and while teasingly attentive, he was seldom as romantic as I hoped. On fine nights we sat on the wall by the gate talking until the curtains in the front room twitched. The twitch was a signal, say goodnight or run the risk of my mother appearing.

Late that year, 1953, a telephone appeared in our hallway. "For emergencies," Mum said. I guessed it was for Dad who was still in hospital but sometimes, when our homework and chores were done, she allowed Doug and me to chat with our friends.

The weeks of the final term flew by. Time spent with Lynn and playing tennis with Peter and his brother, Eric, meant my Sunday visits to Dad became irregular and I compensated by cycling to the hospital on Thursday evenings. I also began an evening art class. My teacher agreed to give me extra tuition as my abysmal results in math and French threatened to lower my aggregate in the end-of-year exams. I needed a high mark and art was my best chance.

Mum's presumption that we keep all previously set standards in the house and garden added to my treadmill of activities. Tempers flared as Doug and I argued over whose turn it was to wash dishes, mow lawns or weed the veggie patch. We squabbled over radio programmes, each switching to our choice, the sound escalating until Mum remonstrated and turned the wireless off. Our animosity reached a point where Doug and I delighted in taunting each other.

Mum and Gran became our adjudicators and punishments were handed out. The disciplines I received seemed harsh and I voiced strong opposition to the expectation, by being the eldest, I should assume a greater responsibility. Mum and I argued over the amount of time I spent away from home and what she called 'my apparent preoccupation in my appearance'— and my increased interest in Lester Pierce. I retorted that as long as I fulfilled my duties about the house and did my homework, I should be free to go. I did not run wild and came home on time. What more could she possibly want of me?

There had been a pause and then Mum said quietly, "Some respect, Ana. And your company now and again."

I tried. I really did. To escape my unhappiness at home I often went to the native park at the end of the street. At first I took my books intending to study but recently I'd found myself sitting idle, doing nothing at all. Now, to make Mum feel better, I stayed home.

In the classroom I struggled to learn, my marks lower than ever. I found the math subjects particularly difficult. None of it made sense. Lynn helped me until my whispered pleas for assistance landed us both in detention for the third time. She thought I should try harder and moved to a seat across the room. I knew Lynn was right and that annoyed me, because if she was right, then I must be wrong. I had tried to cheat and put my best friend offside. Embarrassed and full of guilt, I took the coward's way out and avoided her whenever possible.

At primary school I'd been top of the class, adding and subtracting with the best. It was the trigonometry and algebra that left me feeling stupid. One evening, exasperated beyond measure, I phoned my math teacher at his home and asked him to explain the homework to me. He did and for a short time my marks improved. He also offered me private tuition but Mum refused to discuss the idea, saying the cost was outrageous.

Lonely without Lynn my spirits lifted when passing the Thomas house on my way back from library, I saw my school friend, Ming. She stood on a box picking cherry blossom from the tree where years ago we had climbed and swung like monkeys. As I skidded to a halt in the gravel, she looked up.

"Ana. I've not seen you for ages." Ming opened the wicker gate to greet me, a cloud of pink and white flowers in her arms. Bright patches of pink showed on her cheeks and her brown eyes shone. "Come in. Come and talk with me. It's good to see you." She led the way to a seat in the sun. In our time apart we had grown from juveniles to teens. Yet somehow, Ming still looked very young.

"You're looking better," I said sitting next to her.

"It's called remission. Good days and not so good days. Tell me what has been happening. I want to hear everything."

Somehow we fitted two years of news into two wonderful hours. When I mentioned our new telephone, she became excited. "Us too, I'll ring you," she called as we waved goodbye.

The pressure of swotting for the end of year exams increased. Teachers gave our class extra free periods and left us alone to study. Some boys took advantage of the teacher's absence to fool about, throwing paper darts and making a noise despite the complaints of other students. The noise continued until one afternoon, Padma our top scholar, slammed shut her book, stood and demanded quiet. Jay, the rowdiest boy, retorted she should be the one to shut up because her nigger father had killed himself walking under a train. Padma ran crying from the room. Appalled classmates rose to manhandle the outspoken youth back to his seat. Most of us sat stunned.

Apologies were made and accepted. Nevertheless, the incident made us all aware of how edgy we were and when our form teacher suggested we stop studying and relax before our first paper on Monday, we did not argue.

Although Muriel was older than me, seventeen and a solicitor's secretary, we had become friends. She lived some miles away in the country and drove to and from town in her very own Austin 7. In the days between study groups at Rev.

Warrender's home, we often talked on the phone. During one of our conversations Muriel suggested we go to the pictures together. This weekend would be a good time—if I could persuade Mum to let me go.

Hopeful of earning her approval, I set about spring-cleaning my room. The wet newspaper I used to clean the windows made squeaky noises and Grandma came to see what I was doing. She complimented me. Said the room looked lovely then sat on my bed watching me. After a moment or two, I sensed something different and turned to look at her. Her physical body was as always. She sat erect, her hands clasped neatly in her lap, her small feet in their blue slippers placed firmly on the bedside mat. A strange thin cloud cloaked her upper body and as I contemplated this, Grandma looked up and smiled. The cloud immediately shot through with a rose pink radiance. A moment later she returned to her room taking the colours with her.

This sort of thing, seeing colours like halos around people, happened quite often. I had no idea what it meant. The only clue came from my teacher, Maisie, who told me I had a special gift and must never to be afraid of it. The only person I might have shared this phenomenon with was Dad. But now he was so ill, I did not want to bother him.

Mum agreed I could go to the movies and on Saturday evening she walked with me down to the street where she admired Muriel's car. Our plans to see Clark Gable and Ava Gardner in *Mogambo* had me bubbling with anticipation but Mum's wistful look as she stood alone at the gate waving goodbye made me think we should have invited her to join us. Now it was too late.

Muriel glanced sideways at me as she drove. "I've a surprise for you," she said, her eyes quickly returning to the road ahead.

"What is it?"

"You'll see." With her arm extended out the window, she turned into the parking area beside the theatre. "Come on. I see they are here ahead of us."

"Who?" I looked along the line of people waiting to buy tickets.

"Hurry up." Muriel pulled my arm, steering me around the end of the queue and into the plush reception area. The theatre looked very different at night. Soft lighting cast an orange glow over the heavy oak panelling and fantastic arrangements of exotic silk flowers filled the corners. People stood about in groups or lounged in armchairs, the smoke from their cigarettes drifting up to the ornate ceiling. Eric and Lester stood by the inner door and they each made a sweeping bow as Muriel and I approached. *That was a close squeak. What if Mum had come?*

"Good evening ladies, we have your tickets." With great gallantry, they escorted us into the theatre. An usher took the tickets and led the way to our seats. When the lights went out I was between Lester and Muriel. She leaned over and whispered in my ear.

"Nice surprise?"

"Yes. Thank you."

At half time Lester suggested the two of us go to the café across the street for a Coca Cola. I found a corner seat and Lester went to buy the drinks. By the time he came to sit down the customers had returned to the theatre.

"What have you been doing this week, Ana-banana?"

"Swotting for the exams, I really want a high mark. Some of the others don't seem bothered," I said and told him of the devastating moment in the classroom when Jay rudely reminded Padma of how her father died.

"Her grandfather," Lester corrected me, his voice tight.

"I didn't know that. But I remember the accident. Doug and I were walking home from school. We heard the train whistle then the noise as the wagons ran off the lines. We were way over on the main road and ran all the way to see what had happened."

"I wish I'd been way over on the main road." Lester sucked the last of his drink, his head in hands, face hidden. "Do you mind if I have a cigarette?"

I shook my head. We moved out onto the street, but instead of crossing the road back to the theatre, Lester guided me to a seat in the gardens surrounding the old water tower next door. I sat beside him wondering what Muriel and Eric would think of our disappearance.

Lester leaned forward, his elbows on his knees. The oil that held his hair back an hour ago had given up the effort and his fringe again hid his eyes. He drew on his cigarette and tapping ash from the tip, watched it fall.

"I saw him. I tried to stop him." Lester coughed and threw down his cigarette, twisting his foot in the grass to extinguish the butt. 'He was there, Padma's granddad, by the tracks when I cycled past. I called out hello. But he didn't answer, just stood there with his beads, praying. I had to take a telegram to the Schulz's place. On my way back I heard the train whistle and saw the old man move toward the line. I yelled to warn him but he stepped onto the track. I hadn't clipped my trousers and my cuff caught in the bike chain. I leaned down to free it, and heard the whistle, the wheels screaming on the rails. Showers of sparks sprayed everywhere. Wagons shot into the air. Coal spilled everywhere." Lester paused, twisting his hands as he relived the horror of the accident.

"When the engine finally stopped, the silence was worse. Flames lit the bracken and smoke filled the gully. It was like a nightmare. I dropped my bike and ran back to Mrs Schulz. She phoned the fire brigade. And the police, I think. When I went back for my bike two men were walking alongside the line. One of them shouted and I climbed through the wreckage to look—it was horrible, Ana. The old man I'd seen earlier . . . his head and part of his arm . . . they were cut off."

Lester wiped his sleeve across his eyes. "I felt sick. And I still feel sick when I think about it. Dad says I have to get over it. But I can't. I can see it and smell it and I just want to die."

Without speaking I moved closer and wrapped my arms about his shuddering body. After a bit he blew noisily into his handkerchief then apologized for being such a sook. "No better than one of your Sunday school class," he said with a watery smile. He lit another cigarette.

"Ana, there's something else I want to tell you, before you read about it in the newspapers."

As I waited for Lester to continue, I became conscious of so much: the hard wooden slats of the seat pressed against my back, my coat falling open, exposing my knees to the cold and a twisted clip on my suspender belt hurt the back of my leg. Far above us, the top of the great stone tower cut into a sky sprinkled with tiny silver stars.

Lester waited for my reaction. When I did not speak, he carried on. "I'm in trouble, Ana. I did a stupid thing. Jimmy Oats and me . . . and some others, we went joyriding."

"What's joyriding?"

"We stole a car—and crashed it."

"Was anyone hurt?" I asked, not really understanding the enormity of his confession.

"No. Not really, not seriously anyway."

"What will happen to you?"

"I have to go to court. Dad says he'll have to pay and he's pretty angry. I might be sent to the borstal. I could lose my job." He stared at the ground and sighed. "I'm sorry. I wanted to tell you myself. If you don't want to see me again—" He broke off as the lights came on outside the theatre and people appeared.

"Come on. We must go back." Taking his hand I pulled him across the street. We found Eric in the foyer looking at the posters.

"Where did you two get too? Cosy up in the back row did you?" He gave Lester an affable slap on the back.

"Where's Muriel?" I asked.

"Ladies' powder room." Eric indicated with a nod.

"Thanks. I'll find her."

Muriel stood before a large gilt framed mirror her lips in a pout as she applied fresh lipstick.

"I'm sorry, Muriel. I don't know what to say." Nervous and afraid of upsetting my friend, I wrapped the strap of my bag around my fingers.

"You don't have to say anything, Ana. I'm not your keeper. But please, tell me you didn't do anything stupid."

"Stupid? Oh, no. Of course not. We were talking."

"Nothing wrong with that. Now let's go."

We paused to thank the boys for the night out then returned to the car. Leaning back in the seat I closed my eyes. I wanted to reassure Lester I was not the sort to walk away because he was in trouble. I'd tell him tomorrow, after church.

Lester did not attend church. Nor was he at study class midweek and no one I asked knew where he might be.

By the end of the week only two exams remained. Algebra, which I was sure to fail, and art. Determined to do my best, I buried myself in revision all Saturday. On Sunday I dressed in my best and returned to church hoping to see Lester. He did not appear. Neither did his mother, her place in the choir stalls unfilled.

The day was warm with little wind; a rare occurrence, but I found it hard to be cheerful as after lunch, I cycled slowly to the hospital. My recent visits to Dad had become heart-rending as the morphine prescribed to ease his pain dulled his mind. I could only sit beside him, holding his hand, hoping he knew I was there.

On my way home I stopped by Ming's house. Surprised to find the grass overgrown, the blinds drawn and the front porch littered with newspapers I wondered where everyone had gone. Lonely and sad, I pedalled home to find Mum with yet another migraine, Gran's door closed and Doug's bike gone from the shed. With no one around, I mooned about, my loneliness increasing by the minute. I decided to write Lester a letter and in my best grown-up manner, explained my willingness to remain his friend and the hope he would distance himself from the lads who got him into trouble. I wrote, crossed out and rewrote many sentences until finally satisfied, I copied the whole page afresh and posted it before I could change my mind.

First thing Monday morning I went to the school library to return a borrowed book. Jay and his friend Martin were on duty.

"Hello, Goggle-eyes. I hear Lester Pierce has been fogging up those gig-lamps of yours."

Jay really was obnoxious at times. I chose to ignore him, handed over the book and hurried out.

The morning's algebra exam was every bit as devastating as I expected and I longed for the final bell. That night I went to bed early but was unable to sleep. Through the wall between our rooms I could hear Gran turning in her bed, her unrest accompanied by many small sighs. Sometime after midnight I finally fell asleep.

"Ana. Wake up. I have something to show you."

I rolled over. Gran stood beside my bed. With short sighted eyes I squinted sleepily at the bedside clock, reached for my spectacles and pulling on my dressing gown, stumbled after her as she led the way to the back door.

"Look."

Small fluffy clouds blanketed the entire sky, every one brilliant rose-red. At first awed then overjoyed by the magnificence I stepped out onto the lawn and with arms outstretched, dipped and twirled over the dew covered grass. I felt so light, so happy. When I finally steadied myself, the sun was above the clouds, the pink quickly fading to white. Exhilarated, I returned indoors to where grandma waited, a cup of tea already poured. For the first time since she moved into our home, I hugged her. It seemed the right thing to do.

"Thank you so much, Gran. If I live to be a hundred, I'll never forget today."

Eight

When I returned from school, there were cars parked at our gate but I didn't stop to think. I simply bounded up the steps and in at the back door as usual. The sight of Mum huddled on the couch with my aunts brought me to a halt. All three were sobbing.

"Dad?" I mouthed, barely able to breathe.

"No. Your Gran died three hours ago."

"It was so quick," Mum mopped her eyes then tucked her handkerchief into her sleeve. "Wasn't that incredible?" she asked after explaining how she had been with Gran because a migraine kept her at home.

No more than for me I thought as I sipped tea from the same cup Grad handed me only a few hours before. I'd been in the art room painting when she died; my subject, a morning sunrise, trailing willows, and in the foreground, a large white heron. When Cousin Cyril died I dreamed of a white kotuku that flew, circling higher and higher into the light. I now understood these white birds, like the white horses were omens. I also knew Gran was somewhere nice not too far away and although I felt sad, I did not cry.

When not helping to serve tea or answering the phone, I knelt on the window-seat in my room gazing up at the sky, remembering how it looked at sunrise. I heard Grandma's voice saying, "Wake up, Ana. I have something to show you." I'd promised never to forget this day. Nor would I, not now. Not ever.

At the funeral service, Doug and I shared a pew with our cousins from the farm. We sat close, our shoulders touching. Sunlight streamed in through the stained-glass windows. A mosaic of misty colours spread across pews and the polished oak coffin. In the strange soft light, the casket appeared very small. How could my grandmother be in a child-sized coffin? I soon realised I was confusing her physical stature with her presence. Whenever Gran entered a room, the atmosphere altered. Her serenity compelled attention and whatever she said had value. She listened to me, shared my joys, sorrows and concerns. How I wished I'd given more attention to the advice she offered. I would miss her in so many ways.

Our good neighbour, Lily Stuart arrived to oversee the wake. She came puffing up the steps carrying an extra teapot, electric jug and a mountain of clean tea towels. Ferguson followed bearing a large fruit cake as if it were the crown jewels. In a whisper he confided he helped make the cake and thought he might be a chef when he grew up. All the best chefs were men, he told me with a knowing nod.

After the burial, while the adults conversed indoors, we young ones perched sparrow-like along the wall by the front steps. David and I, Heather, Dell, Doug and Neil – with Ferguson tacked on the end. For a while the only sounds were an occasional sniff or cough as we each dealt with our loss. Dell spoke first.

"Do you remember Gran and Granddad going away for a long holiday and we all went to clean up their garden before they came home?"

"We had a working bee."

"All the hedges were cut and we had a bonfire."

"I lost my new butterfly hair clip."

"I spent hours stacking fire wood."

"Ana fell over and grazed her knees."

"I remember." I pulled up my skirt. "See. I still have the scars."

"I don't remember any of that." Neil looked at us as if we had all gone mad.

Doug turned to him. "You should," he said. "You let the chooks out."

We all laughed then. The eldest, David, who had taken me under his wing during our holiday on the farm, tried to remain serious. "It was no laughing matter," he said. "I was trying to catch them and you kids were useless, running around flapping your arms like lunatics."

I saw the scene as if it had happened yesterday. The six escaped hens, each a flurry of flapping feathers, racing across the garden on stiff little legs. Each time a child appeared in front of one it changed course, charging off again between the rows of vegetables. This to-do had caught the attention of the neighbours next-door.

The O'Reilly boys, older than any of us, were skinny beaky fellows who liked brown ale and ribald entertainment. Their backyard resembled a second-hand goods depot, only messier. There were piles of barrels, bottles and boxes, lengths of timber and old furniture. A bathtub filled with water and slimy weed stood in the centre of what had once been a lawn. The two younger brothers climbed onto a heap of rubbish and looked over the hedge.

Dell managed to return two chooks to the run. The other four crouched, visibly puffed, gathering the strength needed to evade the next onslaught of children. At David's instruction we crept stealthily toward them.

The moment we stooped to grab the hens, the O'Reilly's tipped back their heads and howled like wolves. Startled, the group on our side of the hedge stopped and seeing their advantage, the hens took flight. One reached the run and was let in. David secured another while the last two flew over the hedge into O'Reilly's yard. The two tipsy boys slid to the ground and with their bottles held upright above their heads, wove their way across the yard to where the hens huddled beside the bath tub.

In Grandma's garden we crouched behind the hedge peering through wherever we could find a gap. The boys drained the bottles and tossed them aside. Our attention was on Mrs O'Reilly, who sat on the top step at her backdoor watching her sons. Unaware of her audience, she leant back on her elbows and with her fat legs raised, gave us a bird's eye view of her pink apple-catcher bloomers. The sight was altogether too much and fearful of being caught spying, we stuffed our mouths with fists, handkerchiefs and even jumpers — anything to smother our giggles.

With exaggerated shushing the O'Reilly boys tiptoed closer to the hens, and then lunged. One flew off. The other, finding herself captive shot a stream of hot poo down the older boy's trousers and onto his bare feet. Cursing, he staggered back, toppled into the bathtub and disappeared. Only his hands, still holding the terrified hen, showed above the water. Letting the hen go, he pulled himself up, floundering about as water poured over the side of the tub. There he sat, his face strung with weeds, coughing and swearing, while his younger brother convulsed with laughter.

"Jesus, Mary and Joseph," the younger one gasped. "You do look a sight, Mick O'Reilly." He ambled over, offered his hand and was immediately swamped by a wave of dirty water. "What'd you do that for? I'll drown you, you mongrel," he yelled.

And it was on. With eyes as big as saucers and holding our breath, we crouched, glued to the gaps in the hedge.

"Just what is going on here?"

We spun about to find Dad and Uncle Harry standing behind us.

"You're supposed to be cleaning the bean frame and raking up the weeds. And how did these hens get out?"

Stammering our excuses, we had returned to work. Dad called 'chook-chook-chook' and sprinkled grain at the door of the fowl run. The hens rallied and flew back over the hedge to peck their way into the henhouse.

The moment our fathers returned to the front yard, we downed tools and fell upon one another laughing until too weak to stand, we rolled about on the grass.

"Did you see?"

"Weren't they awful?"

"And the swear words!' we gasped.

"Dell. Heather." At the sound of Aunt May's voice the memory faded. Together we slid from the wall and made our way into the house. "We'll be going home shortly. Collect your things and put them in the car." Aunt May shooed her brood back outdoors.

Everyone was leaving. Dad would not return from hospital. We understood that. That left only me, Mum and Doug. Doug and I were no longer close and Mum's headaches meant she spent most of her time resting in her room. I had no idea where Lester or Ming might be and seldom saw Lynn. I had no one to talk to. Father tried, but he was so weak now, real conversation was rare. I blew noisily into my handkerchief.

"Don't cry, Ana." David patted my back. "I'll miss Gran too, but I know she'd want us to be strong. She bossed me about but I liked her. I once heard her tell my mum that you had talent and if you slowed down instead of rushing into things, you could be anything you wanted."

"Gran said that?"

A wry smile creased David's face. "Give me a lively funny person any day; even if she does put tadpoles in my drink bottle!"

I smiled remembering how, when he found the tadpoles he had chased me and tipped the whole lot over my hair. The slippery little taddies slid inside my blouse and I shrieked in mock horror to let him know that was punishment enough. I had no wish to be dunked in the mucky pond where I found the tadpoles.

"I'm not going back to school next year," David said, "Dad needs help on the farm. That run-in with the bull left him with a lot of pain. He still uses a walking stick. I don't want to milk cows for the rest of my life, but I'll help until he's strong again."

"What would you really like to do, David?"

"Own a large truck. Long distance driving. I'd like that. What about you, what will you do?"

"I don't know. All the careers I like seem so distant. Whenever I make a choice, something or someone makes it so difficult, I just give up. I've no idea what Mum expects me to do."

David pulled something from his pocket. "I almost forgot. I've a present for you. Shut your eyes and hold out your hand."

I did as he asked then felt in my hand, a small smooth wooden object. Eyes open, my fingers slid over the polished surface, tracing the carved shape of a crouched baby rabbit. "David. It's beautiful. Did you make it?"

He nodded.

"Thank you." I looked up at him and felt yet another wrench. Our childhood was over. We were on our way to adulthood.

With the rabbit snug in my pocket I joined Mum and Doug to farewell our relatives, waving until the cars turned the corner. At bedtime, I tucked the carving beneath my pillow and comforted by David's kindness, soon fell asleep.

At school the next day, Lynn came hurrying across the quad toward me. "Did you write a letter to Lester?" she blurted when we met.

"Yes, but how do you know?"

"Some of the boys, Jay, Martin; they have your letter."

"They can't possibly. I posted it."

"I think they found it in a library book."

The rough copy! No. Please, God no. The over emotional words, whole sentences I crossed out as being too forward, too open. I'd have to brave it out.

The torment began the moment I stepped into the corridor.

"We've got your letter, goggle-eyes." Holding my rough copy high, Jay began reading to anyone who would listen. There were plenty who did.

The taunting continued throughout the day. I'd secretly wanted an identity at school but not like this. At the final bell, determined to show neither tears nor anger, I moved to leave the room but Jay blocked the aisle.

"Four-eyes has a boyfriend," he chanted waving my letter just out of reach.

Seizing my chance, I charged at him and snatched the page from his hand. Instead of being fazed as I expected, he laughed in my face. "It's a copy," he hooted pulling more folded pages from his back pocket. He tossed them in the air. "We've lots of copies. Got you, goggle-eyes."

There was no holding back the tears. I clattered down the concrete stairs and into the toilet block. Behind a closed door, my pent-up grief poured out. Huge sobs shook my shoulders. Spent, alone and miserable, I stood before the mirror staring at my red-blotched face. Life could never be worse than this.

True summer warmth arrived mid-November and I felt my spirits rise. Silver birch trees shed their catkins along the pavement and Goldfinches swung from the grass stems bordering the road. On Sunday morning, confident the peaceful atmosphere within the church would provide an increased sense of wellbeing I hurried to join others gathered to hear a lesson based on Matthew 5.39

'But I say unto you, that ye resist not evil: but whosoever shall smite thee on thy right cheek, turn to him the other also.'

They were words my dad might have used to explain how I should put myself in the shoes of others before condemning their words or actions. My chin lifted and I squared my shoulders. I would return unkindness with consideration. I would *not* be angry or upset.

Sunday school over, I crossed the asphalt to join friends on the church steps, the girls already wearing brightly coloured dresses, summer hats and white cotton gloves.

"Hello Gig-lamps. Want your letter back?" Jay materialized and planting himself in front of me, brandished my letter. His buddies smirked behind him.

I remained silent.

"Well, do you? It's here. Look. This one is yours."

He pushed up close, his nose in my face. I wanted to punch him. Hard. Right on the nose. I could have grabbed the letter from him then, but the words of the lesson repeated in my head. *Turn the other cheek.*

"No thank you, you may have it. I don't need it." I told him and praying my cheeks would not redden, continued up the steps to join Muriel.

"What was that about?" she asked.

"Nothing. He thinks he's smart but he's just a silly kid." As I hoped, Muriel offered me a lift home. To show I didn't care, I gave Jay's boys a cheery little wave as we drove away.

I did not know that pretence has a price and that when make-believe takes centre-stage, truth stands waiting in the wings. I pretended not to care — not about Jay's gang of adolescent boys who continued to plague me, or my exam marks, some so low, I barely scraped by. I even refused to allow myself to think about Grandma.

On my way home from school I often cycled past Lester's house hoping he might be there. Once, when Mum was out, I telephoned his number. I thought I'd hang up if someone else answered or plead a wrong number, but neither was necessary as the phone rang on and on. My curiosity to know what had become of Lester was hard to bear. On the pretext of wanting to buy new tassels for the hall curtains, I called at his father's upholstery business.

"Mr and Mrs Pierce are travelling overseas. The boy? I don't know, but he's probably with them," a man told me. Full of hope, I began checking the letterbox.

Our form teacher gave the class a list of the subject options for the coming year. I had no idea what to choose, no notion where I was going or even what I wanted to do. Again I tried talking with Mum.

Exasperated she shook her head. "Couldn't you be happy working in a shop selling things?" she said.

The thought of working locally in the High street had not occurred to me. My earlier plans included university or at least college. Mum's suggestion made me think I was either unworthy or too stupid to be given the opportunity of a real career. This perception seemed grossly unfair after spending two years studying with the top students of my age. Her attitude created ambiguity in my mind and further confused me as to my value as a human being.

Mid December brought unseasonable rain. Caught by a heavy downpour, I sought shelter in the library porch. A moment later Ming's brother, Ian, bounded up the steps.

"Hello. Is it customary for you to bring rain with you?" I asked, remembering how last time we met, squally weather had sent us running to the church porch.

He grinned. "It's good to see you, Ana."

"And I you. I've been to your house several times but there was nobody home."

"We went to stay with my eldest sister in Palmerston North. She's married now and as Margaret was so well, we all went. I'm enrolled at the Horticultural College there. My things are already packed."

"That's great, Ian. I'm sure you will do well."

We were making chat to avoid talking about Ming. Afraid to ask, I hoped Ian would offer news of my oldest friend. He coughed and looked out at the rain.

"Margaret is ill again. The doctors have let her come home. You should come and see her. I know she'd like to see you." Then looking into my eyes, he said, "Come soon, Ana."

In a husky voice I promised to visit. Then as the rain eased, we went our separate ways.

Saturday morning. The long summer holidays only seven days away. Yawning I turned to peer at the bedside clock. My head ached. Another hour, I thought and snuggling back beneath the blankets fell asleep. A loud bang jerked me into wakefulness. Doug stood beside my bed, the remains of a burst paper bag in his hand.

"Time to get up, lazy bones."

"Go away."

"No. Mum says you have to get up. It's lunch time."

I fumbled for my glasses and checked the clock. He was right. I had slept the entire morning but my head still ached. "All right, I'm getting up. Now go away."

Grabbing my blankets, Doug tugged them to the foot of the bed. Brothers!

By the time I reached the kitchen, he and Mum were at the table eating tomato sandwiches. I looked around for mine. Mum noticed me looking and said, "Get yourself something to eat." Instead, I sipped a glass of water and gazed out the window. It was a perfect afternoon to take my sketch book to the park for an hour then visit Ming on the way home. "And you can change out of those clothes, Ana," Mum continued, "I need you to move the compost to the front garden."

"Can't it wait? It will be holidays in a few days. I'll do it then."

"If you got up at a proper time, the job would be finished by now."

"Ming is home. I'd like to see her today."

"No. I've told you before. You are not to go there."

"They're a perfectly respectable family. Why can't I go?"

Doug slipped from his chair and taking the last sandwich with him, sidled out the door. I tried reason. "Mother, I'm tired after weeks of swotting. Now the exams are over I'd like to sit in the park for a while then visit Ming. I won't be late home."

"Ana, you are not listening to me. Besides, young girls should not be in that park alone."

'Why not? I'm quite safe. There are lots of people about, families. Anyway, I know who is nice and who is not."

Mother turned. "What do you mean? Who is not nice? Have men been talking to you?"

"No, Mum. But I know when to stay and when to move on. I can tell by their colours. Light and bright are good colours, dark and dull are not so nice."

"You're talking nonsense. Go and change your clothes. You *will* stay home, Ana."

"That's not fair. I'm not allowed to visit my best friend or go to the park. You don't like Lester and only once let me go to the pictures on a Friday night. Doug has been going since he was ten."

"It is different for boys."

"Why? Because you don't like girls? Well, I'm going." And with that I stormed out slamming the door behind me.

I ran all the way over the hill to the park where I dropped onto a vacant bench. How dare she order me about? I was fourteen, old enough to make decisions for myself. My mind filled with unjust situations, real and unreal. In my imagination I was eloquent as I put my mother in her place. With perfect poise I toppled her from slave driver to her proper role, that of a mother, someone to be relied upon, someone loving and kind.

I could not imagine any of the girls I knew arguing with their mothers as I had done mine. But those girls had no challenges. Life was easy for them. They had no upsets — all they talked about was fashion and what film was showing in town.

Too agitated to remain still I began walking, my mind full of imagined situations where I was in control but benevolent. I left the park and walked through the streets to the church, letting myself in through the unlocked choir room door. Seated in the hushed sanctuary I stared at the empty brass cross. I deserved freedom. Why did I not have it? Angry, I demanded to know what God was going to do about the mess my life was in. Had I not been 'A good and faithful servant'? Was I expected to wait my entire life for the promised reward? Where was the God who saw the sparrows fall? The one who loved us without question? Or so we were made to believe.

Perhaps there was no God. Could it be the stories of love, loyalty and miracles were a hoax, a ploy, a means of getting people to be nice to each other, to lessen the possibility of murders and wars? Why would a loving God take away the people I loved? Both grandma and our funny, lovable cousin Cyril, who had invented marvellous games and told me wonderful stories were gone; my father and Ming unlikely to recover. David, Lester and Ian were growing up and moving away. Worse, I felt estranged from my own mother, and even easy-going Doug.

My anger spent, I found myself pleading for understanding, for the pain and hardship to be taken away. Give me a sign, I begged. God, show me what you want me to do. I waited, kneeling on the carpet, my hands clasped. No flash of light, no crash of cymbals. Nothing. God, it seemed, had let me down.

Outside I turned for home. Along the quiet street misty halos surrounded the street lights. I was tired and hungry and had no idea what awaited me. Would Mum still be angry? With dragging feet I rounded the final corner. Across the gully lights shone from several windows and with a sudden need to be safe at home, I quickened my pace. Easing open the back door, I looked in. Mum sat in her armchair reading the newspaper. The smell of hot apple pie filled the room.

"Ana. I was just about to serve dinner. Come and give me a hand." Together we warmed the plates and served the food. Mum was being so nice and did not mention our argument. Head bowed I offered my apology.

"Mum, I'm sorry,"
"And I, Ana. Now let's eat before our meal gets cold."

A flock of argumentative sparrows woke me early the next morning. Throwing aside the blankets I crossed the room to raise the blind. Sunlight tipped the tops of the trees in the gully creating an aura of gold and green. Washed and dressed in old clothes, I found Doug, still in his pyjamas, sitting on the floor by the radio listening to the children's request program. Honey dripped from the inch-thick slab of toast in his hand, the small blobs falling into the steaming cup of cocoa beside him.

"Morning, Doug."

"Sssh! I'm listening to the *Golden Palomino*. It's my favourite."

I collected my gumboots from the cupboard and pulled them on.

"Where're you going?" Doug's words came muffled by a mouthful of toast.

"To shift the compost."

"I'll give you a hand soon."

That would be nice I thought as I spread the tarpaulin on the path and taking up the spade, jumped down into the pit. For a whole year we threw garden rubbish, lawn clippings and food scraps into a large concrete lined hole in the ground. Then, when the mixture mulched down, we spread it on the gardens. I pushed the top layer and its worms to one side then shovelled the rich smelly compost out onto the tarpaulin. Moments later Doug appeared with the wheelbarrow, filled it and trundled away to the front garden.

We worked quietly so as not to wake Mum. I found the early morning air soothing and when Doug dangled a large worm before me, threatening to drop it inside my shirt and I retaliated with a handful of sludge, good humour prevailed. By the time we finished and I had cleaned the tools, the sun was high in the sky.

Mum appeared carrying her flower basket and we walked together selecting colourful blooms for the house. I picked larkspur and gypsophila, blending delicate pink and blue into a large bunch to take to the hospital for Dad. He liked flowers and had taught me to look at the detail, guiding my pencil as I attempted to draw various plants.

Doug captured a large bumblebee and held it in his cupped hands. Mum and I warned him the bee might sting but Doug just laughed.

"Bees will only sting if they are frightened and I'm not frightening this one. Look. It's happy." He opened his hands to show us the bee calmly wiping its wings. He then blew lightly upon its back until it flew. We stood together, a little group of three, watching as the bee disappeared high in the summer sky.

"What a beautiful day." Mum ruffled Doug's hair. Then looking at me, murmured, "Thank you, Ana," before turning away. Tiny, happy tears clung to my eyelashes.

Shortly after lunch I cycled through town to the hospital, stopping on the way to buy a bar of Dad's favourite dark chocolate as a surprise. The surprise was mine, for when I opened his door he greeted me, smiling and obviously waiting for a visitor. Hellos and hugs over, I put my bouquet into a vase and having popped the chocolate into a drawer, sat beside his bed.

"Lightning bug, have you ever thought of becoming a nurse?" he said without preamble.

"No. A vet, but not a nurse."

"I've been talking with Matron. There's a serious shortage of nurses at present. You might have heard."

"Yes. Reverend Warrender asked his congregation for volunteers to assist with basic ward work. Muriel's mother and some other ladies are helping."

"Matron suggested you might like to work here for the summer holidays. Would you like that?"

"What would I have to do?"

"I'm not sure. Nothing too difficult. You're very young."

"Dad! I'm almost fifteen." We heard a knock and Matron Johnson looked in.

"Hello, John, Ana.' Matron smiled. "Has your father explained why I'm here, Ana?"

"He suggested I might work here over the holidays."

"Not here, Ana. At the maternity annex with the babies. I would be grateful for your help."

The idea of working with babies was so new and surprising, I became embarrassed and stammered. "Yes, Miss Johnson. I'd like that."

"Thank you." Her smile restored my confidence. "Come and see me on Tuesday after school. Four o'clock at my office. You'll find it on the left of the main corridor. We'll talk then. Goodbye John. See you on Tuesday, Ana."

Dad and I looked at each other.

"Well? What do you think, Ana?"

"I'm not sure. It's all so quick. I'll have to ask Mum."

"I've already done that. You'll find her agreeable. Now, love, can you please shift some of these pillows so I can lie down?"

He fell asleep almost immediately. I slipped quietly out into the main ward where bright sunshine created a vision of shiny floors and neat beds. Each locker had the added colour of flowers, magazines or little gifts in fancy paper. There was a low buzz of conversation and an occasional chuckle. It seemed a nice place to work. But when I mentioned this to mother, she thought it her duty to warn me about the other side of hospital life.

"People there are sick, Ana. They are in pain and sometimes very frightened. Not everyone gets well. Some die, even tiny babies."

"Babies bawl and make stinky nappies," Doug put his chip in.

Nevertheless I arrived at the hospital in good time on Tuesday and hurried to the Ladies' room to check my appearance before knocking on Matron's door. My hair stuck out as usual and I tucked it back behind my ears. With my school beret pinned in place, I looked older, more self-assured—on the outside, anyway. Inside, I was all aflutter.

Miss Johnson explained the work and gave me forms to fill in. I agreed to work seven weeks. Her secretary sent me to collect my nurse-aid uniform but I was so nervous I forgot the directions and became lost in the labyrinth of white and brown corridors returning at last out of breath and full of apologies. At the Maternity Annex I met some of the nurses and was shown around the building. During the tour I asked what I hoped were intelligent questions — I wanted to appear keen to learn. My guide, staff-nurse Rangi, quickly dispelled my nervousness. Eager to begin work, I returned to Miss Johnson.

"Well, Ana, do you think you will like working at the annex?"

I assured her I would do my best and sensing she was busy, turned to leave.

"Ana, I want you to know my door is always open to my nurses. Please come if you have any difficulties. I am here to help." She stood and walked with me to the door. "And this is for you. You will need to buy stockings and comfortable white shoes." She held out an envelope.

Surprised, I thanked her and left. At the bike rack I opened the envelope. Inside was a cheque for fifteen pounds. Amazed at my unexpected wealth, and forgetting cycling was forbidden in the hospital grounds, I rode down the drive and out the gate. As I passed the annex my heart bobbed like a kid on a pogo stick, but whether from excitement or fear, I could not tell.

Mum agreed I could finish school early and I took great delight in emptying my locker and vanishing without a word to my fellow students. By slipping away unnoticed I deprived Jay of the opportunity to engender any further hurtful jibes. And, I hoped, left the class wondering.

Some might think I had run away in shame — but that was not so. I simply decided I would no longer be a victim.

Nine

My first days at the maternity hospital were a challenge. Time was divided not by hours, but by minutes and I moved at a pace as near to running as possible. Strangers issued orders, made suggestions and smiled encouragement as I trotted up and down the white corridors, pushing in and out of numerous identical doors, often entering the wrong room. Until I learned to check the obvious; quantity of hair, size, weight and colour, identifying the individual babies was difficult.

As the most junior employee I spent most of the day scrubbing bucket loads of dirty nappies and large amounts of bloodied theatre linen. Armed with an enormous scrubbing brush, my gloved hands forever in cold water, I dealt with unimaginable muck. By the time I learned to shut down my sense of smell and control my retching, it was Christmas.

In three short weeks my new responsibilities had pushed me into a world far removed from schoolgirl chatter. Something I realized when I telephoned Lynn, the only friend to stand by me through the devastating teasing I received from the boys at school. When we spoke on Christmas Eve our usual topics; the kindness or otherwise of teachers, our increased prowess in athletics or the easiest way to clean ink from our fingertips, seemed incredibly juvenile. The widening gap between the very adult events at the annex and the seemingly frivolous chatter of friends set me apart; unable to share my experiences of a place where pain and joy overlapped.

When on duty, the other nurses accepted me and patiently taught me new skills; but I was far too young to participate in their off duty activities. Caught between the old and the new without truly fitting into either, gave me a sense of isolation. I slept longer than necessary and spent little time outdoors.

The New Year celebrations came and went. The daily routine at the Annex now familiar, I found pleasure in accomplishing my many tasks. With so many new experiences occurring, I seldom thought about school or Jay and the way he tormented me. There had been no word from Lester and my heartfelt longing to see him had reduced to pensive curiosity. Sooner or later he would reappear, of that I was certain.

Matron allowed me to see Dad outside of visiting hours. Being able to just 'pop in' was great. Each day after lunch I strolled through the gardens that separated the annex from the general hospital to his room at the end of the men's ward. Most days he barely managed 'Hello' before slipping back into a drug induced sleep. Still, I'd sit beside him telling him of the things I was learning. Sometimes I sent silent prayers to God asking Him to intervene. Surely death was better than this lingering state bereft of everything my dad held dear?

Three more busy weeks rushed by. The new school year now only ten days away but however hard I tried, I could not imagine being back in the classroom.

On a morning when three new mothers all left the hospital before midday, I hurried about helping first one then another until at last they took their leave. Next job, clean the vacant rooms. Rubbish bag in hand, I emptied the bins and turned to the bedside locker. A feathered stork ornament lay on a newspaper, its stand and the tiny baby that hung from its beak in a blanket, missing. Only the sad white stork remained. I dropped it in my rubbish sack and reached for the newspaper. It was folded open at the birth notices. From the column below, a death notice leapt out at me.

THOMAS, Margaret Olive. Aged 13 years. After a long illness.

I scanned the newspaper. It was a week old. Ming was dead and buried and I had not known—not been to see her, said goodbye or attended her funeral. Ming, my dearest friend. Hot tears stung my eyes. Crushing the newspaper I rammed it into the rubbish bag. Second thoughts made me pull it out, save the death notice and put in my pocket. To override my guilt, I set about cleaning the room with all possible speed and energy. I had no time to brood, to cry or even think about my feelings. Bound by routine, I forced myself through the day.

"Come soon," Ian said that day at the library when he bounded up the steps to where I sheltered from the rain. I'd made him a promise I failed to keep. Why had Mum been so adamant I stay away from Ming? Her unexplained dictum caused a flush of enmity.

Yet deep down I knew my mum was not to blame. I had sneaked off to Ming's place on many occasions and could have visited her on my way home from the annex whenever I chose. Instead I selfishly went home to a hot meal and a warm bed. The guilt belonged with me and I would have to deal with that. Mum must have had her reasons. I just wished she had told me.

My work-day over, I cycled homeward head-bent into the cool southerly wind. I remembered the day Ian and I sheltered in the church porch. His words came clear. Ming would be in a better place, her life continuing on a different plane. But today, the concept of these unhappy and difficult times in my life being lessons, failed to ease my feelings of remorse.

"Ana. You're home. Dinner is almost ready." Mum looked happy and came forward as I dropped my bag inside the door. "The matron telephoned me today," she said and sitting down, indicated I should join her. "She is pleased with your work at the annex and has offered you a permanent position. Would you like that?"

"You mean not go back to school?"

Mum talked on. "You can begin full training later if you wish and there will be a room available in the nurses' home in four weeks. You can live in. No more cycling in all weathers. You will have to do shift work of course. Well, what do you think?" Mum looked at me, her eyes bright. She was happy. Why wasn't I?

"I'm not sure. I'm surprised. What do you think? You and Doug would be here alone."

Mum looked down at her hands. "We all have to make changes, Ana. You've always been a highly strung child. I think a regular job with sensible girls will be good for you. You can come home on your days off. Or overnight sometimes. We will see each other."

The idea of being independent was attractive but I had the feeling I was being sent away. Something told me my mother did not want the responsibility of raising a teenage daughter. For her, Matron's offer was the perfect solution.

Would becoming a nurse solve the question of my future? The wages were substantial. Think of the shopping; clothes, make-up, a sports bike. The other girls went dancing on Saturday nights. Picture after picture flashed through my mind as I imagined a life without parental control and money in my pocket. My fingers closed over the slip of paper in my uniform pocket. Contrite, I was about to tell Mum Ming had died, when she rose and returned to the kitchen.

"We can talk more after tea. Run and get washed and changed, Ana. You smell of nappies." I had been dismissed.

With no good reason to refuse, I accepted the matron's offer and moved into the nurses' home. Around Easter the senior girls sat their final exams and moved on. A new group of girls arrived from the general hospital to begin the eighteen month maternity course. The small class quickly reduced to one as the girls returned to assist in the general wards where the shortage of nurses had reached critical point. Our head sister, plump kindly Sister Baird, called me into her office and asked if I felt ready to manage a full ward or nursery duty on my own. Bursting to prove my worth, I said yes. In spite of my youth, not yet 15 years of age, I joined the remaining nurse at tutorials; to give the tutor sister someone to talk to.

My idea of being free of parental control proved a total misconception. Unless given prior permission I had to be present for all meals, in bed with the light out by 10:30 every night and keep my room clean and tidy. At home I'd helped Mum with washing, ironing and mending, things I now did for myself.

Nothing compared to my concerns over the spelling of the new words I was adding to my vocabulary. On the wards, every moment of the working day was one of decision. Dare I leave the milk heating on the nursery stove while I turned a crying baby? Cleaning up boiled over, burnt on milk was not on my list of fun things to do. And while carrying three full bedpans at once might be clever, having to mop up after dropping them was not.

In the staff room, well away from the patients, incidents and opinions were openly discussed. I listened carefully, my knowledge and confidence growing as the weeks passed.

A poultry farm appeared in the paddocks opposite the nurses' home and the sound of fluttering wings brought back memories of the chooks in dunny on Uncle Harry's farm. Remembering my fear of the dark, the hens and my anger when the cat ate the baby rabbits, I laughed. These days strong emotion seldom affected me. I'd learnt to push it aside, or so I thought.

Autumn slid into winter and early morning cockcrow joined the jangle of alarm clocks in the nurses' home. We rose at 5 am to shower and dress, then wrapped snugly in our red capes, hurried down to the kitchen for a hot drink before beginning work at six. A full breakfast was served at eight o'clock.

In the coldest months fewer babies were born allowing the staff to relax a little. We lingered in the warm nursery to coo over the babies, arranged flowers with the expertise of a florist and borrowed magazines from the patients to read in our tea break. The afternoon shifts finished early and during the last half-hour, with a large pot of tea and piles of hot buttered toast, we relaxed at a corner table in the dining room.

On my birthday the cook made me an iced cake. Amid much good humoured teasing, the girls gave me a bottle of 'Anti-Fog' for my glasses. The gift chosen because one day, when we were all rushed off our feet, I had hurried from the heat of the sterilizing room to the kitchen to serve the midday meal. With my glasses fogged over, I picked up the wrong jugs pouring hot custard over the corned beef and adding a generous dollop of onion sauce onto each of the steam pudding desserts. The resulting fuss as meal after meal was returned to the kitchen upset the cook, who gave the staff dinner to the patients and the staff ate baked beans. It was not my most popular moment and earned me the nickname of Mole.

A new class of student nurses arrived mid-year. These competent women had completed their general training and were used to giving orders. With more staff available, my ward and nursery duties were reduced and I returned to nurse-aid status, which meant skivvying for the senior girls. Disheartened, I turned to Elizabeth and Maggie, two senior nurses who had taken me under their wing from my very first day. With their support I resisted the urge to chuck the job in and go home to Mum.

Elizabeth suggested I ask for a late leave pass. A pass allowed us to stay out until midnight two nights a month. Mine came with a caution. I was young, just fifteen. I must not abuse the midnight rule. Confident of signing in before the Cinderella hour, Elizabeth and I made plans to attend one of the weekly dances at St. Joseph's Hall.

A grand occasion required a new dress and with thirty pounds from my savings I bought an electric sewing machine. Circular skirts were in fashion but mother thought them a great waste of fabric. Free from such constraint, I rushed back from the shops with yards of pale pink dimple nylon and a circular skirt dress pattern. Sewing nylon was a new experience for me and far from easy. Near to tears, and suffering my limitations as a seamstress, I phoned Mum for help. With surprising patience she quickly sorted the problem and as we chattered on into the afternoon, she gave me news of family and friends.

Uncle Harry had fully recovered from his run-in with the young bull leaving my cousin David free to fulfil his dream of driving for long distance trucking firm. Aunt Libby was going out with an old school friend. Did Mum think they might marry? Perhaps.

"And the Pierce's are back. They put on a slide show in the church hall." Mum thought the scenery in Europe beautiful and I waited impatiently as she described lakes, cliff-top castles and the landmarks of London. At last she paused.

"That's lovely, Mum. Was Lester with his parents?"

"I didn't see him. I don't think he went overseas."

While not knowing where he was no longer hurt me, I still wanted to know his whereabouts. I promised to join Mum and Doug for lunch the following Sunday and after we said goodbye, I realised how easy it had been to drift away from my family. Visits to my father were also fewer than before. Filled with self-reproach, I searched for something to ease my guilt and remembered it was always me who telephoned home. Neither Mum nor Doug ever called me at the nurses' home.

On the Saturday morning of the dance Elizabeth and I worked hard, wanting to be off duty on time. As I prepared an instrument tray for a circumcision, counting drops of brandy onto the little muslin ball filled with sugar the babies were given to suck, someone called my name. I turned but the room was empty. Thinking I had imagined the voice, I completed the tray and went to collect the baby. Again I heard my name. This time I recognized my father's voice. Goose bumps covered my arms and prickled my spine. Concerned, I determined to visit him the moment my shift ended.

Unless babies are awakened with calm reassurance, there is a risk of them using the full force of their new lungs to express their outrage. In a nursery, one crying baby quickly becomes two, four and then ten. Today of all days I needed to lift this baby without a fuss. I leant over the crib and found myself looking into a pair of wide-open eyes. Seldom had I seen a baby focus his eyes with such serenity. Something in his solemn gaze seemed both timeless and wise. I felt he knew my innermost thoughts, yet I remained unjudged, accepted. Could it be we are born with wisdom and a sense of wonder that becomes lost beneath layers of experience as we age? I certainly felt I had lost something precious along the way. Once, in the security of my early childhood, I had been confident. Now I watched every move, weighed every word, wanting people to think well of me. Not only that, I longed for my own safe place, for someone I could rely on. My upbringing told me that the answer lay in the giving of love, in being willing to assist others. Those who did so, the meek, the generous and caring people, were rewarded—eventually. Gently, I lifted the baby and carried him through the corridors to the theatre.

Shortly after two o'clock I ran up the stairs to my room and draping my new nylon dress over my arm, hurried out again to visit Dad. I pushed open his door and stopped. The bed was empty, the blankets awry. With pounding heart I sought the ward sister.

"Please. Where is my father?"

"He's gone home. Didn't you know?"

"Home? How can that be? He's so ill."

"He asked to go, Ana." The sister spoke kindly. "The ambulance will bring him back at four o'clock. Some people need to see things one last time. Do you understand?"

I nodded. "I'll come back later. Thank you."

There was not enough time for me to change and cycle home. Even a taxi could not get me there before my dad returned to the hospital. Why had Mum not told me? She must have known.

Back in my room I hung my dress back in the wardrobe and sat on the edge of the bed. Tears burned my eyes. I had no idea what to do. In a sudden rage I stamped my feet and beat the mattress with my fists. None of this was fair. None of it!

Someone tapped on the door. Elizabeth looked in. "Do you want me to set your hair for tonight?"

"I don't think I want to go."

Elizabeth closed the door and sat beside me on the bed. "What's happened? Why have you changed your mind?"

"I don't know what to do. My father has gone home for the afternoon. No one told me he was going. Mum must have known, but she never said a word. When I asked Sister Moore, she told me Dad asked to go. That means he doesn't have much time. Why does Mum always shut me out? It's so unfair."

I turned to Elizabeth. She was not pretty; rather plain looking with gingery hair and pale skin, her top lip pushed into a pronounced cupid's bow by prominent front teeth. She laid a hand on mine. I looked down at her fingers, so slender and perfectly formed. The nails neatly filed and buffed to a shine. "You have lovely hands," I said, pushing my own out of sight. Mine were overly large and reddened from constant washing. I also bit my nails. Elizabeth sighed and sat back.

"Ana, it is possible your mother had no more than a few minutes notice of your father going home. He would have to be lucid enough to state his wishes and remain that way for several hours. The drive to your place would have to fit in with that. And they are husband and wife. They were together a long time before you came along and in normal circumstances would have been together long after you moved on in your own life. Perhaps they just needed time together." She paused and with a gentle finger brushed a tear from my cheek. "Why don't you phone your mother?"

What Elizabeth said made sense. I could see how stupid and selfish I'd been. "I'll do that. Thank you, Elizabeth."

Leaving the room I ran down the stairs to the phone box. The phone rang so long I thought no one was going to answer. At last I heard Mum's voice. She sounded as if she had been crying.

"Yes. I'm all right. We both are. Your dad is very tired, almost asleep. He'll be back at the hospital in half an hour. Will you go across? Call me back. Let me know he's all right."

"Of course. I'll call you soon. Bye, Mum."

"Thank you, Ana."

I sighed, a feeling of relief flowing through me. Elizabeth had been right.

An hour later I phoned Mum again. Told her I'd been to see Dad. He was sleeping and looked more at peace than he had for weeks. Before hanging up I reaffirmed our lunch together the following day.

"Yes, Ana. Come before twelve."

The next couple of hours flew by as Elizabeth and I shampooed each other's hair and with much bravado, used a borrowed curling iron. We ironed dresses, cleaned shoes and found unladdered nylon stockings. Later, as we walked to St. Joseph's, we sang the latest songs; *That's Amore, Vaya Con Dios* and *How Much is that Doggie in the Window*?

Inside the hall coloured lights criss-crossed the ceiling and large ponga fronds decorated the walls. On stage, a pianist, an accordion player and a drummer conversed with a small bearded man holding a violin. "He looks like a leprechaun," Elizabeth whispered. As we watched, the little man stepped forward to play, his music so lively I felt compelled to clap.

The dance hall became a mass of swirling colours, the girls' dresses lifting as they twirled lightly across the floor. Some revealed more than they ought. Eager to catch a glimpse of a stocking top and suspender, lads gathered near the entrance encouraged their dancing friends to spin the girls even faster. They nudged each other and grinned, nodding their heads to indicate a pretty girl as they cheered their mates on.

By suppertime I had danced several times with a rather nice boy called John. After the supper waltz, as we chattered over cups of tea and wedges of cream sponge, I saw Elizabeth with a tall lad who bent his head attentively whenever she spoke.

While the supper tables were being cleared the girls fluttered off to the Ladies Room. They emerged, chirping and chattering like a flock of brightly coloured finches, to flutter back to the seats at the side of the hall. As our little group of girls settled, I pointed John out to Elizabeth saying, "That's him. He's offered to escort me home."

John became the immediate focal point. My companions shook their heads.

"No. Not him."

"He's a mick."

"What do you mean? What's a mick?" I asked.

"A catholic."

"So?"

"You can't go out with him. You can't marry a mick."

"Marry! I've only just met him."

"Don't start something you cannot finish."

What were these girls talking about? After the next dance I asked Elizabeth for an explanation.

"Ana, you're so naïve. Catholics only marry their own kind. John would never be allowed to be seriously involved with you." Then leaning close she whispered in my ear. "They're not allowed birth control. Babies. Every year. Dozens of them."

That did it. When he next asked me to dance I pleaded weariness and returned to the annex with Elizabeth and Frank, the nice young man I'd seen talking to her. From the back seat of Frank's car, I listened as they drew from each other information about their work, families, likes and dislikes. If I had not bowed to public opinion, to that old, *What will the neighbours think?* I might have been sharing a similar conversation with John.

Lester and I had shared everything. Even now, eight months after his disappearance, thinking about him created an ache; a miserable longing that blotted out the evening's pleasure and left me feeling very much alone.

Ten

My apprehension grew with every step as clutching my red nurses' cape tightly across my chest I hurried across the grounds to the main hospital. Dad had little time left. What if he had died in the night while I was dancing? He was my anchor, my life without him unimaginable. I persevered in all things wanting him to be proud of me. Inside his door I paused, waiting anxiously for the slightest movement of his chest. The sight of his emaciated form, the yellowed skin pulled tight over his skull, his lips, no longer able to close, brought a shiver to my skin.

"Dad, can you hear me?" I willed him to acknowledge my being there.

His eyelids fluttered then opened. "Lightning bug, you're here. I thought I might see you wearing the beautiful pink dress I've been hearing about."

Relief surged into my throat. Surprise too, for this was surely his clearest speech in weeks. "I'll bring the dress later. You seem so different . . . so awake." I'd been about to say 'So alive' but stopped myself in time.

"I told the doctor, no more morphine. I want—" He drew a sharp breath and gripped my hand.

"What is it? Shall I get the sister?" A trickle of yellow bile ran from his mouth. I knew I should get help but was afraid to leave him. Gently, I wiped his chin with a damp towel and waited. "Dad, it's me, Ana." His green eyes glazed. "What is it? Is there something I can do for you?"

A knock on the door made me jump. "How is he, Nurse Dockery?" Frightened, I shook my head. Sister Moore came closer and without lifting Dad's hand, checked his pulse. "Could you wait outside please, Ana?"

His cheek, dry and cool beneath my lips, smelt faintly of soap. At the door I paused, holding the handle, thinking I heard his voice. Yet when I turned there was no sign of his having spoken. Did he say, "Goodbye, Bug?"

Not wanting to be seen crying I fled to my room. Thirty minutes later, my emotional rush of tears over, I returned to his room. The door was open a crack. Cautiously I widened the gap. Sister Moore, a doctor and a nurse stood close to the bed.

Restless, I paced the short corridor waiting for them to emerge. The doctor appeared followed by the sister. Neither of them looked at me. Surely the nurse would leave soon. I wanted to be with my father. A second nurse arrived carrying an instrument tray. She too disappeared inside the room. Again I paced the floor. Another half hour passed. The door remained closed.

Could I walk in? Pretend I did not know the nurses were there. I decided not to push in. A whole hour dragged by. Sister returned walking briskly along the corridor but before I could speak, she went in closing the door behind her. Exasperation replaced my anxiety. I wanted to know what was happening. When the door opened, I stepped forward. This time I would ask. Sister Moore emerged.

"You still here, Ana?" Her tone seemed to question my sanity and then she was gone, bustling around the corner before I could open my mouth. Defeated, I turned away. Mum asked me to come before 12 o'clock. Already late and fraught with anxiety, I returned to the nurses' home to phone her.

"Hello." I heard quick shallow breathing. Lily Stuart, Mum's friend and neighbour, had answered our phone. "Hello, Mrs Stuart. It's Ana. May I speak to Mum?"

After a moment of silence, Lily spoke. "Your mother cannot come to the phone just now, Ana."

"What's happened? Is she ill?"

Another pause, then speaking slowly, Lily Stuart put an end to years of trepidation.

"I suppose you have to know. Your father died this morning."

Stunned, I stood holding the receiver. Disbelief filled my mind. How could this be? I'd been there — all morning. Why hadn't someone told me? Why did I have to hear the news like this?

I suppose you have to know, she said as if I was the last person anyone would think of telling. Of all the scenarios I imagined, this was not one of them. Shattered, my response mechanical, I thanked Mrs Stuart and said I'd be home shortly. Years of self-conditioning clicked into place. My father might have died but like him, I would be strong, caring and kind.

Hours and days passed; long dark nights filled with the sound of my mother sobbing. Faces, known and unknown came and went. I moved and spoke, looked and listened, but some trigger within had snapped leaving me incapable of registering emotion.

On the day of the funeral, the men from Dad's lodge joined family and friends gathered in the church. The organ music swelled and as we rose to sing *Rock of Ages,* a bass voice led a predominance of male singers. Certain the singer was Lester; I searched the congregation with many a sidelong glance from beneath lowered lids, but failed to see him.

After the service Doug and I waited in the car for Mum and Aunt May. Through the car window we watched Mum accepting handshakes and comforting hugs from the people gathered outside the church. He was our father, but no one had hugged us — another situation where adults seem to think children unimportant.

Beyond the adults, my friends, Muriel and Helen, stood with some youngsters from the Sunday school. Muriel saw me looking and nodded her head, the slight movement conveying sympathy. The eight-year-olds waved. Grateful for the contact, I raised my hand and managed a half smile. Aunt May appeared at the car window. "One does not wave like royalty at funerals," she snapped. "Remember where you are." Humiliated, I drew back out of sight.

I am not sure why, but I believed the apprehension and worry of the past five years would end when Dad's casket was finally buried in the earth. Perhaps because of Dad's love of growing plants, of the seasons and the way he spoke of the earth as being nurturing and kind, I thought for him, and me, the burial would bring peace. Then with gross exaggeration, Aunt May told Mum I waved and grinned at my friends and I was forbidden to go to the cemetery.

Indignant at being treated like a child, I took myself off to the back garden, and in a furious sulk, stabbed at any passing ant. Dad's old cat, Smoke, came to bunt gently against my legs and lifting him into my lap, I bemoaned the injustice of my punishment. My sister Fran came to find me and with soothing empathy, drew me back to the house to help with afternoon tea.

"Being fifteen is hard," she said.

Our best china cups, some floral, others trimmed with gold bands, had to be washed. That was my job. Elbow deep in soap suds, I gazed out the window while listening to the hum of adult conversation about me. None of our cousins came to the wake and Doug and Fergie had disappeared. Mum brought more dirty dishes and I was about to speak when she gave an excited little yelp and pushing past me, hurried outside. Curious, I looked out the window to see who or what had caught her attention. A man, a stranger, stood below me. All I could see was his grey, carefully parted hair curling down over the collar of an out-of-date suit.

Mum stood on the porch step, her face alight. "You managed to come," I heard her say. Then to my amazement, she flung herself at the man. With her arms about his neck, she kissed and hugged him, twined her fingers in his curls and fondled his ears. Finally the man reached up and unclasping her hands from around his neck, stepped back. He held my mother at arms' length and spoke quietly, his words too low for me to hear. Whatever he said did not deter her as grasping his arm with both hands she led him into the house.

My mother was behaving like a besotted teenager an hour after burying my father. I had been sent to Coventry, made to stay away from his burial because I acknowledged a friend. The inequality between the censorship I received and the way others excused my mother, had me wanting to smash all the cups in the sink.

"Breathe, breathe." I'd heard it a hundred times when the birthing mothers became stressed. So I breathed and by the time the dishes were done, my bitterness had eased.

The man Mum greeted so warmly turned out to be her cousin, Beau. They grew up together. I thought fleetingly he might be the man in the photograph hidden in her handkerchief drawer, but the difference was too great. My lean, suntanned mystery man had charming good looks, while mother's cousin was plump and shy.

I soon realized Beau was an amiable person and became resigned — but not forgiving — of my mother for having a dear friend to confide in. I wished Lester had come; he was the only person I trusted to understand my feelings.

Sometime in the night I woke and remembered my dream of Cyril before he died. How I longed to recapture the wonderful infusion of calm that filled my room as he flew with the kotuku that night. There had been no white bird to warn me of Dad's death. All I had were what I thought were his words of farewell, 'Goodbye, Bug.'

A few days later I returned to the nurses' home relieved to be away from all things associated with my dad's death. The following Saturday, my friends, Maggie and Elizabeth, hosted a Bon Voyage party prior to sailing to Noumea for their annual leave. Down in the common room, a piano player thumped out Winnie Atwell tunes to the accompaniment of bongos, raucous voices and tambourines. After a brief appearance, I went up to bed but found it impossible to sleep. As I turned my pillow for the umpteenth time, I thought of Grandma. The night before she died I had heard her sighing and restless in the room next to mine. I should have gone to see if she needed anything but selfishly did nothing.

At sun up I found the corridor outside my room strewn with confetti and toilet paper streamers. Tired and grumpy, I pushed open a toilet door to find Jemima, the classroom skeleton, sitting on the loo. One bony hand rested on the toilet paper, the other held an empty wine bottle in her lap. After my initial shock I shut the door and too tired to even smile, left her for someone else to find.

A taxi arrived for Elizabeth and Maggie and in a flurry of hugs they departed for the bus station. Gran used to say hard work was the best cure for the blues and I followed her advice, applying myself to the tasks of the day.

No matter how hard or how fast I worked, all I could think of were words I wished I had said, things I could have done to assist my dad, Ming or Gran, thoughtful words and acts that might have helped them. Now it was too late. The uplifting atmosphere of church fellowship might have eased my misery. Sadly, my rostered shifts had made the completion of the Local preacher's course impossible and I seldom attended a Sunday service.

At the end of shift, I dragged myself up the stairs thinking only of bed and sleep. The corridor outside my room sparkled, the mess gone, the carpet vacuumed and the floors polished. Someone had collected the bottles from the party and placed them at the head of the stairs, a step from my door. One was half-full of gin. I knew little about alcohol. Mum made it clear; drink caused depredation of both the mind and physical health. Others said it made them feel happy and linked drinking cocktails with romance. In a love story I read, a man and woman had sipped gin slings as they sat beneath palm trees on the terrace of the Raffles Hotel in Singapore. Remembering this sublime scene made me curious. What did a gin sling taste like? Was this my opportunity to find out?

After a quick check of the empty hallway, I unlocked my door and slid the half bottle of gin inside. Then clattering back down the stairs I dropped the rest of the bottles noisily into the rubbish bin.

An hour later I cycled to the public library and sidling in, worked my way along the shelves until I found the section on entertaining. Fearing Aunt Libby might see me and come to see what I was doing, I skimmed quickly through the indexes in search of a recipe for gin sling. The nearest thing was a gin squash. That would have to do. Next stop the grocer's.

Fearful of being challenged I hugged the brown paper bags to my chest to prevent the bottles clinking together. No one must suspect I was planning to drink alcohol. Safely away from the High Street, I reached my room without meeting anyone and there, in secrecy, opened the squash and lemonade bottles, leaving the gin until last. The smell was terrible. How could anyone drink that? Appalled, I held the bottle away from me then cautiously sniffed again. The smell was no better the second time.

Nevertheless, having come this far there could be no turning back. Alone in my room I sipped my first drink. The first two or three tastes made me shudder but then, the more I sipped, the more agreeable it became. Fluffing up the pillows on my bed, I slipped off my shoes, selected a new magazine and settled back to enjoy my elegant gin squash.

For more than a week I continued to pour myself a gin squash when I came off duty. One morning as I weighed each of the babies before carrying them to their mothers, I heard a whisper. The head sister was making an unscheduled check of our rooms. What if she found the gin? Would I be dismissed? Sent away in disgrace? Expecting to be called to the office, I jumped whenever someone spoke to me. The call did not come but I knew I'd had a narrow escape. Late in the night, when all was quiet, I tiptoed to the bathroom and poured the remaining gin down the drain.

Spring arrived. Buds blossomed. Daylight came earlier and darkness later. One warm evening a patient asked me to bring her a cool drink from the refrigerator. I entered the kitchen to find Sister Kathy about to plunge live crayfish, a gift from a grateful patient, into an enormous pot of boiling water.

"Please, drown them first," I begged.

Unable to watch, I poured the patient's drink and had turned to go, when Sister Kathy ran at me with the huge crustacean, jiggling its feelers and claws in my face. With a scream I pushed out through the swing door—and collided with a man coming in. Orange juice arced from the glass. Up, then down, all over his white coat.

"I'm so sorry." Thinking it was a doctor, I dared not look up. His hands clasped my arms and steadied me.

"Ana-Banana Dockery?"

"Lester?"

Lester Pierce stared down at me, orange cordial dripping onto his shoes.

Sister Kathy giggled. "As you two seem to know each other, you'd better come in here and get cleaned up." Still holding the crayfish she indicated the pot room. I led the way, letting the dividing door between the rooms swing shut.

Where? When? Why? I wanted to know everything at once but instead of answering my questions, he asked his own. I learned only of his position as an orderly at the general hospital. He had come to collect drums from the autoclave. I showed him where to find them then watched as he deftly steered the heavy trolley down the corridor.

I called after him. "Lester, were you at my father's funeral?"

"Yes." He turned. "See you, Ana-banana. I'll phone you." With a grin he shook the hair from his eyes and pushed the trolley out into the night.

Lester did telephone, with an invitation to a film and we met, with quiet formality, at the new theatre in High Street. Throughout the evening Lester, touchingly romantic, brushed the back of my neck and in tense moments in the movie, held my hand. I longed for a proper kiss, but while friendly warm-hearted and funny, he kept a slight distance between us. A week later he began dropping by the ward at supper time. I thought he came to see me but then heard he often stayed late, regaling the other nurses with jokes and stories when I was not on duty.

One evening as I ironed a dress ready for an evening out with Lester, Maggie sat nearby watching me. She asked about Lester. How long had I known him? Was our relationship serious?

"Serious. Who could be serious with that clown?" I laughed, not wanting to say I adored him, had done, since I was three years old.

Maggie did not laugh. "Take care, Ana, the man has secrets. I don't want to see you hurt."

"I'm fine, Maggie. I can look after myself," I said and ignored her warning.

At Christmas, when I invited Lester to have a meal with my family, he said he was going away, that he'd see me when he returned. Disappointed by his response, I thought perhaps I had expected too much. After all, I knew nothing of his time away from me. If I ever questioned him, he made a joke or changed the subject. So I pushed aside my niggling concerns and instead of worrying, threw myself headlong into the Christmas festivities.

Near the end of January, when Lester and I had been a casual pair for four months, a girl on the cleaning staff stopped to chat as I hand-washed garments in the laundry. We talked of this and that, small talk flowing back and forth across the room. She stood with her back to me and as I was running water into the tub, I at first thought I misheard what she said.

"I beg your pardon. What did you say?"

"I said that Lester what's-his-name got engaged to one of the nurses over at the general hospital. He gave her a beautiful diamond ring."

"Oh," was all I could say. But I thought a lot. At my worst I felt devastatingly disappointed. In my best moments I wanted him to be happy. Earlier losses resurfaced. Deprived of happiness, I slept poorly and ate little. My head ached and at night I woke crying from dreams I could or would not remember. Finally I became ill and was confined to bed.

Matron came to visit me. She sat on the end of my bed and asked a lot of questions about how I felt when Dad died and if I had cried very much. She listened attentively as I explained the guilt I felt because I had not helped Grandma, Ming or my father enough. I had let them all down. Now it was too late to make amends. When my tears finally subsided she brought me a cup of tea. "Rest and get well," she said, "and in a few days, come to my office and we will talk some more."

Eleven

The bus trundled on into the afternoon, the green hills and fast flowing mountain streams of my home province soon replaced by endless sheep dotted plains. At intervals, immense concrete bridges spanned wide gravel riverbeds. In winter dark water would breach the banks devouring all in its path in its determination to reach the sea.

"Would you like a sweet, dear?" An elderly lady across the aisle held out a bag of toffees.

"Thank you." Soothed by the soft texture of the caramel, I turned back to my daydream state.

"Where are you going, dear?"

I suppressed a sigh. "To Masterton."

"I have a nephew there. He has a bakery on Stanton Street. Do you know it?"

"No. This is my first visit."

"It's a very nice place. Are you staying with family?"

"My father's cousin, I've not met her before."

"Oh dear, you're all alone. Will you be met at the bus station?"

At this rate I might as well tell her how, by the time I was well enough to return to work, Matron and my mother had arranged to send me to an unknown relative three hundred miles away. A new environment with new people would cheer me up they said. Not so. Forever on the verge of tears and highly resentful at being railroaded out of town, I did not feel in the least cheerful.

I had spent the previous night with my half-sister, Fran. "You'll like Cousin Bea," she said as we selected a dozen brown eggs from her hens, wrapping each carefully in newspaper before putting them in a brown paper bag. Together we picked cherries from trees in her yard and putting some aside with the eggs for Bea, made the rest into a pie which Fran later served topped with whipped cream.

From across the aisle, the old lady chattered on. "There he is, the young man travelling to Masterton." She pointed to a man several rows ahead of us. "He's ever so nice. I'll ask him to look after you."

"Really, there's no need."

"Leave it to me, dear. I'm getting off shortly but I'll see him first."

Before leaving the bus, she arranged for the young man to escort me to the refreshment rooms for tea before our journey continued. She was right, I thought as I waved her goodbye, Michael was a charming young man. Good looking too and when we returned to the bus, I happily shared a seat with him. He settled against the window while I placed the bag containing the eggs, my hat and rolled up coat in the overhead, mesh luggage rack.

Michael offered me a magazine. 'Have the girly one,' he said with a smile, passing me the *Women's Weekly*. After an hour of travelling in silence, I laid the magazine aside and dozed. A sudden jolt shook me awake.

"That was close. Did you see the dog?" A buzz passed amongst the passengers and as the driver restarted the bus, a hen's egg plopped into Michael's lap.

Pink with embarrassment, I held out my hand. "I think that's mine."

Without speaking he passed me the egg. I stood, and steadying myself against the seat, replaced it in the bag making sure the top was secure. Then doing my best to control my laughter while imagining the mess had the egg landed on his head, I apologized.

"The trouble is no one will believe me," Michael grinned. "Having an egg drop on me in a bus is really weird. I've copped some pickup lines, but yours is the best."

That made us both laugh and a short time later Michael gave me his phone number and invited me to a dance the following Saturday.

Aunt Bea, as I called her, was every bit as nice as Fran said. Forever busy, she helped at a school tuck shop, worked in her enormous garden and walked Rufus, her indolent golden retriever. Rufus kept me company in the garden as I sat in the sunshine knitting or reading. Our garden at home, all straight lines and formal flower beds, while beautiful, was no match for Aunt Bea's, where gravel paths twisted their way through dense foliage and crossed unexpected open sunlit patches before meandering past thickly clustered shrubs—a garden waiting to be explored.

Michael arrived in a taxi to take me to the dance. His politeness and good humour impressed my Aunt. He also danced superbly. The evening over, he walked me to the door, and with a formal little bow, wished me good night. The following Saturday we went to a film. As we parted, Michael promised to call me mid-week and lightly kissed my cheek.

Filled with new strength and vitality, I wished I could stay longer. Michael was great company, attentive and amusing. Maybe, if when I returned home I wrote to him, he might write back. Mid-week I hung about waiting for his call. Thursday passed, then Friday. My head ached and as a black cloud of despondency rolled in, Aunt Bea suggested instead of waiting, I telephone Michael. His employer answered the phone.

"Sorry, love. Michael's gone to collect his wife and children. They're moving into their new home tomorrow."

"Of course, I forgot. Thank you," I lied, grateful my voice had stayed strong. My insides wobbled like jelly.

"Ships that pass in the night," Aunt Bea said and coaxed me into making scones for lunch.

Be honest, I thought. Michael offered no more than friendship. I was the one building castles in the air. I needed to ground myself; to see this as another of life's little tests. A week later, in excellent health and keen to return to work, I boarded the bus for home.

As I unpacked in my room, Elizabeth appeared. We greeted each other warmly and carrying cold lemonade and a packet of chocolate biscuits, retired to the comfort of the common room to chat. When we ran out of holiday snippets, Elizabeth offered news of a different kind.

"I am thinking of leaving here to work at the new Thames hospital," she said. "It opens at the end of the month. They're advertising for staff at all levels."

"Do you think I could go?"

"Let's try. I have application forms in my room. Come on." Giggling and shoving we climbed the stairs to Elizabeth's room.

A month later we were packing. Mum let me go without fuss. "You are sixteen," she said with a shrug. "I suppose you know what you want."

As a staff nurse, Elizabeth lived in the new nurses' home while I, again a lowly nurse-aid, lodged in a tiny bolthole at the top of the stairs in a shabby, three-storied house. Here, my two years of training went unrewarded. Throughout the staff shortage at the annex, Sister Baird had given me the responsibilities of a regular nurse and I attended all tutorials. I found the demotion difficult to accept and struggled with my hurt pride.

Work on the general hospital took longer than expected and put the new maternity wing back twelve months. The existing ward, an old colonial building with wide verandas and a slate roof, had exposed copper piping with brass fittings in every room. Except for floor polishing, the nurses cleaned everything, including the brass ware and copper pipes, the regime so strict, the patients came second to the cleaning.

Elizabeth and I thought the level of patient care inferior and at times ignored the old fashion rules set by Sister Twist, a wizened old maid who believed in an entirely natural birthing process. Unless directly ordered by a doctor, she refused any form of pain relief for the patients. To sooth the pain of their mastitis, Elizabeth and I made hot oil breast packs for the women. Then someone snitched and we were given extra night duty as punishment. The extremely hot weather and noise from the construction site where concrete mixers turned all day made my stint on nights a test of endurance.

Some of the girls I housed with had frequent fist fights, wrestled on the floor and swore. Whenever I heard a ruckus, I locked my door and stayed quiet until the dispute ended.

Each night at eleven, the house sister locked the door to the nurses' home. Nurses returning late went to the main office and asked to be let in. Several such requests earned the nurse a bad mark. The local girls quickly found a solution. They climbed a tree beside the front door and entered through a bedroom window — my window.

Woken by a noise, I lay terrified as a burly dark skinned man climbed in through the window pulling his girlfriend behind him. His finger to his lips, he warned me to be quiet then opening the door, the pair disappeared into the corridor. On Friday and Saturday nights three or four couples climbed up the tree and in through my window. I tried locking the window but a note was pushed under my door. *Unlock the window or have your face smashed.* Thankfully, the men did not come back through my room. They left by the front door.

A year passed and when Elizabeth returned home to her parents on annual leave, I chose instead a bus tour, travelling further north to the endless white beaches and bush clad hills at the top of the peninsular. Halfway through our second year, the new maternity wing finally opened. Elizabeth and I joined the celebration. I rarely saw Elizabeth now. Not only did we live in different buildings and work different shifts, but the lucky Elizabeth also had a steady boyfriend.

The wards completed, the major construction work shifted to the kitchens. The meals, never very appetising, became inedible. Instead of going to the hospital cafeteria, I ate at a café in the main street. My diet being irregular and barely substantial, I paid little attention to the grumblings in my tummy. The pain worsened and by the end of duty on the third day, I staggered to my bed. Curled in a ball I tried to sleep. At first shivering then dripping with sweat, I finally decided I needed help. Bent double and near blind with pain, I opened my door and called to a girl cleaning her teeth in the bathroom opposite.

"Yeah, yeah," she said wiping her face with a towel. "I'll get the house sister." Renowned for her bullying and rudeness, I knew Moana would not hurry.

I recall being stretchered head first down the stairs but little else until I woke the next day minus my appendix. Four weeks later, shortly before my eighteenth birthday, thin, a little fragile and longing for the comfort of well-remembered surroundings, I boarded the over-night express for home.

At the junction, where passengers changed trains near the end of a fifteen hour journey, an elderly porter came shuffling along the dimly lit platform to unlock the ladies waiting room. Thanking him, I entered. The only seating, a rock-hard leather bench with tufts of horse hair protruding from its corners, filled one wall. The porter, a kindly man, added wood to the open fire and brought me a cup of tea with the saucer balanced on top. The slow train would be here in an hour or two he said. I longed to end my journey, to be home in the familiar cosiness of Mum's sitting room with its big brown armchairs and generous supply of cushions.

In the early dawn, the guard returned with the news my train was approaching. The well named slow train puffed to a halt at every station along the way. Goods wagons were exchanged, shunted back and forth with monotonous regularity until, three hours and thirty miles south, I finally stepped down in my hometown.

I rode in a taxi, my thoughts racing ahead to the comfort of home. I recalled the rather gloomy but snug sitting room. Saw myself surrounded by the undemanding neutrality of familiar décor as seated in one of the big armchairs, my legs curled beneath me; I sipped hot sweet tea from one of Mum's bone china teacups.

Taking the key from beneath the mat, I unlocked the door. Shock widened my eyes. The longed-for bulky armchairs were gone, replaced with small chrome-armed seats and a red couch so rigid and uninviting it might have been stolen from a dentist's waiting room. Instead of soft curtains, a bright yellow blind covered the window. A deep sense of loss clouded my homecoming and tears spilled like rain. I expected my childhood home to remain unchanged, a haven for whenever I felt the need to return. The place I called home had become my mother's house.

Nevertheless, by the time Mum returned from work in the evening, I felt fully refreshed. Her hug was brief but she made me welcome, insisting I sit by the fire while she prepared dinner. When I last saw her, her brown hair showed only a few tentative strands of grey. Today a soft silver cloud framed her face and her usually prim features seemed somehow softer. At first we chose our words with care, keeping our conversation light and pleasant but as the evening progressed we both relaxed. By bedtime I felt accepted as the independent young woman I believed myself to be.

Next morning, with our long autumn shadows preceding us, we walked to church. Fat cushions of velvety moss padded the damp gutters and yellow leaves from the silver birches carpeted the grass verge. Mum pointed out the changes; a freshly painted house, new carports and open driveways.

With Mum leading the way we slipped into the back pew and as the congregation rose to sing the first hymn, more late comers arrived. When three young men, all strangers to me, sat in front of us, I reeled as if struck a blow. My solar plexus turned a somersault. Up and over it went. I felt it flip. It happened. Then, with her shoulder pressed to mine, Mum whispered, "Lester Pierce is home."

Oh! I stared at the man in front of me. Thin, no longer glowing with good health, his lank hair covering the collar of a suit several sizes too big, Lester was barely recognisable. Yet, as he had at my dad's funeral three years before, he sang, his basso profundo filling the church.

There was a second surprise as my friend Muriel, stood at the lectern and reading from II Corinthians 9: 6-8, implored us to give, not grudgingly nor of necessity but with willing cheerfulness. After the service as I chattered with old friends, I felt someone come to stand behind me.

"Hello, Ana-banana. Good to see you. I hear you've been ill."

Lester! I turned at once. "Yes, my appendix burst. Have you been ill too?" My question was hesitant and his reply lost as Muriel and Jim came to join us. I knew Jim. We used to play tennis with Peter and his brother Eric.

"Ana, nice to have you back. You know my fiancée, Muriel Hobbs." Jim's grin stretched from ear to ear.

"Really? How wonderful." Reaching out, I ignored the pain and drew them both into a warm hug.

Mum appeared at my side. "I'm going home in the car with Lily. Do you want to come?"

"I'd like to stay a while if that's all right. I can walk home."

"Are you sure?" Mum's concern was touching and gave me a warm glow.

As I hoped, Lester offered to walk with me and as we walked, we exchanged news. His brief engagement ended shortly after I moved north. He then went to Silverstream to do a senior year as a hospital orderly.

"I got in with a pretty rough crowd and ended up on a marae in Ruatoria," he confided. "It's a pretty wild place." Guys rode into the movies on horseback. Girls carried knives. One morning I woke and decided to come home. I left everything. Hitchhiked and arrived late Friday night. Mum and Dad have been pretty good about it. I guess I'll be home for a while."

"I arrived Saturday morning. I've three weeks sick leave," I said as a swirl of yellow leaves blew across our path and making a sudden dive, Lester snatched a few from the air. "That ought to bring you good luck," I said and when he grinned back at me and sprinkled the leaves over my hair, I felt, for the first time in a long while, truly light-hearted.

Mrs Crombie's dog, Buster, waddled out to greet us. Slow of gait, his muzzle grey, he stood panting, waiting for a kind word. Some things never change and an almost overwhelming gratitude for all things familiar flowed through me as I bent to fondle his ears. Buster had been in my life as long as I could remember, Lester too. Stepping back I stumbled and Lester was quick to offer support.

"You're tired," he said. "Perhaps you should have gone with your mother." He drew my arm through his and leaning down, kissed my forehead. "I'm glad you're here, Ana." Walking in step we turned the corner and looked across the gully to my home on the hill. *So am I*, I thought. *Very glad.*

From the wall by the gate I watched him walk away. Halfway up the hill he turned and walking backwards waved farewell as he had the night he walked me home from the seniors' dance. The night he gave me my first kiss; warm, tender and so well remembered. No other boy had given me the same wonderful feeling of belonging that I experienced with Lester. Now, amazingly, after two years away we had returned home within hours of each other. How synchronous was that? Today's meeting could hardly be a coincidence. Was providence finally taking a hand in my life?

I woke late the next morning; the house quiet, Mum already at work and Doug at school. Cautiously I stretched, testing the pain barrier. My range of physical activities increased a little each day. By the end of the month I hoped to again walk briskly, lift things and take more pleasure in the food I ate.

A note lay on the kitchen table. As I picked it up, my emotional armour slid into place.

There's vegetable soup for your lunch. Back at 5.30, Mum

How silly of me to feel anxious. A few lingering memories made my relationship with my mother somewhat cautious, but not contentious. Determined to remain optimistic and whistling off key, I made toast and poached eggs.

The days took on a routine; a short walk in the sunshine, a rest after lunch and a phone call from Lester in the evening. I thought about my future and in doing so; found I no longer wanted my nursing position. What I did want was to be with Lester. I asked Mum if I might live at home for a while.

"I'll pay board of course and apply for work as soon as possible. Something less arduous than nursing I think."

"Yes, Ana. It will be nice to have your company. I heard the local newspaper is looking for someone in their advertising department. You might try there."

I quickly wrote my resignation and posted it to the Thames hospital.

At midday Lester's phoned. "Great news, I have a job. I'm going to be a baker at Vince's Tea Shop. I start the day after tomorrow. And Mum said I was to ask you to tea. I have Dad's car. I'll come and get you."

The moment we said goodbye I contacted the local newspaper office and two hours later, walked away from a brief interview as the new advertising assistant.

Tea at the Pierces' home became a celebration as Lester and I discussed the possibilities of our future employment.

After the meal we moved to the sitting room to listen to Mario Lanza's *The Student Prince*. While Mr Pierce settled into his armchair with his newspaper and pipe, Mrs Pierce patted the couch inviting me to sit between her and Lester. As the evening progressed I felt increasingly happy and when they sang along with Mario, I joined in. Later as Lester and I sat talking in the car outside my gate, our friendly good night hug becoming a series of long ardent kisses that took us both by surprise.

We talked every day. When I began work, he called by the office each evening and drove me home. His day having begun at 4am he then went home to sleep.

On Saturday nights we went dancing at the Scottish Ingleside. At first we chose slow, sedate dances but as I recovered my agility we joined in the Scottish reels; toe-tapping, hopping, and weaving with the best, having a wonderful time. These evenings offered entertainment as well as dancing and Lester often sang. As his renown as a singer spread, invitations to perform at other functions arrived. Sometimes Mrs. Pierce came along as his accompanist. A big woman, her girth matching her generous nature, she talked and laughed with ease. I liked her very much.

Unlike the church activities that ended at eleven-thirty on a Saturday night, the private functions ran on into the early hours of the morning. Boosted by free alcohol Lester's geniality increased as the evening progressed. Outwardly he appeared an enthusiastic leader intent on generating a good time for all. But later, at the late night café, when he had drunk several cups of black coffee, I glimpsed something else. Hidden behind the man who claimed the centre of attention as a birthright, was a different person, one whose unspoken need made me want to protect and nurture him.

Café owners, Sid and Norah, often paused to chat with us as we lingered over coffee in a high-backed booth. One rushed evening, Lester and I offered to help clear tables and serve meals. Our offer immediately accepted, we both learnt to cook and serve café meals, and from then on, often helped on busy nights.

Our hectic social life and his pre-dawn start at the bakery left Lester little time for rest. Lack of sleep and missed meals made him short tempered and we began bickering over little things. I soon learned he had a knack for twisting my defences. Any attempt to outsmart him ended in failure.

Tired from our frequent late nights and concerned by Lester's changing personality, I felt stripped of creativity. I made mistakes and lost a good customer. My boss strode in demanding I do better or else. Rather than face the 'or else' I resigned. Without missing a working day, I joined the staff of a large department store where I met Sally.

Newlyweds Sally and Noel, only a year or two older than Lester and I, were buying their own home and thinking of having a family. They often invited us to supper; the four of us playing cards or monopoly. It seemed all our friends were either married or making plans for the event and I found myself dreaming of blissful domesticity with Lester.

Six months after our return home Lester turned twenty-one. His parents hired a hall and invited friends and family to join in an evening of celebration. My hopes of a proposal flew high as I hunted the shops for the perfect dress to wear to the party. I found it; the latest H-Line in petunia pink organza flocked with black flowers. It cost three weeks' pay. I thought it beautiful—Mum said ostentatious. She also doubted my ability to dance in the high-heeled sandals I bought. My mum was still quite young. Did she not remember how youthful pride and determination made anything possible?

The party was a great success. The guests, many of them renowned musicians and singers, provided entertainment. A photographer came and Lester joined various groups of people posing for the camera. Those of our age stood relaxed, without pretension. Lester stood as if ready to run. Why, I wondered, did he look so . . . so edgy?

The throbbing beat of *Caravan* filled the hall and gliding and turning with ease in my new sandals I danced, light as thistle down in Lester's arms. We passed the corner where my mother sat with old friends. She looked sad and thinking she might be missing Dad, I went to sit with her when the dance ended.

"Not loneliness," she told me. Then looking down at her hands she expressed misgiving, said she thought me unprepared for a man like Lester. I recalled my own unease at the way Lester posed for the photographer. Yet when I pressed her for further explanation, my mother was either unwilling or unable to put her feelings into words. "I know you care for Lester but he is a troubled man and might not be easy to live with," was all she would say.

I knew that. Lester had done some silly things in the past but with me there to love him he would do better. People changed when they were in love and Lester loved me. He would never hurt me. Filled with the invincible power of youth and love, I felt capable of changing the entire world if necessary. So I smiled at my mum, told her not to worry and put the whole incident aside.

When the lights dimmed for the last waltz, Lester took me in his arms, his mood serious. My heart fluttered with anticipation as adrift in the eddying dancers we moved as one, lost in the music. When the last notes faded we clung together, afraid to break the spell of being the only two people in the world. Lester spoke first. 'Tell your mother I will drive you both home. Then I have to come back and help clean the hall.'

It took me a moment to register his words. Instead of receiving the hoped for declaration of everlasting of love, I was being dismissed, sent home with my mother.

I rallied. "Then I'll stay and help you."

"No."

Protest was useless. Dejected and embarrassed I guided Mum into the front of the car then climbed in the back, fluffing up my skirts and pretending everything was just fine. My foolish fantasy had flopped. On the pavement outside our house, I fought back tears and keeping my voice cheerful, called goodnight as Lester drove away. Later, curled beneath the blankets in the dark, I chided myself for being so childish. There were a lot of relatives staying with Mrs. Pierce. Of course Lester's place was with them.

Lester's Uncle Alec had come from Auckland. He called himself the black sheep because he smoked and drank and bet on the horses. A war veteran, he relied on strong medication to control continuous pain. Penny poker was his favourite game and whenever he visited, we played for hours. He cheated but no one minded. Sometimes we played Canasta or Five Hundred in pairs with much ribbing and fast wit flying back and forth between the players, the losers compelled to buy oysters and chips for supper.

Lester admired his uncle. Together they were incorrigible. They played childish pranks with whoopee cushions and tied Mrs Pierce's apron strings to the handle of the cutlery drawer. One night they hung a sheet over a broom and waved it outside her bedroom window, giving her the fright of her life.

A month after Lester's twenty-first, Alec was found dead in his kitchen, his head in the gas oven. Perhaps his pain had become too much for him. Whatever the reason for this sad act, he would be missed. With Lester driving, the Pierce family made the long journey north to the funeral.

To fill the lonely hours without him I turned to activities at home and with Doug's help, cut the hedges and tidied the gardens working late into the long summer evenings. I sorted through my belongings, giving away toys and clothes I no longer needed. Glassware and china items were carefully wrapped in tissue and packed between the growing layers of linen in the wooden chest in my room. One day they would have a place in my own home. Mum offered some unused towels from her linen cupboard.

"One day you will meet that special someone," she said.

When I replied I thought I'd already met that someone, Mum turned silently away.

Days turned into weeks. Christmas came and went. I ran to answer the phone whenever it rang and my kid brother teased me, saying I was wearing a groove in the steps running up and down to check the letterbox. There was no word from Lester. No word at all.

Twelve

Joy of joys! Mrs Pierce reappeared today. A little murmur ran around the church as she took her usual seat in the choir. At the end of service, I hurried out and found her already leaving by the back gate.

"Mrs Pierce, please wait. Are you pleased to be home?"

She paused looking down at her handbag, her shoulders slumped. I started forward but she squeezed through the little gate closing it firmly behind her. "Yes, thank you, Ana. I wanted to tell you. Lester stayed in Auckland. He's staying with his brother." The words tumbled out in a rush and I saw, just for a moment, a brown and grey haze about her head and shoulders. She had told a lie. Why?

"I'm sorry. I didn't mean to upset you. Please tell Lester I miss him."

She turned away then and crossing the street stumbled, her hand flying out, but before I could run to her, she continued on.

The days dragged by. I called her once, but learned nothing of Lester's whereabouts or when he might return. "Best to give him space," she said. I waited for a phone call, a letter and in a flight of fancy, checked the pigeons that flew into the yard. None carried a message.

Stop fretting, I told myself. Be patient. He'll be back.

Muriel and I stood outside the church in the hot January sun. The day so warm, my bare arms tingled and were turning pink. Around us little groups of parishioners exchanged news and gossip.

"Bother. I've left my gloves inside." As Muriel hurried up the steps and back into the church I waited, fanning myself with my hymnal. I longed to be home, to take a book and lie in the shade of the apple trees and let the perfume from the clove-scented carnations waft over me.

"Hello. A good service don't you think?" I looked up at a tall, fair-haired young man. "Graham," he said and thrust out his hand.

"Ana Dockery."

Muriel reappeared, pulling on her gloves. "Hello," she smiled, "you must be the new schoolteacher. How do you like living in a country town?" While they talked, I sneaked a look at Graham. He was exceptionally good looking.

"I'm boarding with Gloria James. I think you know her." Graham's blue-eyed gaze caught one of my covert glances. Heat rushed to my cheeks.

"Yes. She is doing some machine knitting for me . . ." my voice trailed. Why was I so tongue-tied? I tried again. "Two jumpers, I expect they will be ready this week." Ashamed of my clumsy conversation I avoided his eye. But when he offered to deliver my jumpers to me at home, saying if I gave him my address and phone number he would telephone before coming, I readily obliged.

"You're quiet," Muriel commented as we drove home. "Graham's nice, don't you think?" Her question interrupted my thoughts of a tall fair man who bore a remarkable resemblance to a photograph my mother kept in her dresser drawer.

"Yes, very nice."

Graham brought me my jumpers as promised and invited me to go to the pictures. Flattered by his attention, I found myself wanting to be loyal to Lester and at the same time to test my ability to charm this intelligent and personable school teacher.

On the evening of our first date he arrived earlier than expected. I flew to the bathroom to put on make-up and as I fluffed power over my cheeks, Mum met him on the back porch. Doug joined them and I heard Graham promise him a game of darts next time he called.

"What makes him so sure there will be a next time?" I muttered seeing him nodding and smiling, my mother hanging on his every word as she drew him to the front garden to admire a stately row of arum lilies.

Graham's courtesy was faultless, his wit without sarcasm. I found it difficult not to like him. He introduced new ideas, talked about books and described the lifestyle of people in foreign counties. After our third outing, spent beside the lake making up poetry, I realised Lester and I had barely skimmed the surface of real conversation. Although we shared our feelings, I now saw our exchanges as repartee, shallow chat. I'd made light of situations that bothered him and been afraid to ask questions. Mum, Maggie and others had warned me to take care. What did they see in Lester that I did not? I knew only that he needed me and if my love remained strong, he would change for the good.

With one eye on an approaching storm, Graham led the way as we searched the lake shoreline for flat stones to skip across the mirror-like surface. Keen to outdo each other, we tussled over the best stones and having found one, I raced ahead. Graham caught me about the waist and as he spun me around the first raindrops fell. We ran laughing to the car. Still laughing, I took my glasses off to dry them. Graham leaned over and drawing me close, kissed me. In spite of telling myself I should be loyal to Lester, I responded. After a minute or so Graham sat back, took a deep breath and said, "Whoa, you kiss like a married woman."

I felt I had done something wrong, but had no idea what. I simply responded to a kiss.

"Sorry," I muttered, sitting up straight and laying my bag and cardigan tidily in my lap. Anyway, how would he know how a married woman kissed?

"I think I should take you home," he said and moving away from me, he started the car.

Graham Fitzherbert became a regular visitor to our home and inveigled by his attention, I continued to go out with him. One evening, tired after a long day at work, I slipped off my shoes and walked home barefoot. My back ached. I longed to lie in a warm bath, to relax and let my tiredness slip away. Mum greeted me at the back door, her hair neatly combed, fresh lipstick colouring her lips.

"Are you going out?" I asked.

"No. Graham is on his way round. I thought we might ask him to stay to tea. Go. Freshen up. Quickly now." She was shooing me like one of her chickens. If she'd been wearing her apron she would have flapped it.

In my room I leaned against the dresser staring at my reflection. My face was shiny and there was a pimple at the side of my nose, fat and white. Limp curls clung to the rumpled collar of my blouse. Not a sight likely to impress. Picking up a comb I tugged my hair into shape. I heard Graham call 'Hello' and Mum greeting him, urging him inside, to sit down.

"Ana won't be long," she said raising her voice for me to hear.

Etiquette demanded I wash my face, put on fresh make up and a clean blouse but I could not be bothered. This was me. Why should I pretend to be perfect? Taking a handkerchief I rubbed the shine from my face, flicked back my hair and went to greet Graham.

I knew immediately I had made the wrong decision. Graham's blue eyes lost their sparkle as they travelled from lank hair to grubby toes. I leaned back against the wall, defiant, demanding acceptance. I did not get it. After a moment's small talk, mother asked him to tea but he rose and pleading another engagement, departed without promise of seeing us again.

I told myself I didn't care. He'd been more Mum's friend than mine. And if she was disappointed, she didn't let it show. A few days later when Doug asked where Romeo had gone, I told him Graham was looking for a prissy apron-clad girl and I was not that girl.

Doug decided I needed a new boyfriend and enlisted the help of the lads in our street. They came in a continual stream, borrowing things and asking me to pass messages to Doug. They loitered at the gate and lingered on the back porch. Wherever I moved, lads popped up out of nowhere. Finally I cornered Doug and asked him what had brought the sudden influx of boys to the house.

"I thought you might be lonely. No Romeo and Lester in the funny farm."

"What!"

"Don't kill the messenger!" Doug stepped back, his concern obvious. "Sorry, Sis, I thought you knew."

"Lester? Funny farm? You mean . . .?"

Doug nodded.

"What do you know? Tell me." I guided him to my room where we sat on the edge of the bed. Doug's anxious eyes watched my face as he spoke.

"Lester cracked up when his uncle died. After the funeral he stole his father's car. Drove it without oil and wrecked it. He was drinking — or drunk. Anyway, the police found him in Wellington. Now he's in the psych. hospital."

I stared back at my brother. I knew he would not lie. Lester in a psychiatric hospital? Surely there must be some mistake.

Doug laid a warm hand on mine. "It must have been hard for Lester being so close to two suicides," he said getting to his feet. "Come on. You're shivering." Pulling me up he pushed me through the door to the kitchen where he busied about making a hot drink. Slowly my reasoning returned. Poor Lester.

"Drink up," Doug said placing a cup before me. By the time I finished the tea I knew what to do. I was going to talk to Lester's parents.

The smell of fried sausages and onions greeted me at Pierce's back door. Perhaps this was not a good time. I had half turned to go when the door opened.

"Ana. Please come in." Mrs Pierce led the way to the living room where the table was set for the evening meal. Mr Pierce grunted a welcome from behind his newspaper. Invited to sit, I did so, and for a long moment no one spoke.

"I heard about Lester. I'm very sorry. I came to ask if there is anything I can do." I looked to Mrs Pierce. She appeared near to tears.

"That is kind of you, Ana. Lester is—"

The newspaper dropped noisily to the floor. "Listen, young woman, my son is no good. You best be on your way and forget him." Mr Pierce glowered at me over his pipe. I had the feeling my mouth was behaving like a goldfish. How dare he speak so cruelly of his son? Lester needed help; needed love. Angry, I spat back.

"That's not fair. Lester is kind to me. I love him. And as a father, you should be there to help him."

Behind the smoke screen from the pipe the man's eyes narrowed. "You don't know the half of it, girl."

"I'm listening." Sustained by anger, I determined not to back down. I wanted to know. I had a right to know. My jaw tight, I stared back at him. Out of the corner of my eye I watched his wife fingering the cutlery on the table. Mr Pierce cupped his pipe in his large hands and sucked noisily. Satisfied, he blew the smoke toward the fireplace and settled back in his chair.

"You've got spunk. I'll give you that — for a girl, anyway. But you will get nowhere with that Lester." Mr Pierce shook the stem of his pipe at me. "He cannot help himself. He certainly cannot help a wife and children."

"We've not talked of marriage."

"Just as well. By the time he pays me the money he owes he will be an old man. Now, do yourself a favour and forget him." He picked up his paper and shaking out the creases replaced the screen between us. I looked to his wife who shifted uncomfortably on her chair. After a glance at the man behind the paper she motioned toward the kitchen and stood up.

"Goodbye, Mr Pierce. I really am sorry. I—" Another grunt accompanied by a flick of the newspaper signalled his goodbye. Once we were on the porch, Lester's mother gently closed the door behind us.

"It was kind of you to come, Ana."

"Is Lester all right? Was he hurt?"

"No. No bones broken. He thought so much of his uncle. It was a shock, for all of us." We heard a sound in the kitchen behind us. "Go now. And thank you, my dear."

Cycling home in the dark I realized I still did not know where Lester was or how long it might be before I saw him again.

Six weeks later I received a promotion at work and was now managing the large china and homewares section as well as dressing the company's four large street-front windows. On Friday, after working late to finish a display, I stepped out into a wet and windy night. Away from the lights of town I walked briskly. My arms folded, head bent against the strong wind I rounded a corner and collided with a man. Startled, I looked up.

"Lester!"

Wrapped in each other's arms we hugged, fiercely, tenderly, hugged on and on. We eased apart, looked at each other then hugged some more. At last, our longing satisfied, Lester spoke. "Are you going to make a habit of greeting me like this?" he asked and I grinned remembering how years ago at the annex, I had saturated him with orange juice.

"I would much rather you didn't go away," I replied.

Mr Pierce bought a new car and the old V8 now belonged to Lester. His dad said being responsible for it might teach him a thing or two, especially as Lester was paying off the repair bill. Resigned at last to my being his son's girlfriend, Mr Pierce treated me in a gruff but kindly way. One night after a boisterous evening of table-thumping poker playing at their house, Lester won almost a pound and counted out his winnings from the large cake tin Mrs Pierce used to store hundreds of pennies.

"Look, Ana," he said spreading the coins over the table. "There's almost enough here to get married." His mother and I laughed, but his dad snorted.

"Humph! It wouldn't pay the first coal bill. You'd better forget about that one, my boy."

Later, as we snuggled together in the car outside my gate, I told Lester teasing me about getting married was unfair. In spite of his father's attitude I still hoped for a proper proposal. I suppose I was hinting.

"Dad's right. It costs a lot to be married."

After Lester's candid response, we said no more. Still, I began to save money. Without proof, I assumed Lester also had a savings account.

Mum paused to admire the newly finished piece of embroidery I was ironing and I invited her to come and see my growing collection. While showing her the treasures from my glory box, I chatted, Lester this and Lester that.

"Is there not another man you could go out with? Why Lester?" Mum asked.

"Because I love him."

"Are you sure? Do you think he can provide a home and care for you?"

"Why does everyone seem to think Lester is incapable, useless?" I shrugged. "Anyway there are two of us. I can work. Earn a good wage. We will look after each other." I began putting things back in the box, my pleasure spoiled. If no one else would stand up for Lester, I would. I'd prove the two of us capable of anything. *Just you wait and see,* I thought.

Drowsy after an evening with friends, I leaned back against Lester's chest and with my finger, drew hearts in the condensation on the car windscreen. It was not late but neither my home nor the neighbouring houses showed any lights. Lester slipped his hands beneath my jumper. To keep them warm he said. His ear rubbed gently over my hair. His breath, so close, smelt of popcorn.

"I should go in, Lester." He did not move. My body fitted snugly against his.

"What time is it?" Neither of us bothered to check. Lester's lips found mine. Still we lingered.

"It must be very late."

"I wish we didn't have to say goodnight," Lester mused into my hair, my neck and my ears, "I want to have you to myself, all night."

What a deliciously wicked idea. Desire flowed through every inch of me. To stay together, all night without a curfew. No waiting parents or responsibilities. Just us. Our longing grew as the weeks passed.

One evening, after a night out, our passion fogged the car windows and left me breathless. Holding Lester at arm's length, I begged time out and moving away, sat back against the door, my legs curled beneath me. It was hard saying no but I wanted a formal promise of an ongoing future together. And if mothers the world over were to be believed, then saying 'No' loud and clear was the way to get that promise.

Lester wound down the window and sat staring out into the night. I waited, shivering a little as cold air filled the car. At last he turned. His eyes twinkling and with a smile tilting the corners of his mouth he asked, "Ana Dockery, will you please marry me? Marry me so I never have to say goodnight again."

This was not my first proposal nor the most romantic or even the most promising. But it was the one I wanted and I launched myself into his open arms saying, "Yes, yes, yes."

The following day we stood arm in arm before my mother as Lester, charmingly apologetic for not having spoken to her first, told her of my acceptance. Mum deserved a medal for her performance. She smiled and wished us well, shook Lester's hand and embraced him. Bred to be polite, she had little option.

Being engaged conjured a vision of unlimited freedom and Lester and I both pushed the boundaries of the behaviour our parents expected. Lester now worked at a bakery out of town. He drove out at midnight, returned home mid-morning and slept through the afternoon. Unknown to me, he often stopped off for a drink on his way home, patronizing several of the hotels scattered throughout the local farming community.

Late one Friday afternoon, in that mad fortnight before Christmas when everyone parties, the phone rang at work. The store manager beckoned me behind the counter.

"It's for you. Your young man, I think." He grinned and held the receiver to my ear.

"Hello. You there, Ana?" The slurred words were hard to hear.

"Lester? Is that you? Where are you?"

"Don't rush. I'm looking—"

"What's happened?" Nearby customers moved closer. I tried again. "Where are you?"

"I'm talking on the phone." He sounded surprised as if I was silly for asking the question.

"Lester, are you at a pub!?"

"M-maybe." His voice drifted.

"Wake up. Talk to me. What pub?" No answer. Was that a snore? "Lester," I hissed down the phone, "don't drive the car. Do you hear me? Don't drive the car. Promise?"

". . . promise." The line went dead.

The manager, an understanding man, raised his eyebrows. "He sounded—" I cut him short, nodded and hurried to the back store. As I hoped, the van driver sat at his desk. He delivered around the area every day and knew the hotels. Between us we narrowed the field of possibilities.

"Ring these. Ask if Lester's car is in the car park. You can use my phone," he said.

Third call lucky. I counted the money in my purse and hoping it was enough, phoned a taxi to collect me at 5pm sharp.

Somehow I had to find Lester and get him home within my tea hour.

The taxi driver spotted Lester's 1938 V8 parked with its nose against a phone box at a country pub ten miles from town. Asleep on the back seat, his dentures resting in a pile of vomit on the floor, Lester looked awful. The taxi driver was a hero. He wrapped the inebriated Lester in a rug and warning me of a possible cleaning charge, lifted him into the cab. Gingerly I picked up the teeth and secured them in my handkerchief. We locked Lester's car, not that anyone in their right mind would steal it in that state. The smell was disgusting.

Now what? Taking him home to his parents or to my teetotal mum was unthinkable. Sid and Norah! I shot from the cab before it stopped. The café empty, I ran through to the back calling for Sid. "All right, love, I'm coming." He ambled out to the cab and looked in.

"Silly young bugger," he said shaking his head. Then pulling open the car door, scooped Lester's limp form into his arms and carried him through the shop to the store room. With profuse thanks I paid the relieved cab driver.

Norah bent over Lester smacking his face. His head rolled from side to side. "Come on, Chum. Talk to me." She turned to me. "He can't stay here, Ana." Near to panic, I prepared to plead; only ten minutes of my tea hour remained. "He might be sick. We must put him in the courtyard and keep him warm," Norah continued. A camp stretcher was quickly erected and Lester's incumbent body covered with warm blankets. Norah put a comforting arm around my shoulders. "Run along, Love. We'll look after him. Come back after work. Here," she pushed a hot pie into my hand, "I don't suppose you've had any tea."

Shortly after nine o'clock I returned to the café. When he saw me, Sid rolled his eyes and pulled a face. "Go on through." He indicated the back of the shop with a nod. Dishevelled and miserable, Lester sat on the edge of the camp bed, his head in his hands. Norah came bearing black coffee.

"Get him to drink it. And see he doesn't spill it. It's hot."

It was like coaxing a child. All Lester wanted to do was to die. After the first cup, he swallowed the second and third a bit faster. Around midnight we declared Lester sober enough to be taken home. Norah drove us, her old car coughing in protest after months of rest in the rent-a-garage down the street. A couple of doors from the Pierce house, she pulled into the kerb.

Compliant but unable to stand, Lester clung to the car door. Weak with silent laughter we hoisted his lanky frame, tucked our shoulders beneath his armpits and crablike, edged our way along the street. Inside the gate we made it to the back steps, where Norah held him upright against the wall while I tried the door. It was locked. With an imploring look to the heavens, Norah whispered, "Now what?"

"Lester must have a key." I patted his pockets. He giggled like a girl. "Hush. Be quiet." Then as I felt in his trouser pocket, he grappled for my hand and lisped,

"You musthn't do that. That's naughty. Mustn't touch Pinkie."

Norah's eyebrows disappeared into her hair. Suddenly it was all too funny and leaving Lester unsupported, we doubled up with soundless laughter. Lester slid slowly down the wall to sit on the path, his legs straight in front of him, his chin sunk on his chest.

"Oh look, my shoes, four of them." He reached for his feet but instead fell sideways into a large flowerpot that tipped, rolled off the steps and smashed. A light appeared at the front of the house. Then another followed by voices and footsteps.

"Run!" Norah pulled me out the gate and down the street. We fell into the car as the house door opened to reveal a tousle haired, pyjama clad Mr Pierce.

"We should have waited," I said after we had told Sid and finally stopped laughing. "Poor Lester might still be sitting there. There's no knowing what his father might do."

"Poor Lester, my foot. He's a silly lad. You did more than enough. Let his family sort it."

"Pass the teapot. I need another sip before bed," said Norah and lifting her cup she crooked her little finger. "Pinkie," she said. Again the sound of our laughter filled the kitchen.

Not all Lester's drinking escapades were amusing. Once, when his parents went away for a few days, I offered to prepare his evening meals. I went to his house after work, cooked a meal then woke him from his day's sleep. After eating we'd wash up and he would drive me home. Except one night I arrived to find the house empty. I cooked a meal and waited.

At last his car roared up the driveway. Doors banged, the house door opened and a happily inebriated Lester came in followed by a shifty little man. Unshaven and unsavoury, the stranger stood without speaking as Lester stumbled over, planted a sloppy kiss on my cheek and disappeared into his bedroom. Expecting Lester to reappear, I placed the meal on the table and with the barest civility invited the man to sit down. When Lester failed to appear I went to get him. He lay face down sound asleep on his bed. Unable to wake him, I was on my own with a strange and unpleasant man.

The man kept insisting Lester had invited him to stay the night. Leave you here, alone, when Lester goes to work? Not likely. I gave the fellow a meal—and hid all the big knives in the kitchen. When told he must leave, he argued, repeating he'd been invited to stay. Whenever I moved, he moved. He walked a single pace behind me. Nervous, I had a desperate need to go to the bathroom. What if he followed me? There was no lock on the door.

I tried several times to wake Lester. I even put ice on his face and neck but he slept on. As I washed the dishes, the creepy little guy stood beside me wringing his hands the whole time. I had to get this man out of the house. It took a lot of argument but finally he agreed to take a taxi to a hotel. I willingly paid for it all. Anything rather than have him in the house. After he'd gone I checked all the locks making sure the house was secure.

I then turned my attention to Lester. Along the top of his bed was a row of large biscuit tins each containing an alarm clock. The amplified sound of their ticking filled the room as I pondered my situation. Should I stay and wake him in time of work or phone his boss and say Lester was ill?

The phone in the hall rang, making me jump.

"What are you doing there? Do you know what time it is? It's after midnight. You are to come home at once."

I tried to explain to my distraught mother about the creepy little man, Lester's inebriation and how I was unable to wake him. Her response was to burst into tears. That really upset me. Sniffing, and with tears running down my cheeks, I rifled Lester's pockets taking enough money for a taxi fare then setting all four alarm clocks five minutes apart, I locked the door behind me and went home.

Mum lay alone in her big bed, a box of tissues beside her. She looked so small and lost I felt a rush of something close to pity. I apologized, telling her I'd been so concerned about keeping Lester, the Pierce's property and myself safe, I hadn't thought to telephone. When I told her how the man behaved, she blamed Lester for putting me in a dangerous situation. Blamed him for a lot of things, pointing out his reckless behaviour and telling me I had changed from a generous, thoughtful girl to a headstrong and inconsiderate creature who had forgotten her family. Unable to continue she sobbed on while I sat beside her feeling wretched.

I did not disbelieve my mother. I knew Lester was different to other young men. What I did believe, was that I could help. That with a steadfast and loving partner, Lester would change; settle down.

The point was, I thought as Mum's sobs subsided, any trust between us had worn away. The erosion began the day she told Doug and me our father was going to die; when she folded her hands beneath her apron and refused to comfort her children. She let me down when I really needed her. There was no trust. No loyalty. Each time our needs clashed the old wound reopened and layer upon layer of thick scaring sealed the pain inside. I'd told myself I did not need a mother.

From that night on, Mum tightened her control of my activities. While I was living in her house, I must abide by her rules. I railed against the mandate, saying I must be the only engaged person whose time with her fiancé was controlled by her mother.

"Where is your ring?" Mum scoffed. "When do you plan to wed? Have you set a date? That Lester has no money. How will you live?"

I had no answers. I came home at the expected time, said goodnight and went to bed. But later, when the house was quiet I climbed from my bedroom window and ran, shoes in hand, up the street to where Lester waited in the car.

To atone for his foolishness, Lester gave me a tiny heart shaped locket on a gold chain and promised he'd never again drink to excess. The necklace was beautiful, his apologies sincere and I forgave him.

Throughout Dad's illness, our mother had withdrawn from family life and spent a great deal of time alone in her room. Now the pendulum swung the other way. Hyper active and often enraged over small incidents, we never knew what to expect of her. One Saturday morning she burnt a batch of biscuits and in her anger, used words that left Doug and I stunned. Our mum never swore. When we offered pacification she verbally abused us. Defeated, we left her blaming the universe for the numerous inadequacies in her life while scraping black biscuits into the rubbish tin.

"Everything I do or say is wrong," I complained to Norah. "Even young Doug is receiving regular tongue lashings. Mum is hot then cold. If she's not angry, she's crying. I don't know what to do for the best."

"Sounds like menopause. My sympathies are with your mother," Norah said.

Unable to help, I simply kept out of Mum's way. I bemoaned my miseries to Lester and expressed my longing for us to have our own home far away from parental tyranny.

"Perhaps we should run away. Elope. My dad's got a big ladder. Shall I bring it round?" he joked.

"Idiot. My window's four foot from the garden."

Lester began to sing. *'James, James. Hold the ladder steady. James, James. I am packed and I am ready.*

I thought he was teasing me and continued to laugh, clapping in time with the song. Suddenly serious, he looked at me. "We could you know. Just go."

"Where would we go?"

"To Eric and Brenda."

I felt my body go still as I recalled Eric and Brenda. Brenda's mother had fought their marriage, refused to attend the wedding and destroyed Brenda's wedding gown. Steadfast in their love, the couple married anyway and then moved far away. I looked into Lester's eyes. He was serious. Dare we?

Once the idea took hold it became not a matter of *could*, but *when* we would leave. The following night Lester received twenty pounds for singing at a reunion dinner. The MC offered him several more well paid engagements. If we waited three weeks we'd have a substantial sum of money. Three weeks it was.

Excited, edgy, and unable to share our plans with anyone else, we phoned each other three or four times a day. We did not last the three weeks. Eight days later, without the help of a ladder, we eloped.

Thirteen

We drove through the night singing, the car radio at its loudest. Each time we passed through one of many small towns to forge ahead beyond the lights, Lester thumped the horn, the triumphant sound cast out into the night followed by laughter, our sense of freedom and independence increasing with every mile. After five hours of driving, Lester's attention wavered. Too tired to eat, we climbed into the back seat and curled beneath a shared rug, slept until dawn.

The following afternoon, the lift being out of order, we trod the stairs to the third floor of the city newspaper building.

"I hope he's here."

"He will be." Lester squeezed my hand. At the top of the stairwell where telephones rang and voices shouted over the clatter of typewriters, we found Eric's office. Alongside his name *Eric Larsen Chief Reporter,* someone had drawn a cowboy hat with an arrow through it.

Eric rose from behind a large desk to greet us. "Well, well," he kept saying, "this is a surprise. Let me phone Brenda." His communication was brief. "I'm bringing home a couple of guests. They will stay the night. Expect us at my usual time — and Brenda, cook something nice."

Sweet, calm Dresden-like Brenda welcomed us at the front door of their home. Within her warm and long hug were all the things I felt were missing from my life; serenity, purpose and loving friendships. She showed Lester and I to the room prepared for us and we quickly settled in. At dinner, Eric opened a bottle of wine and with the guys exchanging puns and wisecracks like they used to, Brenda and I relaxed and listened.

As the evening progressed Eric's chauvinistic attitude became more obvious. He demanded constant attention from Brenda and made cruel and unnecessary remarks about his gentle and very pregnant wife. He reminded me of the colonials in India. Men who insisted the natives iron their newspapers and even their bank notes. Eric had Brenda fetching and carrying, catering to his every whim and when I offered to go in her place, he insisted I sit. I was a guest and no guest of his would pour tea.

"He likes giving orders doesn't he?" I whispered to Lester as we prepared for bed.

"Yeah. Back home he played the field and rated his conquests. I was surprised when he married. Poor Brenda."

Invited to stay, we did. With so little money, we had no option. One morning Eric patted the couch beside him suggesting I sit with him. When I chose not to move, he came to sit on the arm of my chair. His hand fondling my knees he reminded me how, as a mixed pair, we had fought our way up the tennis ladder. He wanted to know if I had fancied him, perhaps had a schoolgirl crush on him?

What I wanted was to hit him. But Lester and I needed his hospitality until we found a place of our own. So I smiled and agreed with him, saying it had indeed been so. "Things change," I told him. "You're married and I'll soon marry Lester, the man I love." I talked fast, extolling my happiness and Lester's virtues until Eric abandoned his obnoxious pestering and moved away. He did not bother me again and preferring to forgive and forget I did not tell Lester of the incident.

Unlike my twenty-one year old fiancé, I needed parental consent to marry. In a letter to my mother I chose my words with care and Lester added a note promising to love and provide for me. I enclosed the necessary consent forms, crossed my fingers and hoped for the best. Lester wrote to his parents and while waiting for replies, we searched for work and a place to live.

Eric provided helpful local information. Two bridges spanned the broad river that split the city in two. At peak hour congested traffic crawled over the bridges. To live and work on one side of the river seemed best and we concentrated our search to where the long, single street of shops lay sandwiched between the river and miles of sandy foreshore. Each day I collected the morning newspaper and found in the classifieds, a semi-furnished beach-front cottage with a six month lease.

The owner's directions led us past the main swimming beach with its kiosk, playground and tent sites to a quieter area where a pink two-storied house stood out from a row of bungalows. The high wooden gate creaked as Lester and I pushed through. Tucked behind the wall, in the front corner of the garden, was a vine-covered cottage. An elderly gent proceeded by three black and white cats came to greet us. "Please, go in and have a look," he said with a bow to me. "The family uses the place in the summer, hence the six month lease. There is furniture and blankets, some pots and pans."

Slipping off our shoes, we stepped into a long narrow room. The bare concrete floor felt smooth and cool beneath my feet. To one side two large cane chairs piled with faded cushions flanked a small table. The first of two main rooms contained a dining table and chairs, the second a large bed and a chest of drawers. Leafy green vines trailed across the windows and from somewhere outside the shimmering light of reflected water rippled over the ceiling. Entranced, I stood in the centre of the room. One of the cats bunted back and forth against my calves. I bent and lifted it. Fat and heavy, its coat glossy, the cat purred loudly as it kneaded my shoulder. Things thrived here. I could feel it.

"Do you like it?" Lester asked. I nodded and he came to hug me — cat and all. A polite cough from the doorway interrupted our long kiss.

"The shower needs attention. If you come with me I'll show you the bath and the washhouse." The owner led us across the garden to a large corrugated iron shed. Tendrils of morning glory and potato vine had explored every chink; covered the exterior and snuck inside. Beside the shed was a large pile of driftwood. "We all collect wood to fire the copper," he said.

A huge copper filled a corner beside a pair of wooden tubs and in the gloom, at the back of the shed, sat the biggest bathtub ever. The tap, a large brass lion's head encrusted with blue-green patina, stared with dull eyes at numerous small spiders whose silken trapezoids extended the length and breadth of the bath.

"It won't take much to clean it up. You're welcome to use it." He turned from the entrance, the cats running ahead, tails high. At the opening I paused. There was no door. Well, we could always swim in the sea.

The gentleman's daughter arrived. She invited us to tea and after fresh scones and jam we signed a six month lease on the cottage.

"Have you been through to the beach?" she asked. "Follow the path at the side of the house." We rose, shook hands then waved goodbye as Mr Samuels and his daughter went indoors leaving the cats basking in the sun.

Eager to see the beach, we hurried along the path to where clumps of toetoe lined the boundary, their feathery plumes flying in the sea breeze. Before us lay the limitless Pacific Ocean; to our right pale sand stretched to a distant headland gauzed in blue-grey sea mist. In the other direction red safety flags marked the swimming beach. Beyond them at the wharves, oscillating cranes, dwarfed by the towering landmass of Lookout Point, moved at a stately pace. At first speechless then exhilarated by the open space we ran, leaping, our arms outstretched, along the water's edge.

Our little cottage overflowed with love and happiness. Lester found work as a nursing assistant at the old folk's home while I served behind the counter of the corner shop three mornings a week. Every morning rain or shine, we walked on the beach.

Lester lost his night-shift pallor and gained weight. We danced to music on the radio, read books and encouraged each other to try different foods. At night we slept, spooned between the sheets.

After three weeks of anxious waiting, letters arrived from Lester's parents. A twenty-pound note fell from his mother's letter. On a page filled with large spidery writing, she wished us well and reminded Lester the door was always open at home. In a footnote she hoped he'd write regularly. Lester sat tapping the other envelope against the table, reluctant to read his father's words.

"Come on, I can't bear the suspense. It's only words. Whatever he says, we can work through it," I said leaning over to hug him. Lester opened the envelope. I paced the small room, brushed imaginary dust from the radio and straightened a calendar on the wall. At last he refolded the pages. "Well, what does your father have to say?"

A subdued Lester handed me the letter. "You read it," he said.

To My Youngest Son, Lester,

The manner of your departure has been a great shock to your mother. However, we have talked over the situation and are trying to understand.

We appreciate that we were a great deal older than the average parents when you were born and have not perhaps been as close as we might. We have done our best to instil in you the basics of honesty and reliability. In this, I may have failed.

I expect you to honour your debt to me. There is still three hundred and forty pounds owing. As you now have the added responsibility of a wife, I will lower the monthly payments to six pounds. I expect regular payments.

I have spoken with Mrs Dockery and we are agreed that in the circumstances, you should marry. I trust you will write often to your mother and reassure her of your welfare.

Your father
N. Pierce

"Mum has agreed. We can get married. This is wonderful news." Jubilant, I spun about the room, pulled Lester to his feet and hugged him.

I waited impatiently for my mother's letter. It came four days later written in beautiful neat script, blue ink on pale blue paper and every dot in place. She was, she wrote, sending me the things from my room as I requested. The balance of my wages would cover the cost of transporting them.

To save any further embarrassment she had signed the consent forms — *to save any further embarrassment?* She thinks I am pregnant! Well, Mum, you are so wrong. I didn't run away because I had to, but because I wanted to. I'll jolly well show you. Lester and I will have a most wonderful loving marriage, one that will last forever.

I made light of my mother's words; refused to admit to being hurt. She had not asked if I might be expecting a child, she simply assumed I was. We, because it included Lester, had been unjustly accused. Mrs Dockery, you are in for a surprise. Slowly, deliberately, I tore her letter into tiny bits, carried it to the beach and standing knee deep in the waves, let the wind take and scatter the pieces.

We arranged to be wed in the Methodist church on Friday, April 18th. Lester booked us a single night at a recently opened hotel and invited Brenda and Eric to join us for dinner. I borrowed Brenda's sewing machine and set about making my wedding dress. Stitched with pride and care, the pale pink, satin brocade gown was ready to be hemmed a full week before my big day. Eager to finish, and unwilling to wait until Lester had a day off and could take me to Brenda's in the car, I instead asked Mr Samuels for the loan of his wheelbarrow. He thought it a huge joke as with the carefully wrapped dress, my sewing kit and the sewing machine on board, I wheeled the wooden barrow toward the gate.

"Wait a moment!" He rushed off and returned with an oilcan. Still laughing he gave the big iron wheel a good squirt before waving me on my way.

My arrival with the barrow made Brenda laugh too. Time flew as we chattered, measured and pinned. We forgot about lunch and Eric until we heard his car at the gate. Brenda's cheeks paled. Bundling the sewing into the spare room, she hurried to the kitchen. As she hastily filled the kettle and made sandwiches, I opened the door to Eric.

"Hello. You're early today. Look," I pointed to his car. "Is that tyre flat?"

"Which one? They look fine to me."

"Sorry." I dawdled back up the path asking questions about the plants in the garden. Eric became impatient.

"I'm hungry. Brenda will have lunch ready," he growled.

I hoped this was true. It was, for as we walked into the house, Brenda came from the kitchen carrying a laden tray. After eating, Eric asked for a second cup of tea.

"Half a cup will do," he said as Brenda rose awkwardly from her chair and went to refill his cup. I could see she was tired. She returned, placed the half cup of tea beside Eric and sank wearily back into her chair. He never seemed to thank her. A moment later he turned to pick up the cup.

"I asked for a cup of tea."

"Half a cup," I corrected. He ignored me and glared at Brenda.

"I want to drink my half-cup from the top half of the cup. Take this away. Get me another."

Surely he was joking. Brenda struggled out of her chair.

"Let me," I reached for the cup.

"No. It's her job. Let her do it." Eric's voice cut like a whip.

"Get lost," I hissed and taking the cup, headed for the kitchen with Brenda close behind. "Why do you let him treat you like that?" I was shaking with anger. Brenda laid a cool hand on my arm.

"It's all right, Ana. I understand him."

I didn't understand either of them.

Lester and I chose to keep our marriage as close to the conventional service as possible; except there were no guests. I arrived at the church by taxi. As I alighted, the driver, a cheerful bloke, stuck his head out the window and called, "Would you like me to wait in case you change your mind?"

Awed by the size and hushed atmosphere of the church's vaulted interior, I hesitated at the door. Lester, Eric and Brenda appeared doll-like in the far-off front pew. The minister appeared beside me.

"I thought I might walk with you in place of your father," he said offering his arm. Gratitude for his understanding coupled with a momentary rush of sadness had me near tears.

Together we stepped into the carpeted aisle. A hidden organist sent familiar chords billowing to the rafters. My spirit soared; my new life as Mrs Lester Pierce was about to begin.

We emerged from the church into a shower of confetti thrown by two giggly young ladies from the women's auxiliary. "A wedding is not a wedding without confetti," they called as still giggling, they disappeared around a corner. Eric was in excellent form organizing photographs and driving the car. Later, when the four of us settled in the cool, smoke-dimmed comfort of the hotel lounge, the barman grinned down at us — Brenda, eight months pregnant and me in a gown as close to white as I dared, my bouquet of roses on the seat beside me. Leaning closer he asked, "Which one of you two is the bride?"

Brenda shook her finger. "Cheeky," she said as he passed us each a free drink.

During dinner as Lester and Eric told hilarious stories making us laugh so much it hurt, a waiter brought a bottle of champagne to our table.

"From over there," he said. Across the room, our landlord and a large group of people raised their glasses. Nodding and smiling, they wished us well. Happiness filled, I caught Lester's eye. Holding my gaze he reached out and pulled me close.

"Together for ever," he whispered.

Our meal over Lester and I went to our room to change. As I dried my hands in the bathroom I heard a sharp metallic *ping*.

"No!"

Lester came running. "What is it? What's the matter?"

"My wedding ring. It's gone down the plug hole."

My handsome husband leaned over the bath, his hair falling over his eyes as usual. "It might fit," he said, doubt in his voice. "Don't cry. We'll find it. It could have gone anywhere."

We began looking. Lester, wearing a skimpy pair of yellow under pants and socks to match, climbed into the bath to check the gap between the bath and the wall. I, wearing a lace slip and panties, lay on the floor and peered beneath the bath.

That was how the housemaid found us.

"Sorry. I come back later." She was backing out the door when I called.

"Please don't go. I've lost my wedding ring." I scrambled to my feet, Lester hopped from the bath and the diminutive maid came slowly to stand between us.

"There," she pointed to where the gold ring lay beneath the lip of the soap dish. "That your ring?"

"Thank you so much." I wanted to hug her, but instead hugged Lester who placed the oversized ring back on my finger saying, "We must get that fixed."

Laughing, we told our friends about losing the ring and still laughing made our way out to the car where I moved a pile of library books making room for Eric and Brenda to sit in the back seat.

"Library books?" An incredulous Eric lifted the books, reading the titles. "You're taking library books on your honeymoon?" In the front seat Lester and I exchanged smiles. Our time together was one long honeymoon and started with six glorious weeks in the little cottage by the sea. A short time later, amid profuse thanks, we wished our friends goodnight and then drove to the jewellers. Rather than risk losing the ring,

I left it at the shop. The owner promised us it would be the right size by lunchtime on Monday.

By the time we reached the car parked down the street it was nine o'clock. All along the street shops shut their doors and turned out the lights; closed for the weekend.

On our return to the hotel, Lester suggested a nightcap and we lingered in the lounge bar studying the other guests and trying to guess what they did for a living. After three nightcaps I felt somewhat light-headed and leaned against Lester as we climbed the stairs. He opened the door and flicked the light switch. No light. Still holding each other we stumbled across the room in the dark and fell onto the bed. The springs groaned. We bounced a little, testing. The bed springs twanged in response. For a moment we sat very still.

Then, fuelled by our three nightcaps, we jumped on that bed. We stood up and ran across it. We somersaulted and danced. We fell in a heap helpless with laughter then rose bouncing time after time, the cacophony of bed springs accompanying our every move. At last, exhausted by our exuberance, we lay still. Calm now, our kissing and touching slow and gentle.

"Wait," Lester whispered and motioning me to get off the bed, he pulled the mattress to the floor. As I drifted into sleep I wondered at our childish behaviour. I also hoped Lester had locked the door.

We woke early and straightened the room. Today we planned to drive up the coast to Tolaga, an area new to me but one Lester loved. He spoke glowingly of its isolation and pristine beauty and I was eager to see it through his eyes, to share his pleasure. Lester went to collect a picnic basket of food to take with us. While waiting for someone from the kitchen to bring the basket, he talked with a man cleaning in the bar. A bell above the bar rang, stopped and rang again. The man saw Lester was curious.

"That's nothing," he said. "You should've heard it last night. It's attached to the bed in the bridal suite. We thought they were gonna come through the ceiling. I'd like to shake that young fellow by the hand. I wonder how he feels this morning."

A maid brought the picnic basket. Lester slid from the bar stool. "Pretty good, I expect," he said as he sauntered out the door.

Our official honeymoon began with a succession of new and wonderful landscapes. The narrow gravel road followed the course of the river, winding along steep ridges with so many twists and turns, we thought they would never end. Rugged bush covered the hills, the dark canopy strung with banners of glistening white clematis. In some places massive scars gouged the cliff-face, the land torn where rocks had tumbled to the river and been dragged to the sea. Unlike anything I knew, this was a wild place, barely touch by man.

Tens of miles from the last habitation, we rounded a bend and spread before us saw a sweeping bay, a tiny cluster of iron roofs and boats pulled up on the beach.

A perfect horseshoe backed by a line of low hills, the bay was a jewel. Set in a band of silver sand, the sapphire sea sparkled in the sunlight. An ancient, gnarled pohotukawa tree sprawled over sand and sea. A silver-green pier, its faded timbers near invisible against the shimmering water, jutted from the beach.

Arm in arm, with the breeze intertwining strands of our hair, we waded in the crystal clear water. When we turned the sun was at our back and as its warmth seeped deep beneath my skin, I felt my shoulders relax and my body soften. How long had I held myself stiff, afraid to let go? Months? More like years. Here in this beautiful place, with a man I loved and who loved me, I was discovering a deeper sense of freedom; the freedom to be myself.

All too soon our idyllic weekend ended and we settled back at the cottage. My savings spent, we now budgeted with care. Lester ate good meals at the hospital. I seldom cooked for myself, preferring fresh fruit, salads, bread and cheese.

Two large wooden crates arrived at the door. Dragging, pushing and skewing, I shifted them into the sunporch and with the poker, levered off the lids. Mum sent me everything: all of my clothes, pictures, a mirror and the contents of my glory box. Even a half burned candle from my dresser. She added my books from the shelves in the living room and shoes from the washhouse cupboard. At first elated, but then as I dug deeper into the crates, a feeling of finality took hold. By sending me everything, my mother had wiped me from her house. There could be no turning back. Cradling a cushion Grandma made for my tenth birthday, I quietly wept for what might have been.

Fourteen

We enjoyed five blissful months at the cottage before my meagre hours of work at the corner shop ended and I joined Lester on the staff at the Aged Care Home — not as a nurse but as a seamstress mending bed linen. Eager to please, I worked fast. So fast I unwittingly cleared the sewing room and put an end to my employment. Our lease on the cottage expired and we moved into a spacious flat, one of four in a large, well-kept house situated on a quiet avenue across the river. Away from the cool sea breezes, and unused to such hot summer weather, we both lacked our usual energy. While I searched for work, Lester took extra shifts. Even so, we sometimes ended up with more week than money.

An outbreak of H bug spread throughout the country targeting the young and the elderly. Newspapers reported deaths from the disease. Appalled to hear the staff at the care facility used neither gloves nor masks and that hand washing between patients was rare, I first lectured Lester and then begged him to take care. Two weeks after our discussion he collapsed; an ambulance rushing him to the isolation unit of the nearby hospital. For forty-eight hours he hovered, then rallied. The crisis over, I visited often.

In preparation for my fourth visit, I curled my hair, applied makeup and dressed in my favourite white blouse and navy crepe suit, set out on the long walk to the hospital. The sky looked most peculiar; a kind of mustard yellow, the clouds brown. I walked briskly hoping to dispel the uncommon stillness of the empty street. Caught in sudden spate of wind and heavy rain, I pushed on holding my umbrella before me. Unable to see ahead I stumbled into something soft. Off balance, I teetered.

Whipped from my hands, my umbrella landed in a tree where it hung, twisted and torn while I, soaked to the skin, stood ankle deep in horse manure.

I trudged on through wind and rain up the big hill to the hospital. In the foyer I paused to catch my breath, an ever growing puddle at my feet. Passers-by gave me strange looks; little wonder, with my hair plastered to my head and my lovely white blouse streaked blue. Worse, my skirt had shrunk to my knees, but not my petticoat. I squelched my way down the corridor, six inches of exposed wet lace clinging to my legs, my wrists protruding from the now three-quarter length sleeves of my jacket. In the rhythm of my steps I imagined an exchange of words with my mother.

'You are so stubborn, Ana.'

'Define stubborn. How is stubborn different from determined? You say stubborn. I say determined. What does it matter? I'm here.' I bent to kiss Lester on the lips.

His face a picture, he stared up at me. "What is that awful smell?"

"Horse manure," I said and told him of my eventful walk to the hospital. Tears in his eyes, he begged me to stop as laughing hurt more than he could bear.

Lester's illness frightened me and during his stay in hospital I dithered between finding work and wanting to spend time with him. Unprepared for the role of breadwinner and with few budgeting skills, I barely knew where to start. While living in the nurses' home or with Mum there had been no overheads. Now the costs of rent, power, gas and food needed to be met. Each morning I borrowed a newspaper and after checking the job column, attended several interviews without success.

Two weeks after Lester's admission to hospital, I sat in a patch of sunlight on the balcony eating my breakfast. I chewed slowly, determined to savour the last slice of bread. After today it would be potatoes — or flour; there was little else in the cupboards.

As I ate, I remembered breakfast-time in the red and cream pantry at home. Newspaper spread on the wooden benchtop. Dad cutting thick slices from the loaf, spreading them with bacon fat: the little marble inside the kettle bouncing as the water boiled for tea; music from the radio. Sometimes Dad would dance a soft shoe shuffle, the metal clips on his plaid slippers clicking in time to the music as he side-stepped across the kitchen floor.

A tremendous sense of loss, flip-side of the happy memory, washed through me and my tears flowed. Please, I begged, my face turned to the sky, show me what to do.

The gate clicked. Below me our landlord, John, stood gazing about the garden. When we first moved in I cleared the unattended weed-infested mess and planted geranium and daisy cuttings. All had flourished. As I watched, John cupped his hand about a pink rose and inhaled its perfume before disappearing beneath the balcony to rap on the front door. Slowly, I got to my feet. How was I to tell him I had no money to pay the rent?

"Hello, Ana. Beautiful day isn't it. I've been admiring your garden. How's that man of yours? Is he home yet?"

"No, he's still in hospital." I felt John's brown eyes checking me in a kindly way.

"I've come to ask you to dinner this evening." John and his wife Loren lived a few houses down the street. Were they going to tell me I must leave the flat, softening the blow with dinner? Whatever the reason, the chance of a good meal could not be ignored.

"Yes. Thank you. And please thank Loren." I waved from the door step, my smile fading the instant I turned back indoors.

As I busied about with broom and duster, I had an idea. Someone might buy some of my things. There wasn't much: some pretty Royal Albert china, a set of crystal glasses and a boxed carving set. I fetched the watch Fran gave me when

I began high school. Reluctant to let it go I sat, running the links of the silver strap through my fingers. I lifted a gold chain bracelet with a padlock clasp; my father's only gift. Of all the items on the table, I treasured the bracelet most. I hoped one day to have a child, a little girl who might also delight in the gift of a gold bracelet.

"Ana, are you home?" Linda from the back flat called up the stairs. Baby cradled in her arms, her rotund figure rocking as she crossed the room, she dropped onto a chair opposite me. "My mum has had a fall. I need to go to her place, today, now. Can you look after bubs for me? I'll pay you."

"There's no need to pay . . ."

Linda cut me short. "Don't be silly. I'll be back by four. I've left her things in a bag in your hallway." Linda laid her sleeping baby on the couch and packed her in with cushions. "She should sleep two hours. Thank you. Bye. See you at four." She clattered back down the stairs leaving behind a familiar sweet milky smell. After a moment I rose and returning the gold bracelet to its usual place at the back of my drawer, went to collect Linda's bag.

Tucked in a corner of the bag alongside the clean naps I found a toy horse made of white towelling. A gold bell hung from a ribbon about its neck. With Lester so ill and me without funds, the white horse magic had returned just in time. Linda offered money and tomorrow I'd have more from the second-hand dealer. The white horse was a sign of better things to come. Filled with hope, I packed the saleable items into my shopping basket and setting it aside, spent a contented afternoon with the baby.

Promptly at five I tapped at the door of John's house. He came from the glasshouse across the lawn, wiping his hands down the sides of his pants.

"Ana, I'm pleased you've come. I have something to show you." He led the way through a hole in the hedge and into the property next door. Pushing aside branches and the creepers that festooned them, I followed him to the back porch of a weather-beaten house. "I bought this property last week. Old man James lived alone here for years. The inside is worse than the garden."

I pulled a face wondering what this had to do with me.

"I've seen what you've done at the flat, Ana. The wonderful way you fixed the garden, the little bits of decorating inside, and the place is always clean and neat. I wondered if you'd help me clean and paint this place. It'll be hard work I know. You can have the flat rent free and I will pay you two pounds a week. I think six, maybe eight weeks. What do you say?"

I had no words. My fears about the outcome of this meeting rocketed into relief and joy. Close to tears I dared not speak.

"Ana? I'm sorry. Am I asking too much? I thought . . ." his voice trailed away.

"No. I'd love to help. Look at this Judas tree and the magnolias. There's crazy paving, a birdbath . . . *and* a pond. It's like that book, *The Secret Garden*." I eased my way through the undergrowth. "This wistaria must be a hundred years old!"

"Don't get too carried away. You haven't seen inside yet."

I didn't care. I could do anything. No mess would be too great. Lester might help too, when he came home.

Loren provided a delicious meal insisting I take home the left over dessert and a fruit loaf. Before going to bed I unpacked my shopping basket, returning things to their usual places. *White horse magic triumphs again.*

The following week Lester relapsed suffering a series of rigors. Five days later he was still subdued. I attributed this to his poor health and sat quietly, holding his hand instead of chattering on as I usually did. But when a pretty blonde nurse holding a bundle of magazines came to stand beside his bed, his hand slid from mine. His eyes lit up, the magnetism between them palatable. On my walk home I pondered Lester's obvious interest in the blonde nurse. He was still seriously ill. I reasoned that feeling close to someone able to give practical and caring help was natural and pushing aside my suspicious thoughts, worked harder than ever on John's new property.

A defensive and moody Lester returned home three weeks later. He brightened only when talking of the blonde nurse, Pamela. She, it seemed, was a saint. I assumed this attitude to be part of his diminished health. I fussed over him, reluctant to leave him alone while I continued to work with John at the old house. One evening, tired and hungry after a full day of painting kitchen cupboards, I returned to find Lester had eaten the food set aside for our evening meal.

"How can you be so thoughtless? We can't afford more food. We're barely scraping through. You know that." To show him how little cash we had, I opened the tin of housekeeping money. It was empty. "You took the money too?" Incredulous at finding the money gone, I seethed, my anger growing.

"I needed petrol for the car." His response petulant, he continued, "to take Pamela back to the hospital."

That blonde Barbie doll had been here, in our home? I sat back in my chair. "I think you'd better explain that."

He gave me his story without hesitation. Lester had a knack of shifting any possible blame from himself to the accuser and I heard how Pamela came to return a pair of slippers she thought belonged to him.

"They weren't mine but it was only polite," he said, "to drive her back to the nurses' home." Charming and apologetic, he came to kneel beside me, holding my hands and telling me I was the only girl he wanted or cared about. In the end I felt guilty for misjudging him.

Later, as I lay beside him in the dark, I knew one of us must find full-time work very soon. I also needed to tell him his father said, if we were unable to make the payments, we could return the car. He had linked us together making it a shared obligation. In other circumstances I'd have been pleased and proud but there was something unsettling about being jointly responsible for Lester's financial affairs.

The work on the James property complete, John invited us dinner and told me to bring the rent book. Loren cooked roast lamb and encouraged us to second helpings of crisply baked kumara, potatoes and pumpkin. After eating we gathered round the piano. Loren played and the men sang popular ballads, John's true tenor a pleasant surprise. It was a happy occasion made happier when John took the rent book and asked what the date was.

"April the first, April fool's day. How could you forget?" Loren chided him. John scribbled away in the book.

"There," he said handing back the book, "your rent is paid to the 1st of May. You deserve that. You did a wonderful job of work, Ana. Thank you." He planted a kiss on my cheek.

That night, for the first time since Lester's illness, our shared loving was tender and complete. His head pillowed on my breast Lester nuzzled me, his lips soft and warm. "Do you know, Mrs Pierce," he murmured sleepily, "we've been married almost a year."

A few days later I accepted a nursing position at a small maternity hospital seventy miles away. After a hurried round of goodbyes to John, Loren and our neighbours, we packed our belongings onto a hired trailer and drove to our new home. Everyone there was friendly; neighbours, townsfolk and the staff at the hospital, all made us welcome. As I settled at the cottage hospital, Lester, with avid spiel, began selling life insurance. On our first payday Lester and I amicably allocated household finances. He agreed to pay the rent and look after the car while I assumed responsibility for the rest.

I loved our new rental home with its large garden. A hen house and run filled a back corner and I bought four black hens; Celeste, Cleo, Clara and Clunk, the smallest, but who laid the biggest eggs.

On our first wedding anniversary we celebrated with a candlelit dinner and raising our glasses, drank a toast to a long and happy future together. Our lives glowed with promise—and the irritatingly saintly Pamela lived far far away.

Flushed with new vitality and keen to socialize, Lester joined the local amateur operatic society. With a major role in the current production of South Pacific, Lester became Lezz and loved every minute of his new popularity. This large and garrulous group of people drew us into a whirl of social activity. The cast rehearsed on empty stomachs. Then, late at night, filled some favourite café where they wined and dined before driving to someone's home to carouse into the early hours of the morning.

My shift work excluded me from much of this conviviality. Instead I made friends with the woman from the Ladies Auxiliary. With them there was no compulsion to wear the latest fashion or to have my hair sculptured every week. Besides, I was happier at home with my knitting than out on the town. Lester/Lezz bought pale mauve shirts and ties to match. He required a winter coat, a hat and new shoes. Then a new wallet, leather gloves, an expensive fountain pen and sheepskin covers for the car seats. No longer fit to press his trousers; I now sent them to the dry cleaners.

From the way Lester spoke at our infrequent meals together at home, I believed he was doing well in his job. He seemed to have plenty of money and often took me out to a film or a restaurant for dinner. Whenever we managed a day off at the same time we drove into the magnificent hill country beyond the town or to a beach and picnicked, just the two of us, together, a couple in love.

When the *South Pacific* season ended, the cast agreed to an additional three performances in a nearby city. I asked the charge sister for special leave to attend but my request was refused. The results of last year's Christmas parties apparent, the wards overflowed and extra beds lined the corridors to accommodate the influx of spring babies and their mothers.

Lester agreed to transport some props for the show in his car and on Thursday afternoon he held me close as we kissed goodbye.

"I must go," he said but instead driving away, he sat behind the wheel staring through the windscreen. Sensing something amiss and wanting to hug him again, I stepped forward to prolong the farewell. In the same instant he backed from the driveway, returning only a brief salute as I waved goodbye.

The house felt empty without him and I wandered from room to room before deciding to work in the garden; work being the best cure for the blues.

Our lovely home was an estate property soon to be for sale. As occupiers, we had first option and I worked hard to maintain both the house and garden. My savings were growing and with our rent money going toward a deposit, we'd soon be in a position to buy. I wanted to put down roots, to plant a tree and watch it grow; right here, in this town, among friends. We planned to have a dog and later, children.

At sunset I returned the garden tools to the shed. The hens clucked as they scurried to peck handfuls of wheat tossed into the run. Indoors in the warm I cooked myself a meal and ate at the kitchen table, the flow of popular music from the radio dissolving the last of my earlier loneliness. Later I filled the bathtub and lay soaking in the scented water letting the day's tiredness melt away. Wrapped snugly in my dressing gown and ready for sleep, I reached beneath my pillow for my nightgown and found an envelope.

Much too bulky to be a comforting note from a loving and briefly absent husband, the sight of it caused a sudden fear. Inside were two folded letters. The first came from a firm of solicitors. Typed on heavy paper, it reminded Lester of his obligation to pay thirty pounds rent a month until such time as he paid a deposit to purchase the house. In the six months of occupation, no money had been received. Pay one hundred and eighty pounds within seven days or further action would ensue.

He paid nothing? I sat heavily on the edge of the bed and stared at the letter. No wonder he always had money for clothes and entertainment. My hands shook as I unfolded the second note.

By the time you read this letter I expect to be many miles away. I found the letter from Dad. I will return the car to him. I do love you but like Dad says, I'm no good at being responsible. You'll be better off without me. Lezz

Disbelief came first. Then anger.
"You bastard." My fist slammed the bedside table. "You bloody bastard. How could you? How could you do this?" I strode back and forth. Pounded the walls and called Lester all the names imaginable. Pulling the pillows from the bed, I screwed his pyjamas in a knot and flung them across the room. Again I thumped the wall. "I hate you," I screamed at his photograph on the dresser, hot angry tears scalding my cheeks. "I hate what you have done."

Long after midnight, I sat hunched over a cup of tea. Tea leaves circled my cup like marauding sharks and I stabbed them with a spoon as they passed. Empty of anger and tears I tried to marshal my thoughts. I needed to talk to Lester. Presumably he would perform with the show tomorrow night and again on Saturday before returning the car to his father. It was too late to telephone anyone tonight and I had to be at work at 6am. Everything would have to wait until tomorrow afternoon.

Next morning staff-nurse Rama and I sipped hot coffee together during our break.

"Are you all right Ana? You look peaky. Not suffering from morning sickness are you?"

"No, just very tired."

Sister appeared at the door. "Nurse Pierce, there's a phone call for you. You know I don't like staff taking personal calls but this man is most insistent."

I hurried to the office and picked up the phone. "Hello"

"Is that you Ana? Mike Roberts here." Mike was the operatic group's producer. "How is Lezz? What happened? Is he badly hurt? We were cut off when he telephoned. I've been worried."

Something in my stomach formed a hard cold lump. "I thought he was with you. Has there been an accident? Is he hurt?"

Silence. Mike no doubt thinking as fast as I was, then, "Lezz arrived here yesterday afternoon. Dropped off the props and said he'd stay the night with a friend rather than at the hotel. I refunded his accommodation money. This morning he phoned. Said he'd had an accident in the car and couldn't take part in the show. The call was cut off. That's why I rang you. Ana, I'm sorry to be the bearer of bad news. Perhaps his friends will know more."

"Yes. I'm sure they will." What friends? I silently screamed. I don't know his friends. Aloud I asked Mike, "What about the show? What will you do?"

"I'll have to take his part. The show will go on. Will you be all right, Ana? Call me if I can do anything to help. Cheeri-pip."

"Bad news?" Sister asked as I replaced the receiver, her usually stern face showing concern. Unsure of what to say, I told her Mike thought Lester might have had an accident in his car.

"You must call the police. You may use the phone."

I made the call telling the police what Mike told me, then added details about Lester and his car.

"Don't you worry, Mrs Pierce, we'll find him for you. We'll be in touch."

The ringing of the theatre bell sent sister and I scurrying down the hallway. Babies have no respect for others when making an entrance into the world and my own worries were pushed aside as we battled to save premature twin boys. Before leaving the hospital I went to look again at the two tiny babies, now breathing on their own. Sister came to stand beside me. "I hope you have good news soon. Unless you advise otherwise I shall expect you here in the morning. Good day, nurse."

Out on the street I turned toward the bank in the town centre. With a hundred pounds in my purse I then hurried to the solicitor's. A pleasant middle-aged woman called me into her office. "How can I help you, Ana? May I call you Ana?"

I nodded then apologizing for the neglected payment, took the money from my purse. Placing it on her desk, I asked her to accept it as an initial payment. Mrs O'Shea studied my face.

"Why are you here alone? Why did your husband not come?"

Momentarily surprised by her perception I avoided her eyes. "He's missing. I don't know where he is."

"Tell me," she said and passed a box of tissues.

Outside the office I hugged my purse containing the one hundred pounds. Mrs O'Shea had handed back the money. "You keep it. Wait until things settle down. Come and see me then," she'd said.

Feeling more confident now, I hurried home, changed my clothes and fed the hens. As I returned to the house a car pulled up at the gate. A short stocky man, his arms covered with tattoos pushed open the gate. I met him at the door. Unsmiling, his words gruff, he asked to see Lezz Pierce.

"He's not home."

"When will he be back? I'll wait."

"He is out of town." That was true. "Can I help you?"

"Only if you pay the thirty quid he owes me."

'Thirty pounds! What for?"

"Petrol. Repairs to his car. I own the garage on North Street." He thrust an account at me. The invoices extended over three months and stopped four weeks ago. Lester must have gone elsewhere for his petrol. Did that mean there were more unpaid bills?

"I'll pay this. But I must have a receipt." At least my brain was still functioning. My body was putty.

"Fine, lady. Let's do it."

After the man left I leaned against the passage wall sobbing until further unnerved by loud knock at the front door. Unable to face anyone, I took a moment to splash my face with cold water before greeting the uniformed policeman waiting on the step.

"Mrs Pierce? May I come in?" Over coffee I answered his questions. Although his words were kind he promised nothing. Not even hope. "You do understand," he said, "if your husband has chosen to leave and we do find him, we require his permission to inform anyone of his whereabouts."

"That's terrible," I told him holding back more tears.

"Now don't worry, Mrs Pierce. I'm sure there is a good reason why your husband has been unable to contact you." He pushed his notepad into a pocket and with a brief nod, departed.

My work at the hospital filled the weekend. In the lounge room a group of prenatal mothers played cards and made jokes about their husbands' inability to cope during their absence. At least you know where your husbands are, I thought, as repeated visions of steep ravines and fast flowing water filled my mind.

On Monday my shift changed, work began in the afternoon. My actions automatic; I spoke only when necessary, ate little and slept less. The waiting, not knowing, was unbearable. I woke at dawn on Tuesday. No more shilly-shallying around. I needed to do something. First in line at the Post Office, I placed a call to my mother-in-law.

"Box two for Pierce." The girl at the counter indicated the far phone booth.

"My dear Ana, I'm so pleased you rang. I've been trying to write you a letter but didn't know what to say and couldn't say enough in a telegram. How are you, dear?" Mrs Pierce spoke so fast her words became jumbled.

"I'm all right. Is Lester with you?"

"No dear. But he is in good care."

"Good care? What do you mean?"

"I don't know it all. We found the car in the drive on Saturday morning. There was a note that just said 'Sorry'. We waited;

expecting you to come. But you didn't, so Neville phoned your mother. She was away and Doug knew nothing."

Thank goodness. At least my mother doesn't know he's missing.

"That's when Neville phoned the police. They finally came yesterday afternoon. They said . . . ." I heard the catch in her voice. "They said Lester had been transferred to a psychiatric hospital. He may be there for some time."

"Why? What happened? People can't be locked up for nothing."

"We don't know, Ana. Neville is going to talk to the Police later today." Her sobs grew louder.

"Mum, I'm so sorry. Can I come to you? I feel so far away here. I want to see him. I miss him so much." After cursing Lester for being stupid and thoughtless I still loved him.

"Yes dear, come soon. And please," she said quickly as the pips sounded, "phone me if you have any news."

When I handed in my notice, the usually rather grumpy and strict Sister tallied up my sick leave and holidays saying in the circumstances, I was free to go. If I called back after lunch, my pay would be ready. Discharged, I found a second-hand furniture shop and arranged for someone to come to the house for our larger belongings.

Back at the house I pulled the packing cases from storage and began filling them. Later in the afternoon I collected my wages and said goodbye to my nursing friends. To my surprise they gathered for afternoon tea and gave me a gift; a very pretty cake plate. On the walk back to the solicitor's office, I felt strangely calm. After telling Mrs O'Shea all I knew, I again offered a hundred dollars. For a long moment she looked past me at the wall.

"No, Ana, put the money back in your purse. My advice is for you to pay nothing. If anyone demands money from you, tell them to contact me. You must not worry. Look after yourself and your husband and leave the rest to me."

So great was my relief I think I floated down the street. At the café where Lester and I had often sat holding hands in the candlelight; sipped red wine and eaten delicious food, I paused and on impulse went in and sat down. André came with coffee and black forest cake. My being there was a gesture of farewell to all the good times, to the people I would not say goodbye to.

"André, do you know anyone who would like four laying hens?"

"Me," he said with a grin.

Fifteen

A single streetlight turned summer drizzle to silver glitter. The bus departed, tail lights blinking and for a moment the glistening black bitumen turned fire engine red. Alone in a hometown street after an exhaustive fourteen-hour journey, I turned wearily toward my in-law's home. As I walked, I sang quietly to myself, *God will take care of you,* but on this occasion the words failed to comfort me. Light rain continued to fall. Miniscule diamonds studded my boucle coat. Similar pretty, unexpected sights normally raised my spirits but the shame of returning alone with so little, was a burden heavier than the suitcases I carried.

Mum Pierce answered my knock and welcoming me in, held me close. Mr Pierce took my cases and led me to the living room where a wood fire glowed in the grate. As we sat sipping tea and eating chocolate cake, I felt their concern, not just for Lester, but also for me. They asked no questions and appeared unsurprised by their son's behaviour. He'd clearly been unstable for a number of years. Why did no one tell me? And if told, would I have believed them? Probably not.

Before washing the breakfast dishes next morning, Mum Pierce hovered at my elbow asking if I'd like to telephone the psychiatric hospital for news of Lester. The phone rang so long, I thought it too early, the office not yet open. Finally the receptionist answered, her response brief, my questions cut short. "Your husband is in good physical health. No visitors during the first four weeks but his psychiatrist wishes to see you."

Two days later I boarded the overnight train to Frankton. Alighting in the early morning, I found a bus and travelled on through rounded green hills to the country township of Te Awamutu. Too late for the daily bus out to the hospital, I hired a taxi and arrived with an hour to spare. Set amongst aged trees, extensive lawns and garden beds, the mellow red brick buildings looked more like a manor house than a mental institution. There were no locked gates or even boundary fences.

After several errors in direction I finally found the right office. A plump receptionist apologized. "Doctor Zeigler has been delayed. Please come back at noon."

Two hours to wait. Back I went, through the maze of buildings to the canteen where I drained a pot of tea and ate a large sticky bun. Replenished, I wandered out into the sunshine, found a seat and sat down.

Two men rode a bicycle into the shade of a nearby tree and taking spanners from a hollow in the trunk, removed the wheels from the bike. To my surprise, they then scrambled up the tree and secured the wheels in the branches. After pushing the tools back into the hole and leaving the remainder of the bike against the tree, the men came to sit beside me. Intrigued, I asked why they had taken the bike apart.

"Nobody gonna steal our bike," one said as they both rose and solemnly shook my hand before ambling toward a distant tennis court, swinging imaginary racquets as they went.

Twenty minutes later I wondered why I had travelled so far to learn so little. A small bespectacled psychiatrist explained Lester's condition as having no specific name but related to paraphrenia. When asked why Lester did not take his prescribed medication, my response was a round eyed, "What medication?"

"As an admitted patient, your husband must remain at the hospital for a minimum of three months," the doctor told me. "Come again in four weeks. You can see him then. Now, please excuse me." Gathering up his notes, he departed. Stunned by the lack of communication, I hesitated for a moment and then hurried after him but the corridor was empty.

Rather than pay a second expensive taxi fare I decided to wait and take the local bus back to the township. Dejected, I returned to my seat in the sun. A group of smiling nurses walked by, keys swinging from their belts. They chattered amongst themselves, complaining in a half-hearted way about getting sun-burnt while walking their patients outdoors.

Without stopping to think, I went back to the reception centre and asked to see the matron. A large motherly woman, she listened to my story, gave me forms to fill, and ten minutes later welcomed me onto the nursing staff. She stipulated only one condition; no one was to know I was married to a patient.

On the way back to my in-laws the next day I thought of the two men and their bicycle. Of the easy going nurses and asked myself, "How hard can it be?" I should have asked, "How naïve can I be?"

I had the perfect solution; a home in the nurses' hostel, a good income and with Lester nearby, I quickly settled in. Two trained nurses, Zoe and her fiancé Paul, befriended me and when I confided my secret, they arranged for me to meet with Lester.

Each day another nurse and I walked a few of our elderly female patients to the tennis courts and back. One morning as we strolled through a secluded area, I saw Paul guiding a group of young men toward us. Among them Lester, shuffling along, his head bowed. The pain of seeing him in such a wretched state hit me with the force of an avalanche and when Paul called me over my legs felt strangely weak. Lester stood motionless; his arms limp at his sides. I waited, fighting back tears, hoping for recognition. After a long moment of nothing, I reached out and took his hand. "Lester. It's me, Ana." For the briefest moment his fingers tightened about mine. Then without speaking he turned away.

Overwhelmed by intense love and pity my impulse was to go after him, to hug and hold him. To reassure him I was there to help. Unable to watch him stumble across the grass back to Paul and the other men, I too turned away — and was struck by a frightening possibility; that of being married to a man unable to reciprocate love.

Days passed. Once, as I hurried in from the rain, Lester waved from an upstairs window and I rode through the day on a wave of happiness knowing he had acknowledged me and wanted my attention. Weeks later, together with Zoe and Paul, we began meeting secretly in a secluded corner of the grounds. While Lester kept abreast with most conversations, he talked haltingly, as if explaining things to an invisible person.

"This is awful. He used to be so clever bright and funny. How long will this last? Will I ever have the real Lester back?"

"He will get better," Paul assured me. "As he adjusts to his medication, his detached attitude will lessen." But weeks became months and still Lester remained emotionally remote, untouched by anything I said or did.

I worked on a closed ward, each of its four main sections separated by extremely heavy locked doors. Each nurse carried a key, unlocking and locking the doors when passing through. The windows were heavily barred, the rooms functional, without decoration.

The inmates were the decorative interest. They wore, or did not wear, all manner of clothing. An ex opera singer wanted long dresses and lengthened her skirt with any available piece of fabric, be it a tea-towel or a piece of sacking, she tied it to the hem of her dress. Others hated their clothes and having flushed them down the toilet, pranced about naked until captured and redressed. One lady pounced on every scrap of paper. Declared it her lost knitting pattern and proudly showed me the imaginary garments she made for her grandchildren. Another taught me more swear words in five minutes than I had heard in my life. Yet another gave me a black eye, claiming I stole her cigarettes.

There was much I did not understand. Like the beautiful young mother, separated from her baby and husband. Locked in a concrete cell with only a paillasse on the floor, she ate with her fingers, no cutlery allowed. She cried for her baby, begged to see her husband and was refused both.

"Why?" I asked the senior Sister.

"Severe depression. She tried to take her life. Given half a chance, she'll try again." My heart ached for the girl. Surely she needed love not isolation.

When my shift changed, I found myself doing wakeup call in a twelve bed ward. The smell made me gag; every bed wet and most dirty, as were the patients who overnight smeared the walls with brown finger painting. Two other nurses and I showered and dressed these inmates and after settling them in the day room, returned to the ward to drag the straw mattresses outside. The straw was emptied into a heap for collection, the covers sent to the laundry. New paillasses arrived and we made the beds with a single blanket. No pillow. No sheets.

At first I was horrified thinking these people were being treated like animals. I soon realised it was the best possible. These people could not change. When we opened the ward in the morning we rarely saw an upright bed. The wire frames leant crazily against a wall, or rested upside down in the middle of the floor. We once found them stacked three high with a bunch of naked people perched on top. My companions laughed.

"Look at them," Vera chortled, 'clustered together like sleepy hens disturbed in the night. You have to laugh, Ana. If you don't you'll end up crying and that's no good at all."

It was a strange unreal world and when, after fourteen weeks, Lester and I left the hospital, I felt I could never again take the future for granted.

Throughout my relationship with Lester I believed my love strong enough to change his reckless ways. Given time he would settle, become a responsible husband. In spite of knowing his illness included unpredictable mood changes and behaviour, my determination to be a constant, loving and supportive wife remained unwavering.

With no home of our own and Christmas a week away we returned to the Pierce home. Lester's older siblings and their children joined us, the overflow from house sleeping in tents on the back lawn. Lester did his best to fit into the family fun, but sometimes the continual noise and activity upset him. One moment he'd be planning some prank, playing cards or conducting as the children sang rounds of *Here Comes Santa Claus*: the next, nowhere to be seen. I often found him sitting in the garage, his expression vacant. If, when I tried to jolly him along, he did not respond, I would sit with him as introverted and silent, he stared at the floorboards. Only once did he turn to me. Dry sobs shaking his body, he buried his head in my lap, that vulnerable needy part of him I had glimpsed in the fun filled days before our elopement, finally breached.

Slowly his affable and enthusiastic nature re-emerged. Together we planned a new future. The subject of bankruptcy was broached and Lester agreed. January rolled into February and when I found employment as a ledger keeper in a town thirty miles away, we moved from his parent's house. A kind benefactor allowed us to buy a nice little house, no deposit and £3 a week. Amazed and grateful we scoured the second-hand shops for furniture, added two striped cats and a budgerigar and settled in. Lester found employment with a family-owned food packaging business. We bought bicycles, joined the church and were happiness filled.

Within twelve months the overgrown area around the house became smooth green lawns. Colourful blooms filled the flower beds, vegetables flourished and feeling secure, I planted a tree, a large weeping elm in the centre of the lawn beyond the kitchen window. By the second spring, when the brilliant lime green of new leaves tipped the umbrella shaped branches and Dutch irises bloomed blue against the laurel hedge, I sensed a change. A new and unfamiliar atmosphere was rippling through our home.

Lester and I loved dancing, especially old-time dancing; the fox trot, Valencia and Viennese waltz. Shortly after arriving in town we discovered a monthly old-time dance with an eight piece band providing wonderful music. Rich in pomp and ceremony, the dress code was strict. The women wore full length gowns and elbow length gloves; the men, bow ties and tails. Help was available to learn new steps and when we expressed a wish to try more exotic dances like the Tango, Samba and modern quickstep, we were given experienced partners. My instructor, a portly middle-aged gent guided me in a stately and dignified manner, while Lester was partnered by a tall, gypsy-like woman whose colourful and flowing garments accentuated her long red hair. This woman invited Lester to extra lessons at her home and as she was old enough to be his mother, I thought nothing of it. I did not know she had a young daughter; a quiet, enticing little mouse who lived in her mother's shadow.

The extra dancing lessons with the gypsy extended to three evenings a week. Lester became an excellent dancer and Mrs Gypsy, as I called her, invited him to join a demonstration group as her partner.

"Where is Mr Gypsy?" I asked.

Lester shrugged. There was, he informed me, only Mrs G. and the girl.

"What girl?"

"Her daughter, a timid little thing with straight hair that falls over her face. Wouldn't say boo to a goose. I sometimes feel sorry of her."

"Why is that?"

"Well, you know. Everyone is there, dancing, having fun and she just sits watching from the corner. I tease her a bit. Try to make her laugh."

"Does she not dance? How old is she?"

"I don't know. Fifteen? Sixteen? And no, she doesn't dance."

I felt left out sitting at home alone so often, but when I asked if I might attend the demonstration nights, there was no available transport. Disgruntled at being pushed aside, I bought wallpaper and paint and redecorated the spare room.

A week later I arrived home from the office and prepared the evening meal as usual. When Lester did not arrive, I put the meal aside and waited. A car pulled up at the gate and from the bedroom window I saw Lester hop from the driver's seat. A young woman then slid across behind the wheel and drove away.

"Who was that?" I asked as he came in the door.

"Mrs G's daughter, Tyler. I'm teaching her to drive."

"She's learnt quickly. She seemed to manage very well." I could not keep the sarcasm from my voice. "You're late and your meal is cold. I'll heat it up."

"Don't bother. I'm going out," he snapped, and striding into the bathroom, closed and locked the door.

Twenty minutes later, clean-shaven and dressed in fresh clothes, he called cheerio and without explanation was gone. I sat alone in the quiet house, the cats curled on my lap, thinking about Lester's behaviour. Fed up with the way he tootled off night after night, I decided to have a bit of fun. *Just you wait, Lester Pierce.*

Taking two crystal glasses from the shelf I swilled them with brandy essence and placed them on the table with some flowers and a lighted candle. I put on make-up and my best dress and dabbed perfume on every pulse. My skirt swirling to the rhythm of romantic dance music I waltzed through the house, bumping the kitchen table as I passed. A cascade of violets fell from the vase and scooping them high above my head I let them fall into my hair. Eyes closed, lost in the music, I flowed through the rooms and up the passage — to where my feet tripped on a pair of shiny shoes. I looked up into Lester's amazed face.

"'ello, you're 'ome," I slurred and danced off again, back down the passage toward the kitchen. Lester followed.

"You're drunk," he said.

"Am not."

"Who's been here?"

"I think I had a visitor." The cats sniffed at the spilled violets.

"There are flowers in your hair!"

I was being accused now. "So?" The music stopped and my little play ended.

"Why would you do this?" Lester's angry voice filled the room. "You are behaving like a slut." He strode back toward the front door.

"Wait. It was a joke. I hate being alone so often. Please, wait." I ran after him. The door banged in my face. "Les," I shouted tugging with all my might. The swollen door should have been fixed long ago. Now it stuck fast. "Lester. Come back." From the window I stared after him, listening to his fading footsteps.

Next evening, nervous but determined to remain calm I cooked his favourite meal, prepared an apology and waited. He came and our conversation, at first stilted, became easier. He wanted to be cross with me but was unable to maintain his self-righteous attitude. Instead he leant across the corner of the table and pulling me to him, kissed me awkwardly on the lips. I adjusted my position and by the time we returned to eating, our meal was cold.

Sometime during the night I half-woke and feeling Lester's warm back pressed against me, knew he was awake. "Can't you sleep?" I asked.

"Ana, what would you think of a married man who had an affair?"

My eyes flew open and I lay very still. "I'm not sure. I've never thought about it. Why do you ask?"

"No reason. Just thinking."

"Then stop thinking and go to sleep. We have to get up in a couple of hours."

Lester sighed and soon fell asleep. I lay staring into the darkness. Would he? Out four or five nights a week, he had ample opportunity. I'd been happy to let him go. Glad he was no longer introverted and brooding. Well, I'd have to find him an interest closer to home.

I suggested we dig a sunken garden outside the living room window but he laughed saying it would probably become a swimming pool when the first rain fell. "How about building a bookcase in the alcove beside the fireplace then? Or painting the ceilings pale green?" I asked searching for a project to keep him at home.

"Yuck. Anything but pale green."

"All right. You chose a colour."

"Burnt orange."

My turn to say yuck.

Lester did stay at home for a few nights, but he became unpredictable; withdrawn and silent one day, all hyped up the next. I thought he might have stopped taking his medication and I checked, tipping the tablets onto the table and counting them. He caught me and was furious.

"Am I not to be trusted," he shouted. Red faced he raged on.

"You're frightening me. You should see a doctor, Lester."

"I'm fine thank you very much. It's you who needs the doctor, you who imagines things. You're the paranoid one." He strode back and forth across the room shouting. Several times he came close and shook his fist in my face. Unable to reason with him I turned away. It was then he grabbed me. Spun me round to face him and holding the collar of my dress, pulled my face up to his.

"Don't you ever walk away from me." He spat the words. Dropped me onto a chair and slammed from the house.

Near midnight he returned. He'd been drinking and fell into bed without speaking. In the morning, after a silent breakfast, he placed his tablets and a glass of water on the table.

"Watch me. I'm having my tablets." He made a great show of letting me see the tablets in his mouth before swallowing them. "Happy now?" he sneered.

I wanted to fight back but feared I'd only further antagonize him. I felt terrible and made no attempt to kiss him goodbye when he left for work. Again he returned late smelling of beer, his mood just as nasty as it had been in the morning.

The doctor offered little help and reiterated what I already knew. Unless Lester was willingly to take advice there was nothing to be done. He did ask if I thought Lester might harm me or himself.

"No. He is just being verbally nasty," I said.

"What about at work? Is he getting on all right there? Do try to persuade your husband to come and see me, Mrs Pierce."

Unable to ask about Lester's behaviour at work without telling his employer why I needed to know, I let the matter drop.

Several weeks passed. Away from the office I filled every minute at home with cleaning and gardening, pushing myself into exhaustion. Night after night I lay awake listening, waiting for Lester, who now stayed out until the early hours of the morning. Even when he was safely home in bed I could not relax and rarely slept before daybreak when I fell into a troubled sleep filled with frightening dreams.

I returned to the doctor. Yes, Lester was taking his tablets. No, he was not any better. It was me who needed help. Unable to sleep and lacking appetite I felt utterly miserable. Valium. It softens the sharp edges but the problems remain. The situation was untenable. Lester and I lived as brother and sister and tolerated each other out of necessity. Perhaps a holiday would help. The more I thought about the idea, the better it became.

Sixteen

Had it been possible to hug someone over the phone, I would have hugged Mr Pierce long and hard when he agreed to loan Lester his car for a weekend. The car was my bait, as Lester was unlikely to refuse an opportunity to drive his beloved V8. My idea worked and two weeks later, we set off for Lake Waikaremoana.

I love the mystery that emerges from the darkness at dawn. When the world is colourless it is easier to imagine everything consists of molecules that ebb and flow with life, that all is change and substance fleeting. Nothing stays the same.

Like old times we sang along with the car radio until the remoteness of the area cut the radio signals and the music turned to static. By midmorning our first view of the lake appeared and we gawped, awed by the magnificence of the vast inland sea of sparkling water. The miles of loose gravel road, too narrow and winding to risk stopping, clung to a sheer rock face that towered above us and to our right, dropped to the lake far below. Vehicles crawled like ants along this ledge, miniscule in a rarely disturbed and incredibly beautiful landscape.

A little further on we followed a steep side road down through a tunnel of greenery to emerge on a small, sandy lakeside cove where swallows wove invisible nets over the water. The area so isolated, Lester made a joke about us being Adam and Eve and suggested skinny-dipping in the lake but the water was icy cold. As he passed me the picnic basket from the car boot, our eyes met and he smiled; one of his soft warm smiles that had been missing for so long. In return I dropped a light kiss on his forehead. His response, at first so urgent and demanding, made me feel vulnerable and little afraid. Through an exchange of kisses, the tightness of his grasp relaxed. Taking my hand and with the car rug slung over his shoulder, he led the way into an ocean of shiny yellow buttercups where the passion of our reunion eclipsed my months of waiting. We emerged from the field sleepy eyed, and arm in arm, returned to the little beach for a picnic lunch of thermos tea and cucumber sandwiches.

Far across the lake and barely visible was a small patch of white we guessed was the hotel. An hour's drive later, the white splodge grew to a sprawling single-storied hotel with wide verandas. Dense bush lined the road and native birds, previously unseen, flew back and forth. I recognized tuis and bell birds, but there were others I did not know.

The step from bright sunlight into the cool dim interior of the hotel was a step back in time. Ghosts of Noel Coward's plays filled the dim, oak-panelled hall lined with gilt framed oil paintings and potted palms. We unpacked in our room, the first inside the main doors. Then eager to explore, wandered through the spacious high-ceiling rooms and found the dining room, lounge and bar. All offered gracious well-padded comfort.

Outdoors a series of steep steps led us down through the bush. Alongside the path a small handwritten sign said Kiwis lived nearby and if we came in the night, we might see them. On the lakeshore an elderly man wearing baggy overalls and a Dutch cap offered us a rowboat. There was no charge, he said, but we must return before dark and not fall in the lake as the water was so cold people died.

Undaunted by his warnings and surrounded in every direction by soaring cliffs and with a protective arched shield of blue above, we glided across the water in an indescribably serene landscape. We rowed from cove to cove, idling away the afternoon. Hot and pleasantly relaxed, we sat back to back on a rocky outcrop, our bare feet dangling in the cool water. Lupin pods split in the heat. Our surroundings so quiet the seed bouncing over the rocks sounded like hail on a tin roof.

We returned at sunset and climbed the steps to the wide verandah over-looking the silver-blue waters of the lake. A waiter brought tea and as we sipped from delicate cups, another couple joined us. Immersed in the surrounding stillness and reluctant to break the feeling of peace, we spoke quietly. Honeymooners, Mark and Mary seemed nice people and when, as we parted to change for dinner, Mark suggested we meet in the bar later in the evening, we agreed.

Dressing for dinner took longer than usual as we paused to hug and kiss.

"We'll be late for dinner."

"Who cares?" Lester manoeuvred me gently back against the bed. I felt the edge behind me. My knees gave way and I leaned back.

Bong-bong! bong-bong-bong! That was not a dinner bell. On and on it went. Scuffling sounds and high pitched women's voices came from the hallway. A man shouted, "Shut the bloody door." Our love making forgotten, we peered out into the corridor.

At the far end overhead sprinklers showered the hall with water. Wet people in various states of dress scurried out onto the verandah. A waiter appeared, raised a large black umbrella and in sprightly hops moved up the hall knocking on doors.

"Please be calm. There is no fire. Calm, please. No fire." At the top of the hall he dropped the umbrella and running back, hoisted a painting from the wall. Staggering beneath its size, he brought it to the dry area near us and leant it against the wall. He went back for another and as Lester moved to help him, the noise stopped. The sprinklers slowed and water dripped onto sodden carpets.

Staff arrived with mops and buckets. An apologetic young man came to tell us that owing to a misadventure, dinner would be an hour late. Those caught by the sprinklers gathered in the bar and in excited voices told their stories. The barmen provided good cheer free of charge and what began as a catastrophe became a memorable moment to be shared at dinner parties for years to come.

I drew Lester from the bar and following a line of fairy lights among the trees we made our way down a steep path to the lake edge. In the dark, water slapped the gently bobbing boats tied to the pier and from across the vast lake, night birds called. We stood close, returning kiss for kiss. *What bliss.* My idea of a break away had been right. Aquiver with expectation, I imagined the romantic night ahead.

After dinner I slipped back to our room to freshen up. The bedside lamp cast a rosy glow over the bed. The maid had turned back the covers. A red rose and gold-wrapped chocolate lay on a pillow. Already weary after such a long day, I sighed, wishing Lester here with me instead of in the bar socializing.

Wrapped in a warm stole I returned to the lounge. Lester and Mark bent over a pianist who sorted through a pile of sheet music. Song followed song. Everyone joined in well-known choruses, some getting up to form a kick line. By midnight I could barely keep my eyes open. Cigarette smoke filled the room and voices became babble.

"You and I seem alike, Mary. Neither of us sings and we both prefer lemonade to alcohol."

"Mark does enough for both of us," she said. "I hope it will change now we are married."

"Shall we ask the boys to stop now?" Mary nodded and together we made our way to the piano and taking our husbands aside, pleaded a need for sleep. An inebriated fellow appeared and draping his arms about our shoulders said the night was young and his song not yet sung.

"Stay," he pleaded.

"One more," said Mark. "You girls run along." And chucking Mary beneath the chin told her, "Make yourself pretty, Chick-a-biddy."

Lester grinned. "You too," he said to me before turning back to the piano.

Mary and I unlocked our adjacent rooms, said good night and parted. In the bedroom I hurriedly changed into my dressing gown, removed my makeup and cleaned my teeth. Seated on the edge of the bed I brushed my hair, counting the strokes until it shone. Feverish with anticipation I inspected my image in the mirror. A week ago stress had dulled my complexion and shadowed my eyes. I looked better now. Nervous, I fussed about, straightening this and that, hanging up my clothes. The music and singing ceased and I settled back in an armchair doing my best to appear at ease.

More music. A conga, the steady rhythm growing in volume as feet stomped and voices shouted. On and on it went, fading at times, only to grow in strength as the line crossed the hallway and wound out onto the verandas where the hollow thump of many feet all but drowned the singing. Finally it stopped and I waited for the sound of Lester's return. People called goodnight. Doors opened and closed. Another half an hour passed.

I heard Mary's door open and close quietly, her soft steps going down the hall. She returned alone and behind the closed door, sobbed as if her heart would break. I longed to go and comfort her but was afraid to interfere. What was keeping our men so long? When the hands of my watch passed two o'clock, I crawled into bed. Disappointed, tired and miserable, I tried not to cry.

A short time later Lester crept in. He skirted the bed, bumping into things in the dark. I turned on the lamp. Finger to his lips and swaying on his feet, he warned me not to wake Ana.

"I *am* Ana."

"Sorry."

He struggled to remove his shoes and I reached across the bed to help, when he jerked upright and sent a stream of projectile vomit straight to my chest. A second jet covered the bed and extended to the floor by the door. Filled with disgust I knelt on the bed surrounded by the revolting smelly mess. It filled my lap and dripped from my arms. Lester's eyes rolled and he fell back against the pillow, out cold. Taking off my lovely new nightgown I rolled it in the sodden bedclothes and pushed the whole nauseating bundle in the wastepaper bin. Then heaving and straining, I hauled the insensible Lester to a cleaner part of the bed. A few minutes later, washed and dressed in my warmest clothes, I took a pillow and went to sleep in the car.

The night air was bitter and my hands shook as I opened the car door. Curled on the back seat, shivering with cold and perhaps shock, my teeth chattering and my stomach tense with nausea, I hugged the pillow and tried to calm myself. After what seemed an eternity I looked at my watch. I had been in the car less than ten minutes. The minutes dragged by. Unable to control my shivering I decided to return indoors for extra clothing.

As quietly as possible I edged back across the car park in the dark and into the front hall where l felt my way along the wall to the bedroom door. Stupid me, I'd locked it, the key inside. My first definable emotion hit me — helplessness. I was alone, in a strange place in the dark. At the far end of the hall, a dim light showed. Terrified of being discovered sneaking about the place, I stole silently past the potted palms toward the light. An open door revealed a guest room with two single beds. Uncertain, but thinking this might be a spare room for late guests, I climbed into a bed fully dressed and for the remaining hours of darkness lay listening to every sound, fearing someone would come and find me in their bed.

At daybreak I heard light footsteps and rolling from the bed stepped into the hall as a maid disappeared toward the kitchen. I followed her and asked if she had a master key to my room. The bedroom door open, the smell of vomit hit us.

"I'm sorry. My husband had too much to drink. I'll clean up the mess."

"No. That is my job. Come with me." She led me to the kitchen, made me hot coffee and toast and told me to sit tight. "I'm used to this and will have it fixed in no time," she said.

Half an hour later she came to tell me Lester was in the shower and our room ready to use.

While I silently packed our belongings, Lester dressed then went outside for a cigarette. I watched him pace the car park, cigarette smoke drifting above his bowed head. He looked awful, pale and gaunt

Not waiting for breakfast we set off for home. From the open car window I gazed down at the lake. The water no longer sparkled. Yesterday's serenity had become a choppy sea. Grey cloud smothered the surrounding hills. Tears of regret burned my eyes. I'd spent my entire savings on the trip. Saturated in grief I pined for what might have been. What if I were to jump from the car? Let myself fall, arms outstretched, down into the water. Down I'd go, down, drifting down into stillness and peace. No one would miss me. I had no purpose. I was useless. No help to Lester. No use to my mother.

"Ana, I need to stop. Look for a place to pull over will you?" Lester's voice made me jump and pushing aside my misery, I turned to look at the road ahead.

"We're close to the river where we stopped yesterday," I said looking around. Only yesterday, it felt like a week. There had been so many new experiences; time had become distorted in my mind. At the layby I read as Lester slept. An hour later we drove on. Lester's haggard appearance did not improve and when we returned the car, his concerned mother wanted us to stay the night.

"Thank you, but no. If we hurry we can catch the bus, get home and have an early night; wake bright and fresh for work tomorrow."

What a joke. I felt anything but bright and fresh the next morning. There were bills in the letterbox and no money in the bank. Inwardly I seethed. My jaw tense, I prepared breakfast and waited for an apology. His head resting in his cupped hand, his hair covering his eyes, Lester pushed cereal around in his plate. He did not attempt to eat. Laying down the spoon he gulped half a cup of tea and stood up.

"Don't you want anything?" I asked, the emphasis on anything, meaning food.

"Yes. I want plenty. But not from here," and snatching up his lunchbox, he stumped down the back steps.

For a long time I sat without moving. What did he mean? He wanted plenty, but not from here.

Seventeen

From the day we returned from that disastrous weekend away, our verbal exchanges have been polite — nothing more. Lester has spent a lot of time brooding and when I try to draw him out, he complains of tiredness and goes to bed.

This evening, while listening for sounds of his return home, I watched the cats chase moths, leaping and pouncing in the stream of light stretching out across the lawn. I scooped peeled potatoes into a pot and glanced again at the clock. Lester was seriously late tonight and when the phone rang I hurried to answer it.

"Hello Ana. Is Les home?" The caller was not Lester as I hoped but his employer, Bill.

"No. Not yet. Shall I ask him to call you?"

"No. Don't worry. He'll probably come here first."

"He's not back from his round?"

"Now, like I said, Ana, don't worry. He's probably had two flat tyres or something. Things happen. I'll check around," and with a promise to relay any news, he hung up.

Instead of eating I made coffee and carrying the mug with me, sipped while wandering about the house straightening cushions and rearranging ornaments. Eight o'clock. Nine. The phone book open on my lap I searched for Bill's home number. Lester's absence, though not uncommon, was tonight worrying me. Startled by a loud knock at the front of the house I dropped the book and hurried to pull with all my might on the swollen front door. It opened with a rush and as I stumbled back, Mrs Gypsy pushed past me into the passageway.

"Where is he?" she demanded.

"Lester? I don't know."

"Rubbish. You're his wife. Where is he?"

"I really don't know. He hasn't come home. Please, come and sit down. Why are you so upset?"

"Tyler has gone. She's only sixteen. And he is old enough to know better, the two-faced rat. Well, he'll support her and the baby. I'll see to that."

"Baby! You think Lester . . .?"

"Of course he is. He's been there, part of the family for months, a year, more. Tyler has no boyfriend." We stood staring at each other, struggling to understand what might have happened.

"Mrs? I'm sorry I don't even know your name."

"Leila. I'm sorry too." She dropped onto the couch and for a moment covered her face with her hands. "I shouldn't have come barging in like that. If you don't know where your husband is, then we must assume he and Tyler are together."

An insidious helplessness crept over me. I wanted to cry, run, hide — anything other than be here. Instead I offered to make fresh coffee.

"No thank you. I should go. Can we agree to be in touch if either of us has any news?"

"Of course." We exchanged phone numbers. Leila patted my arm.

"Chin up. We'll find them," she said.

Despair dulled my mind. My thinking ragged, I huddled close to the coal range, my arms tight across my chest. A sudden clear thought sent me rushing to pull aside pillows, to search for a note. I opened drawers. Checked the mantle shelf, the coffee table; even the bathroom. There was no note. Lester's belongings all accounted for, our suitcases undisturbed on top of the wardrobe. Unwilling to believe he had walked out again I spent the night making excuses for his behaviour. I should have tried harder, been a better wife.

When I woke, my entire body ached. At work, hidden behind the ledger machine, I wept silent tears. Around midday, Bill passed the office window and I straightened in my chair hoping there might be news of Lester. A moment later the manager put his head around the partition and beckoned me out into the corridor. "Bill has news for you. You may go, Ana. There is no need to hurry back."

His words set me on edge and when Bill held out a large hand and said, "Come along. Miriam and I will take you to lunch," I felt so shaken I returned first to my desk and took a moment to compose myself before collecting my handbag.

In the hotel opposite the office, Bill ordered drinks while his petite wife found us a table. When he returned with our glasses, I waited anxiously for him to speak. He seemed to be having trouble getting started.

"I'm sorry," he rubbed his chin and began again. "Ana, I'm sorry but it appears Lester has done a runner. We found the van at a country hotel. He spent the afternoon there then hitched a ride south. We've traced the truck driver. He dropped Les at the Wellington docks around midnight last night." Bill took a long drink from his glass and put it down before looking at me. "Les also took a large sum of money paid to him by one of our clients. Now, wait," he held up his hands, "I can deal with that. There's no need for the police."

"He's alone. He's not with Tyler." My teeth knocked the edge of the wine glass as I sipped, eyes closed, relieved to know he had travelled alone. Bill and Miriam looked at me.

"Who's Tyler?" Miriam asked.

I told them of Mrs Gypsy's visit, explaining how she thought Lester and Tyler had run off together. "Lester didn't plan this. He took nothing with him. Nothing at all," I ended.

After lunch, instead of returning me to the office, they drove me home. Miriam walked me to the door where she hugged me close. "Call me if you need anything, anything at all," she said.

I turned the key and shouldered open the door. As I entered, Blue Boy the budgie shrilled a welcome and the cats came running. At least I am good for feeding cats I thought as I placed their bowls on the floor. "My mum would have to agree with that," I said aloud looking down at the cats' sleek little bodies.

My mother did not need to know about Lester's disappearance. His parents did, but not today. I needed to think. First I called Leila. Unconvinced, she suggested Tyler and Lester planned to meet somewhere.

"None of Lester's personal belongings are missing. I'm sure if he planned to set up house with anyone, he would at least take his clothes." I stopped speaking. Fear gripped me. My legs went weak and a chill spread through me. The doctor had asked if I thought Lester might harm himself. Would he? Oh help. What was I to do?

"Ana, are you still there?"

"Sorry. I have to go."

Sunk in wretchedness I tried to eat. Shame isolated me. I had failed to keep my man happy. Would he take his own life? Buck up, I told myself. You're useless like this. You must stay strong. It's a test. Do your best.

My effort at self-encouragement failed and after a sleepless night I crawled wearily from my bed, dressed and hurried to catch the Saturday morning bus to my in-laws' home. I planned to tell them Lester had again gone to Wellington but to say nothing of Tyler and the missing money.

On the return journey I turned my head to the window. My cheeks damp with tears, I saw nothing of the countryside. Mr Pierce had reacted angrily, telling me not expect him to care for me. Stung, I retorted I was capable of caring for myself. I had a good job and would manage. I had hoped for understanding, for suggestions of what I might do, where I might begin. When I said I intended to search for Lester, Mr Pierce's response had been to snort and wish me luck.

When we left the psychiatric hospital two years ago, I accepted Lester's illness as a challenge, a test of my ability to cope. I enjoyed the highs and forgot the lows. Now I held my breath waiting for the next downhill plunge, each lower than the last.

The days stretched into weeks. The Salvation Army's missing persons pinned Lester's photograph to noticeboards in Post Offices and in the Wellington hospitals. Each ring of the phone, each knock at the door sent my heart leaping. Was he alive or dead? The stress of waiting became unbearable. I began to think even if he were dead, it would be better than not knowing.

The first morning of a long weekend I woke lethargic and out of sorts. Grumbling, I prepared to drag myself through yet another long day when suddenly, I was running to the bathroom to throw up. Opting to skip breakfast I sat on the back steps nursing my queasy tummy. Cheered by the autumn sunshine, I set about trimming the hedge at the bottom of the garden. Long stems of wandering jew entangled the branches and as I knelt to pull them free I found, in the thick of the hedge, a bottle of pills. Further along I discovered another. Enough of the snail nibbled labels remained for me to recognise Lester's medication. What then was in the bottle in the kitchen; the tablets he had made such a show of taking each day? Indoors, I emptied the current pill bottle onto the table; each tablet stamped, Aspro. He'd fooled me. Lied. I thought his behaviour impetuous, irrational perhaps, but not scheming or deliberately dishonest. It hurt to know I had been deceived.

I settled into a lonely routine of doing whatever needed to be done. Work at the office, gardening and housework. Whenever I walked a street my eyes scanned passing faces, hoping to see my husband; each familiar set of the head and shoulders followed until their owner turned and disappointment brought tears to my eyes.

On Saturday I walked to the Indian fruiter's in town and as I waited to cross the road, a car pulled up and Leila stepped out. Tyler sat in the passenger seat, her gaze averted as her mother called, "Hello Ana. Have you had any word? As you see, Tyler is home. She's been a very silly girl. There is no baby, only wishful thinking. I'm sorry. Really very sorry for the concern Tyler and I caused."

"You mean she made it up — there was no affair between her and Lester?" I think had I been closer to the car, I would have hauled Tyler out and shaken her until her teeth rattled.

"Nothing serious. Lester tried to coax her out of her timidity. He teased her and my guess is Tyler misunderstood. The silly girl went crying to her father in Auckland. He seems to have talked some sense into her. I hope you hear good news soon, Ana."

"Little brat," I muttered to myself as I quickened my pace over the pedestrian crossing. "She's not a mouse she's a vixen. All this time I thought Lester had run away because he thought Tyler—. Perhaps Tyler had an abortion? A mother would lie about that. It doesn't matter," I mumbled on while selecting apples and oranges. "Trying to imagine what other people might or might not think creates problems. Lester behaved badly. He stole money and left his employer with a lot of problems. His actions have put me offside with his father and made me sick with worry. I should be grateful Tyler is now off my list of concerns." At the counter I paid for my shopping and determined to enjoy the sunny day, turned for home.

As I walked up the path to the house the telephone rang and I raced in through the back door to answer it.

"Hello, Mrs Pierce. Captain Smith, Salvation Army missing persons." I held my breath. The pleasant sounding voice continued. "We have some news for you. A man very like your husband but calling himself Jim Morley, recently moved from Wellington to a bed and breakfast place in Wanganui. Do you have pen and paper handy?"

I wrote the address, checked the spelling and after thanking him, jumped and twirled with excitement.

Action at last. No more hanging about. I called the office manager at his home. A kind man, he offered me two weeks leave, more if I needed it. On Monday morning I paid the rent ahead and cleared the accounts. My neighbour agreed to take the budgerigar and to pop over and feed the cats for me. I also booked a seat on the midday bus.

By late afternoon I'd found the B & B and settled in. Instead of a dark and dingy house with narrow stairs in a poor part of town as I imagined, bright pink and red geraniums lined the path to a spotless interior. Across the road in a small park, children played on the swings. Everything had gone so well, I felt it was meant to be, an omen of good things to come.

I waited at my window for the man called Morley. The receptionist told me he returned from work around five-thirty each evening. By six o'clock, three men had walked up the path between the geraniums. None looked at all like Lester. There was a light tap at my door and the housekeeper's smiling face appeared.

"Mr Morley is downstairs. Will you come and meet him?" Anxiety closed my throat. Would Lester be pleased to see me? The man at the desk was of similar height and build to Lester but there the resemblance stopped. He stepped forward, a puzzled frown creasing his brow.

"You wanted to see me?"

"Yes. But there has been a mistake. I'm sorry," He looked more perplexed than ever. "I'm sorry," I repeated and returning to my room, lay curled on the bed wondering what to do next.

The room was dark when I woke. Changing into my nightwear I slid back into bed and slept fitfully until the breakfast tray and morning newspaper arrived at my door. I drained the teapot and nibbled at the toast. The sight and smell of sausages and eggs turned my stomach and covering the plate, I quickly moved it to the dresser.

Included in the newspaper was a pull-out section on the new Waikato University. Zoe and Paul lived alongside the university's extensive grounds. After Lester's stay at the psych. hospital Zoe and I remained good friends. We regularly exchanged news-filled letters. If I continued south and stayed overnight with my sister, Fran, then travelled inland, I could visit Zoe. Why not? Gripped by the idea of a real holiday, I pushed worry aside and phoned the bus depot.

Soothing warmth spread through me as crouched before the open fire in Fran's living room, I lifted logs with the poker, coaxing the flames higher. This brown and traffic worn area provided comfort and ease. Throughout the day Fran's four boisterous children filled the place with their friends, the phone rang, the radio blared and a large black dog trotted in and out. Now, as Fran tucked the children up for the night, I left the fireplace and carried a tray of glasses to the sink. As I swished hot soapy water over a stack of dirty dishes, I wondered at the differences between Fran and our mother and me.

Mum gave an impression of quality and refinement, of being aloof from lesser mortals. Fran was a people-person; her home, forever in a constant muddle, overflowed with love. Despite the chaos, Fran remained calm. She drew people out, asked direct questions and got answers. If asked for an opinion she responded honestly and openly. She, it seemed to me, lived life to the full while Mum and I, in our spotless tidy homes, hardly lived at all.

When the dishes had been put away I telephoned Zoe. Her tired voice answered my call.

"Sorry Ana. I was asleep. Give me a moment to wake up." We laughed a little. Zoe was a renowned heavy sleeper.

"I'm on holiday. I wondered if I might come to visit you later in the week," I said.

'I'd love to see you but I'm packing. We're moving house. Or rather I am, Paul's in hospital with a fractured leg. One of the patients threw a heavy cabinet at him. Lester tried to help but this giant of a guy knocked him out."

"Lester! My Lester was there?"

"Yes." Zoe sounded puzzled.

"Zoe, I'm sorry about Paul being injured but please tell me about Lester. He's been missing for ten weeks. He left without a word and we've been unable to find him."

"He was at the hospital; came in as a volunteer patient. Paul first saw him the day the big guy went berserk. Our two were taken to the general hospital. When Les was discharged he told Paul he was moving on. We assumed he was going home to you."

"When did Lester leave?"

"Two weeks ago — more. And you've not heard from him?"

"No."

"You must be beside yourself with worry. I wish I could be more helpful. I could check at the hospital, see if he gave an address. Where can I contact you?" Zoe waited while I gave her Fran's phone number then said goodbye.

Fran called from the living room, "Come and join me."

"I should be glad but I feel even more bewildered," I concluded after telling her the news.

"Surely you're reassured knowing Lester went voluntarily to the hospital —made an effort to help himself."

"Yes I am. But, Fran, one of the doctors told me some people are smart. They hide in an institution and plead mental illness to avoid responsibility. Others pity them, make excuses for them. I think he was trying to tell me I should make Lester stand on his own two feet.

"And Lester stole a lot of money when he left. His employer is not pressing charges but Lester doesn't know that. The man is hopeless with money. I've been paying his bills for years. I've been trying to do the right thing for so long, I can no longer think straight," I ended.

"The right thing? Who are you trying to do the right thing for?" Fran regarded me over the top of her spectacles.

"For Lester and the people he has hurt. His parents and other people he owes money to."

"Why do you feel you should be the one to put things right?"

"Because of all that stuff we were taught. Do unto others. Turn the other cheek. Walk the extra mile, all those things that supposedly make us worthy human beings."

"And while you are so busy patching up other people's lives, what happens to yours?" She held her darning needle aside, waiting as a kitten settled itself among the socks bundled in her lap. I gazed back at her. My big sister was so easy going; so quietly assured within herself and in her surroundings.

When had I ever fitted in? I wanted to be a hero for my father and failed. I gave up my dreams of a career and moved from my childhood home to please my mother. With a heavy sigh I poked the fire, half hoping a white horse might appear and my worries vanish. I tried to explain to Fran.

"I feel like a balloon, floating loose, being driven this way and that. And all the time I have the ambiguity of both fearing and longing for the inevitable pin pick that will end it all." I sat on the floor hugging my knees. "Lester and I . . . I believed we were soul mates, destined to be together. I thought our difficulties stemmed from his illness, but he lied to me. If only I could accept Lester has chosen a life separate from mine . . ."

"Let's assume Lester is perfectly happy where he is. That he is not coming back and you are free to make choices for yourself. What would you like to do, Ana?"

"I think I'd like to start afresh, somewhere new. I like the regular hours of office work and I'm good with figures — hopeless at spelling. I could rent a semi-furnished flat; one with a small garden." As the idea took shape I spoke faster, my enthusiasm building. "I'd go to pottery classes. Improve my typing skills. Or take care of children. People pay well for good child care."

"Are you confident you can support yourself?"

"Yes."

"Then why don't you do it?"

Why not indeed? Better than sitting around in limbo-land waiting for Lester. Fran and I chattered on. We made tea and toasted the future, chinked our teacups and still laughing, made our way to bed in the early hours of the morning. A soft brown teddy lay beside my pillow and I cuddled him. Was I really as free as Fran suggested? Free to leave Lester and go my own way? Everyone knew a woman's role was to love and nurture, to support her husband in sickness and in health, to honour and obey. It was instilled in us from birth. Women the world over required a man to provide for them and the children of their union. Men, on the other hand, were a law unto themselves. To keep them happy and at home, wives had to be generous, loving and forgiving. The church proclaimed this, as did mothers, grandmothers and romance novels. Women were surrounded by the concept that love conquers all. But did it? Divorce was rare but it happened. There had been times I felt helpless, unable to forgive Lester. Times when love failed to bridge the spaces between us and I wanted to scream at him, *What about me? What is to become of me? Don't I have rights?* As a child I heard women whisper behind their hand. 'There's a woman who can't keep a man.' Would I too be labelled a failure?

"Not if I can help it," I said aloud to the bear and turning over, flicked off the bedside lamp.

The children woke me, coming to say goodbye before leaving for school. Five minutes later I was again being ill in the bathroom. Fran called from outside the door.

"Are you all right, Anna?"

"Yes," I replied looking at my white face in the mirror as I pinched my cheeks and chewed my lips trying to raise some colour.

Fran offered me coffee with breakfast.

"No thank you. I've gone off coffee. For some reason its makes me feel ill."

"And you don't know why?" Fran looked at me in amazement.

"No Fran. No. I am not pregnant. It's just not possible."

"If you say so." Fran busied herself at the sink.

The black dog came and laid his big glossy head on my lap. I fondled his ears and he gazed up at me with soulful brown eyes hoping I might share my breakfast.

"He knows a soft touch." Fran smiled and passed me the bus timetable. "I can drive you to the bus but I must be at school by ten o'clock," she said.

"That's fine, Fran. Thank you for all you've done. I feel so much better after talking with you. I'll write and tell you what I decide to do."

We hugged at the bus depot and as Fran drove away I felt very lucky indeed to have an older and wiser sister.

Eighteen

Jan 20th 1961
Dear Fran,

I love this place. Beautiful trees, oaks, walnuts and maples grow in extensive parklands bordering a river broad enough for a paddle boat. Large department stores vie with delightful little boutiques and the continental coffee shops have the most tempting array of tasty treats. My indulgences have caused me to gain weight. My clothes no longer fit; I need a safety-pin to extend the waistbands.

My holiday home is a B & B close to the Anglican Cathedral. Mrs Wolfe, who manages the B & B, has taken me under her wing. Her helper recently had a fall and broke her wrist. I offered to stand in and now assist with serving breakfast and cleaning the rooms, all finished by ten in the morning. For this I have free lodging. Isn't that wonderful?

Zoe and I went to the hospital to see Paul. Sadly they have no idea where Lester might be. Yesterday I went to the Police Station, told the Sergeant there all I knew. He promised to check with the hospital and let me know if more information was available. My fingers are crossed.

I will stay here for the remainder of my holiday unless news of Lester brings a change in plan.

Much love,
Ana

Jan 27th 1961
Dear Fran,

So much has happened I hardly know where to begin. I love Hamilton city and decided if I could find work, this was the place for a fresh start. The very next day I found employment as a records clerk with an electrical company. Can you believe that? The manager, Fred, is a perfect gent with a quirky sense of humour. The building is new and quite posh. I have my own office next the Fred's. Three other men work in the storeroom. They are all nice.

Fred drove me in his car to look at accommodation. (I told you he was nice.) I have chosen a flat close to the cathedral and within easy walking distance of the office. My new home is the back half of a large well-kept house. There is a sitting room, twin bedroom and spacious kitchen. I have my own bathroom and share a laundry. Everything is provided. I even have a piano.

My elderly landlords have an enormous garden with vegetables galore. I am to help myself whenever I wish. In my wildest dreams I could not have asked for more. There is more however. I've met people from home and been invited to visit them.

Moving house went so smoothly I felt it was meant to be. Stan and Norah took the cats. We had not paid very much off the house and the owner agreed to take that money as rent and annul our agreement. He was very nice about it.

While I was packing, Doug came over. He has his own car now. Our little brother has grown so tall, Fran. Together we dug up the elm tree and tied it to his car. He will plant it at Mum's place. As he was leaving he gave me a handful of money. 'Here,' he said. 'You might need this. When I think of how Lester has treated you, I want to punch him in the jaw.'

Our kid brother has certainly grown and I loved his show of protective manliness.

There has been no news of the elusive Lester. My sad days are less. I am feeling better.

Please write soon.

Love,

Ana

Feb 6th 1961

Dearest Fran,

You were right. I am expecting a child. I'm almost four months pregnant. You will remember that as a child, I hated green beans. Now they are my passion. I cook them by the potful, add a dob of butter and eat the lot.

Fred guessed when he caught me eating green apples at my desk. He told me his wife had craved raw cabbage and once ate a whole one on the way home from the shops.

A doctor has confirmed what I should have known. I am happy with the idea of being a mother, but uncertain as to how I will manage. Fred has assured me I can work for as long as I wish.

Feb 7th

Yesterday's letter was interrupted by two detectives who wanted to know where Lester was. One asked a lot of questions while the other prowled around the flat. He seemed to think Lester was hiding in the wardrobe or beneath a bed. After they left I realised they had not said why they wanted to speak to him.

I did not sleep well. The air is hot and sultry with a storm threatening. My head aches and I have eaten all the green beans.

Love you lots,

Ana

A trickle of sweat ran down my aching back as hemmed about by pedestrians, I waited for the traffic lights to change. A similar group of people stood on the opposite side of the road and as I looked them over, I saw Lester. I was sure it was him. The way he walked with his cigarette held turned to the side and the quick flick of his head as he shook the hair from his brow made my heart leap. Bumper to bumper traffic kept me on the kerb. A step ahead of the buzzer I pushed through the throng, searched the street and shops but failed to find him. Upset and hotter than ever, I found a phone box and calling the police station, told the detective I'd seen Lester in the street. The man's terse response left me stunned.

"You're seeing things. It can't be your husband."

"What! How do you know? How can you be so sure?"

"Because Lester Pierce is in the Rotorua lock-up waiting a court hearing."

"In goal! What has he done?" I gripped the receiver with both hands unable to believe I had been wrong. Worse, Lester was . . .

"He stole a car among other things."

"Oh God." I tried to think but thoughts would not form.

"Mrs Pierce, are you still there?"

"Yes. Would I be allowed to see him?"

"I don't see why not. Call the duty Sergeant first. He's the man to talk to."

Rather than wait for a bus, I took a taxi home and called the duty sergeant in Rotorua.

"Visitors welcome," he assured me and gave me directions from the bus depot to the station. At the corner shop I selected cigarettes, sweets and a paperback then added a book of crosswords, a writing pad and pen. Back home I wrapped the gifts, added a tin of homemade biscuits and placed them ready in my basket.

I chose a loose fitting dress, the perfect garment for a long journey in hot weather. Lester would not know it was a maternity dress. I decided not to tell him of our unplanned baby.

However desperately I might want him to fulfil a father's role, I first needed to know his state of mind. A mother carried her child for nine months but dutiful, lawful and financial support of a child came mainly from the father and lasted twenty-one years. Please, I prayed silently, let me see him. Let us talk.

Momentarily intimidated by the high pillared entrance of the Rotorua Police Station, I paused and drew a deep breath before climbing the steps and pushing open the door.

"Ah, Mrs Pierce, Just a moment please." I waited, hugging my basket, fear and hope vying for first place in my mind. A door at the rear of the room opened.

"This way please. What do you have there?" The Sergeant indicated my basket and smiled as I listed the contents. "He's a lucky man, your husband. Let me carry this for you," and walking ahead he led me down several corridors to a small room. "Wait here, please," he nodded toward a bench seat and returned my basket.

There was nothing to look at. Scuffed brown linoleum, half-panelled walls of a lighter brown and a single light bulb that hung from a once cream ceiling now covered in fly spots. How did the flies get in? There were no windows. Footsteps sounded in the corridor, one heavy and regular, the other light and shuffling. The Sergeant reappeared and stood aside to reveal Lester framed in the doorway.

For a long moment our eyes sought the familiar and registered the changes. Lester's skin was pale, deprived of sun. He wore a fresh shirt open at the neck and his trousers bagged at the knees. He had no socks and his shoes no laces. His nervous grin was lopsided and his voice soft. "Ana-banana," he said.

I turned to put my basket down and as I turned back an incredulous look appeared on his face. His mouth hung open and he stared at my stomach.

"Are you? Ana? Oh jeez, you are. We're going to have a baby." He turned to the man beside him. "Will you look at that? My wife's expecting a baby."

The Sergeant's large and friendly hand clapped Lester's shoulder. "All the more reason for you to get yourself sorted out," he said giving him a quick shake. "I'll be back shortly."

We sat at opposite ends of the seat. My secret out, I felt exposed and shy and rather than talk about myself, I listened. Surprisingly frank about his wrongdoing and genuinely sorry for running away, Lester wanted to make amends, to provide for the baby and me.

As he talked, I tried my best to hold a measure of reserve; to keep the months of lonely desperation clear in my mind and not be won over by his apologies and promises. I failed. After ten minutes in his company I was as much captivated as when, at the dip in the road behind the creek, he had given me my very first kiss. I longed to feel his arms around me. To feel his breath on my hair, his heart beat next to mine and as I teetered on the brink of surrender, the Sergeant returned.

We rose and I unpacked the basket, placing the gifts in Lester's arms before kissing his cheek. "Write to me," I whispered.

"I will. I love you."

I love you. He said he loved me. I sat in the bus, my hands resting on the tiny bulge at my waist, reliving every word, every look of our time together. Later that night I lay in bed thinking about him. Might he, I wondered, be lying awake thinking about me.

Propped against the pillows in the early morning light, I wrote to his parents. I thought it best to be honest and told them, in a straight forward manner, how Lester stole money from a drinking companion, then took the man's car which he later wrecked and abandoned. The court case was set for the end of the month. Adding words of hope I sealed the envelope.

From my bed I watched rain clouds scud across the sky and imagined my mother's reaction to the news her daughter was pregnant and her son-in-law in gaol. "Oh Ana," she would say clasping her hands, "Whatever will the neighbours think?"

For as long as I could remember there had been a distance between my mother and me. I recalled sitting on the floor as a toddler, wanting to be lifted up, held close and comforted. My attempts for attention ignored, I instead picked threads from the pompoms on her slippers and had been given a smart smack on my hands.

One day, years later, she appeared in the doorway of my room and to my surprise, flung a small book across the room at me. "You'd better read this," she said her voice knife-edged. "And when you've finished, burn it." She was gone before I read the title, *Sex and the Adolescent*. I did read it and looked at the diagrams, but at ten years of age, failed to make sense of it.

As a housekeeper, educator and provider my mum was faultless. Our environment was spotless; we were well fed and clothed. Perhaps I was an unwanted child. When I arrived she already had my older half brother and sister to care for. And the child that followed me had been aborted. Killed; she told me that. The idea of taking the life of my unborn child to better my own was unthinkable. My baby would be loved, held and cherished. Always.

My mother's imagined argument was reasonable. *Open your eyes, Ana,* she would have said. *Lester will never be reliable and the longer you prop him up the more misery you will create for yourself. How will you mange alone, with a child? You're young, twenty-two years old. What if you wish to marry someone else? What young man would want to care for another man's child, especially one with a history of mental illness? Have you thought about that?*

Yes, I have, but I want to give Lester another chance.

You are refusing to see reason. By now you should have a home of your own and a place of good standing in the community. What do you have, Ana? Nothing. No ambition and no consideration for what other people might think or how badly your unimpressive life reflects on your family. Have you any idea what people think of you at home?

Rolling onto my back I stared at the ceiling. More than ever I determined to prove myself a good wife and mother. I did not need advice from Mrs. Rose Dockery. My love for Lester remained strong and while he might never be a truly responsible person, I wanted to give him every opportunity to do his best. Did I not vow, in church, to be there for him in sickness and in health? A promise I felt incapable of breaking even though he failed to uphold his half of the oath.

After all, I was a grown woman not a child; a fact that created ambiguity within me. Part of me felt a strong determination to uphold my marriage vows, to support Lester, whatever his need. On the other hand I felt I'd been plunged into adulthood far too soon and for some reason, denied much needed parental and marital support. Why? What in the great scheme of things was that supposed to achieve? No sooner had the thought formed than I heard the words, *This is a test. Do your best.* Determined to do just that, I tossed back the blankets and stepped into a new day.

A letter arrived from Lester. He offered apologies, saying his past behaviour was inexcusable and would not happen again. Letters continued to arrive — three to my one. But after being transferred to a distant prison, the tone of his letters changed. His boyish enthusiasm became pages of retrospective meandering and as I had no wish to make suggestions or promises about things I might later regret, I carefully avoided any speculation of the future.

Lester wrote about his new cell mate, Buster. A father of two, Buster was full of advice for pregnant mums. Recommendations about the best foods, the need for exercise, fresh air and adequate rest poured into my mail box. Lester's concern for my welfare was touching and with his release now three weeks away, it was time for me to decide my future expectations. An initial time of space between us seemed prudent.

What is it they say about good intentions? Mine all fell through a crack in the floor. Lester spent his first night out of prison sleeping on the couch in my flat, the second in the spare bed and the third with me. That night the baby kicked for the first time. Whether from joy or derision, I will never know.

No amount of washing and airing in the sun could remove the prison smell from Lester's clothes. Together we shopped for new gear then threw his old clothing in the garbage bin. I insisted he take a fortnight's break before looking for work. Those two weeks cleared his prison pallor and restored his ability to relate to people. While in prison, Lester took prescribed medication, but it seemed overly strong, making him slow and hesitant. With the help of my doctor a new medication was found; a change for the better noticeable in a few days.

On Sunday afternoon we strolled through the gardens at Victoria Lake and as we turned for home, a bright red and yellow carriage drawn by two white horses bowled by. A sheet of newspaper, lifted by the breeze, wrapped itself about my legs. Lester bent to pull it free.

"Hey look at this." Pushing the paper toward me he pointed to an advertisement in situations vacant. I only had a quick glimpse before he pulled the paper away turning it back and forth searching for the date. "Yesterday, I've time to apply. Come on," he urged and taking my hand tugged me toward home. For a moment I held back, looking after the white horses.

Any doubts about leaving the flat and Fred's lovely air conditioned office to begin again in a small country town where Lester secured the job of running the forecourt of a large garage were quickly pushed aside when we were offered a three roomed cottage rent free.

The garage owner also arranged credit with the local furniture store enabling us to buy essentials. His attractive darkhaired wife came with a laden basket filled with homemade jam, cake and fresh vegetables from their garden.

The cottage, empty for years, hid behind a sprawling ten-foot high hedge and beneath the hedge lay all manner of rubbish. Truck tyres and bits of car bodies, a broken trailer and an assortment of drums half filled with oily water, rolls of wire and a dog kennel.

The young mechanics came and with a frontend loader removed the heavy items. Lester borrowed a ladder and armed with a slasher, trimmed the hedge. The ground was dug and lawn seed planted. I enjoyed house painting and in spite of my pregnancy, painted the place inside and out. The neighbours stopped to chat and shook their heads in wonder at the transformation of the little cottage.

Our home, at an intersection one block from the shops and across the main road from the garage, became a halfway house. Whenever staff wives came to town they stopped by for a cup of tea and often left their children with me while they made a quick trip to the shops or visited the doctor. Surrounded by their undemanding friendship I felt supported, safe and happy.

The season changed. Liquidambars turned red and gold. Spikey chestnuts littered the ground and drew school children to the trees behind the library next door. As the weather cooled I turned from painting to sewing tiny white garments, and embroidering them with delicate flowers and baby rabbits. I mastered fancy knitting patterns and after wrapping the finished garments in tissue paper, stored them in a suitcase beneath the bed. I haunted the auction rooms until I found a bassinette and a pram; made curtains for the nursery and practiced breathing in readiness for the birth.

Lester's parents arrived and settled in a nearby caravan park, ready to move into the cottage and care for Lester while I was away. With everything ready, we waited. Four, five, six days overdue. Mr Pierce took one look at the old pram I so proudly purchased and offered to line it. He was really quite nice in a bearish sort of way and I watched with interest as his large hands deftly stitched the lining into place. He added a fringe and a strap to keep the baby safe. When it was done I bravely kissed his forehead. Embarrassed, he brushed aside my thanks and with his bulldog cheeks quite pink, retired behind his newspaper.

The strain of waiting for an overdue baby made me restless. One night I woke screaming in pain, my legs tense with cramp. I fumbled for the torch. Lester's side of the bed was empty. The torch beam found him cowered behind the door, his arms crossed protectively over his head. He blinked sheepishly. "Are you all right? What happened?"

"Cramp," I moaned. "What are you doing over there?"

"You screamed. I thought you were being murdered. And sure as hell, what got you wasn't going to get me!" He came to wrap his arms about me. "Sorry," he murmured in my ear. Though unlikely to win medals for bravery, he proved excellent at easing cramped muscles.

Now a week overdue, I decided to give the baby a nudge and throughout the next day drank quite a lot of castor oil, floating it on cups of hot milk. Still nothing happened. Much as I loved my in-laws, having them in the cottage every day was hard; hard for them too. After another cup of castor oil I had a burst of energy and cleaned all the windows. At sunrise next morning I woke Lester. It was time to go.

By breakfast time my contractions had stopped. For two days I mooched about the hospital waiting. On the second evening I fell asleep while reading a magazine, then woke with an urgent need to go to the bathroom. Off I trotted down the long corridor following a line of tiny nightlights. On wobbly legs I returned to my bed. No sooner was I back than I had to go again. Coming back I felt faint and using the wall for support, reached my room and rang the bell.

A sister came immediately, checked me and demanded to know why I had not rung earlier. Still questioning my sanity, she pushed my bed into the theatre. Mystified, I protested. What was wrong with her? I had no pain. The doctor appeared pulling on his gloves. A mask was pushed onto my face.

"Breathe and push."

OK I felt that one.

"Again. Now. Deep breath and push."

"One more. Well done. You have a perfect baby girl."

We did not have a phone at the cottage, so the night taxi driver was sent to wake Lester who arrived at my bedside with his jacket and trousers pulled over his pyjamas, his hair on end and the biggest smile imaginable across his face. Excited, he hugged and kissed, patted and praised me. Finally he settled.

"No wonder they felt funny," he said looking down. He'd put his shoes on the wrong feet.

Each day brought new surprises. Cards, gifts and flowers filled my room. They came from neighbours I knew only by their smiles, from the butcher and the lady at the book shop. Even the grumpy little man at the mart sent a card. It seemed the whole town was there to welcome our daughter, Clare Louise. I held her close, delighting in her tiny weight and warmth as she nestled in the crook of my arm. I smoothed the fuzz of fine hair that covered her head, touched her delicate pink ears and felt her tiny fingers curl about one of mine. She had slipped into the world without fuss. I thought of the births I had seen, of the women who screamed and begged for relief, of the stalwarts who refused drugs and the many, many more who did what they had to and then held out their arms to welcome a new child. The same child who as often as not, had been cursed along with the man responsible through the many hours of pain. How our daughter could have been born so easily, was a mystery.

After ten days of cosseting, I became restless and spent the last four days at the hospital in a state of longing. I wanted to be home with Lester, to sleep with him in our bed. On my last night in the hospital he came to visit.

"Mum and Dad would like to stay a couple more days. Is that okay?"

"Of course. We can have them over for lunch. To say thank you for all they've done."

"Well," Lester began, "I said they could stay with us. No point in going back to the campground for one or two nights."

"But where will they sleep? We only have our bed and the box couch."

"Dad bought two safari beds."

'What! You mean those little wire things that are six inches off the floor?"

Lester nodded.

"Lester, your dad weighs seventeen stone. Your mum's not much less. And has arthritis. They cannot sleep on the floor. They will have to have our bed. You and I will sleep on the floor. It's only for a couple of nights . . ." My voice trailed, lost beneath my disappointment. Going home to just the three of us, Lester, Clare and me, had filled my mind for days.

"Okay. That's good." He yawned and stretched. "I'm so tired. Sleeping on the box couch is terrible."

"I'll be home tomorrow. Off you go. Get a good night's sleep."

The following night while the in-laws occupied our double bed, Lester and I lay in separate sleeping bags on the kitchen floor with Clare asleep on a pillow between us. The clock ticked steadily in the darkened room. In the light that shone from beneath the bedroom door, I could see Clare wrinkling her nose as she slept.

"Look," I whispered. Lester raised himself on one elbow and tenderly traced the baby's cheek with his finger.

"She's beautiful, delicate, pink and white. Like cherry blossom, don't you think?" Lester looked at me, his expression both loving and protective. I leaned over to kiss him — and the light went out.

In the sudden darkness there was an almighty crash followed by a shriek, bumps and thumping. Pushing open the bedroom door, Lester fell over his father who lay on the floor at the foot of our now tilted and broken bed. Jammed between the wall and the bed, Mum Pierce fought to disentangle the sheets. She finally emerged, her toothless mouth clamped shut, pins falling from her hairnet. Her big bosom bobbling, she struggled to hold her laughter behind closed lips. It was useless. Gasping and patting her chest she rocked with mirth.

"Oh, Neville. You do look a sight."

"Take a look at yourself, woman," he retorted.

Lester helped his dad to his feet.

"I'm sorry. I've wrecked your bed. I walked across it to reach the light cord." Hitching his pyjamas he retied the cord then rubbed his head as if searching for lumps.

"Give me a hand to unscrew these broken bed legs. Then we can all spend the night sleeping on the floor." Lester gave his father a good humoured push.

Our baby Clare slept through it all.

Of course we laughed when telling our friends of Clare's first night at home. But behind my smile was a resentment that would not go away. For once I had earned a place in the limelight but lost it in the ensuing fiasco. Deep down I blamed Lester for depriving me of that moment.

The young mothers who formed my close circle of friends envied me my child who slept all night and whose occasional crying was easily soothed. Yet I felt tired. No matter how carefully I arranged the day, Lester and I hardly ever had time to talk.

I missed the modern comforts of the Hamilton flat. In the cottage I cooked on a coal range, had no washing machine, not even a tub. I hand washed our clothes, baby washing, bed linen — everything, kneeling on the floor beside the bathtub, wringing everything by hand.

Winter turned to spring and through the day Clare slept in the garden beneath a canopy of crab apple blossom, her pram covered with a net to keep out the insects. My two best friends each gave birth to a baby boy and the safari beds were pulled from storage to accommodate Joan's lively lads at our house.

While she was in the hospital, her husband bought her a new washing machine. Early one Sunday morning I rolled out to investigate noises on the back porch and found, resplendent in pink crepe paper bows, Joan's old washing machine. I was so happy, I bawled.

Clare gurgled as she attempted to grasp her toes. I reached over, about to tickle her when my neighbour called across the fence, "Ana, come and see what my son sent from Japan." She unrolled a bamboo scroll to reveal a white heron, one delicately clawed foot raised, the movement so accurately captured by the artist; I half expected the bird to step forward.

The sound of an approaching siren grew louder and my neighbour crossed to her gate. "There's an ambulance at the garage," she said rolling up the scroll. I watched the heron disappear. No! A white heron. The deaths of Cousin Cyril, my grandmother and Ming sprang to mind. Snatching Clare from the rug I hurried out the gate and across the road. Behind a group of onlookers Lester and an ambo knelt beside an older man. Relived to see Lester was safe, I moved closer. The man on the floor worked in the lube bay. When the ambulance left, I asked Lester what had happened.

"Heart attack. But I remembered what to do." Clare stretched from my arms wanting to reach her father. "Come on, Blossom Child. I'll walk you both home," said Lester and proudly carrying his daughter, led the way back across the road to the cottage.

The boss asked Lester to run the lube until a replacement could be found. Unsuited to methodical and mundane work, Lester struggled, but did his best fearing dismissal if he rebelled. Weeks passed. Saturday trading arrived and the garage now opened six days a week. Instead of receiving extra money for the Saturday, the staff were given rostered days off, an arrangement that caused dark mutterings among the men, especially those with young families.

After watching the Christmas parade with a group of friends from the garage, we all returned to the cottage to share an evening meal. While five small children packed about with pillows slept in the double bed, the conversation around the table turned to Saturday trading, the dissatisfaction over longer hours and promises of money that never came.

"It's a pity we don't have a union representative," someone said. "I bet it would be quickly sorted if we did."

A lively discussion followed and by the time the sleeping children were lifted and carried out to the cars, Lester had been nominated spokesperson. His job, to contact the union and make enquires.

Instead of the expected letter or phone call, the union rep came in person, parked his car in the boss's car space and strode into the workshop. The lads downed tools and listened. The boss, forced to park halfway down the street on his return, was furious. Everyone knew of his stomach ulcer and how quickly he became tetchy but when the union man wrapped an arm about Lester and called him brother, the boss exploded. His face turned from red to purple. He shook his fists and yelled. He called Lester an ungrateful young pup and a few less complimentary names. Believing he had the backing of the staff, Lester retaliated. The sound of their angry voices drew shopkeepers and others, including me, into the street. Beside himself with rage, the boss hurled an oilcan, turned on his heel and marched to his car. The union man disappeared and as the oil dripped from Lester's shirt, he realised his prudent mates had snuck quietly back to work.

Lester felt he had been right in contacting the union and wanted to stand his ground. The other employees, preferring not to be looking for new jobs at Christmas, calmed him down. The boss made his feelings very clear. Instead of paying the usual Christmas bonus, he bought an eighteen-foot cabin cruiser and parked it on our only patch of grass at the cottage.

Rather than live with the humiliation, Lester decided to go back to milking cows. Like most Taranaki youngsters he'd worked on dairy farms. We said goodbye to our friends and moved out of town. Clare and I thrived on country life. I found pleasure in the colours and textures of the fields, in the trees and the sky. I loved the deep, silent nights, the dawn chorus of birdsong and the way the cows lifted their heads and slowly plodded homeward at milking time. There was satisfaction in baking my own bread and in learning to budget for a monthly trip to town instead of running to the shops each day.

For me it was a pleasant winter in a modern house. Long cosy evenings spent curled reading or knitting before the open fire. Both Clare and I loved the crisp frosty air and walked miles across the paddocks. Lester was not made of such hardy stuff. He developed a cough and then pneumonia. Before he had fully recovered, his mother died and Lester again retreated into silent brooding.

We were different, Lester and I. He required constant involvement with people, a platform to stand on and a steady flow of new projects that rarely, if ever, reached completion. He was not suited to country life and hiding my reluctance, I suggested we leave the farm and return to the city.

I could adapt, I told myself. I'd done it before, I could do it again. Now pregnant with our second child, I made it very clear to Lester, once we settled back in Hamilton, I would not move again before the child was born.

Nineteen

We settled in a new housing estate where friendly folk walked from door to door across unfenced back yards. Clare stopped shuffling along on her bottom and took her first baby steps. One sunny morning as I coaxed Clare to walk on the back lawn, our next-door neighbour came to say hello. Diane and I became the closest of friends. Both pregnant and expecting our babies within the same week, we swapped cake recipes, knitting patterns and shared our hopes and dreams.

Lester became a salesman, driving for a large soft drink firm. The product sold itself. As well as delivering to a popular seaside area, he ran a mobile shop at carnivals, markets and sports meetings. He loved to interact with people. With his eye on the annual sales award, he worked every day that summer. His enthusiasm reached manic level and I watched helplessly as, my caution ignored, his wave of elation founded on the gritty sand of reality.

To celebrate the arrival of 1963 the council organized a pop concert on the beach front. When it finally ended in the early hours of the morning, Lester stacked his truck with crates of empty bottles ready for the long drive back to the depot. Weary, he failed to fully secure the load and with the radio playing, heard nothing until a police siren sounded alongside. Behind him lay a trail of splintered crates and broken glass. After collecting the crates and sweeping a long stretch of road, he arrived home at daybreak. Restless, he roamed about the room. He talked, retelling the incidents of the previous night many times over. When I finally coaxed him to bed he immediately fell asleep. Gathering his clothes I took them to the laundry.

As I flipped them into the machine something hit the rim and I pulled from his shorts pocket a small unlabelled bottle of blue tablets. Clare arrived to tug at my skirt and scooping her into my arms, I left the bottle on the windowsill.

Throughout the morning Lester tossed and turned, often sitting up to call out but at no time becoming fully awake. Nor did he respond when I tried to sooth him. Worried, I went next-door for advice and Diane returned with me to stand beside the bed. Lester lay twitching, his skin grey, foamy spittle dribbling from his mouth.

Diane looked worried. "I think you should get a doctor. If he can't come I'll drive you to the hospital." While Diane carried Clare down the road to stay at a neighbour's house, I phoned the doctor. He arrived a short time later and I hovered anxiously as he examined Lester.

"Does your husband take his prescribed medication regularly? Would he take more than necessary?"

"I doubt it. He dislikes taking them."

The doctor stroked his beard. "I'd like to move him to the hospital. You say he works long hours. Does he take tablets to stay awake?"

I was about to hotly deny the suggestion when I remembered the tablets in Lester's pocket. "Just a minute," I said.

The doctor unscrewed the cap and tipping the pills into his hand first sniffed then tasted them. "I wonder where he got these," he said sliding the bottle into his pocket.

When Lester regained consciousness the following afternoon, Diane and I were at his bedside. His eyes opened and he blinked.

"Tweedledee and Tweedledum," he murmured drifting back to sleep. The crisis over, we giggled and patted our respective seven-month pregnancies.

For several days I worried about our future, the pills and the possibility of Lester losing his job. I did not want to move house. At times Lester judged himself perfectly rational and no longer needing medication. Sometimes, when we argued he'd storm out of the house.

One night after leaving home in a huff over some trivial thing, he called me from a phone box. "I've been standing on the bridge rail over the river. It's a long way down."

"I know, Lester. Are you coming home now?"

"No. I'm a terrible husband and a bad father to Clare. You'd be better off without me. I make life hard for you. I'm no good."

"Lester, I love you. Please come home."

"I've made up my mind. Give Clare a kiss from me. Tell her daddy loves her."

"Do you love me too?"

"You know I do. That's why I'm going to jump."

"No Lester. It is why you're *not* going to jump. Clare and I need you here."

"Don't do this, Anna. I told you. My mind is made up."

One o'clock in the morning, not a good time to go knocking on my neighbour's door. Nor did I wish to involve the police as Lester often threatened suicide but never followed through. Knowing this did not lessen the paralysing fear that robbed me of all coherent thought. I paced the house in the dark, my bare feet soundless on the carpet. Each time I passed the front windows I stared out into the night, willing Lester to return. An hour passed. When the phone rang I hurried to lift the receiver.

"This is Jane Mallory, Salvation Army." In a voice low and comforting she continued. "Your husband is here with me. He's quite safe. I've invited him to stay the night. I'll call you in the morning."

Captain Mallory drove Lester home in a bright red Mini. The moment he stepped through the door I moved to hug him. His face buried in my shoulder, he pleaded forgiveness.

"Tell me, tell me I am forgiven," he begged. It was always the same. My condonation required but difficult to give. For once a thing is forgiven it is gone forever and cannot be used to prop up any future argument. These stressful episodes left me emotionally drained. I longed for an ordinary life. Even boring would be better than this seesawing of emotions.

Four weeks from term, I packed for my stay at the maternity hospital. One could never be too sure. Babies liked to choose their own birthday. Easing my back as I straightened up, I looked about the room with pride. In spite of his erratic behaviour, Lester earnt good money and our home was nicely furnished. Better still, supportive friends surrounded us and with our babies due in the same week, Diane and I shared everything. Grateful for the happier side of my life I gave myself a warm hug and quietly singing, *You are my Sunshine*, prepared the vegetables for dinner.

The moment I saw Lester I knew he was bursting with news, but waiting for the right moment to tell me. After the evening meal when we settled with coffee at the kitchen table, I asked what it was he wanted to say.

"How did you guess?" He grinned and added sugar to his coffee. "I've been offered the assistant manager's job on the coast." Lester stirred his drink. There was a catch to this. I could feel it. Something he knew I would oppose.

"And?"

"I have to begin immediately."

"How immediate?"

"Monday."

"Four days! You want me to move in four days. No, I cannot. No, Lester. Not this time." I rose from the table and with my back to him, sliced bread for his lunch next day.

"Ana. Listen, please. You don't have to move straight away. I'll go ahead. Find us a house. The company will pay our moving costs. You can have packers in. You don't have to do it yourself."

"No." I took my anger out on the loaf and only stopped when I heard the knife grinding through the bread board.

"Ana —"

"No. I told you when we came here. I will not move. I have friends here. So do you. Diane and I have planned so much together. Everything is arranged. The hospital booked. I've a good doctor. I don't want to move. You're asking too much."

"Come and sit down." His hands on my shoulders he guided me to a chair. "The manager is a nice guy. I've met him. He needs someone urgently and I offered. It's an opportunity to better ourselves. My pay will almost double and there's a company vehicle." He sat opposite me, our knees touching. Taking my hands he soothed them gently between his own, his eyes fixed on mine, "Will you think about it, Ana?"

I nodded glumly. The move was one of choice, of promotion. For Lester anyway, and with two children to care for the extra money would be useful.

"Very well, I'll think about it."

To keep Lester happy, I agreed to move. He came with news of a nice new home he'd chosen but when we arrived we found it stripped bare, all carpets, curtains and blinds removed. Even the light bulbs had been taken. At five o'clock each day, ear-splitting thunderstorms caused power cuts and evenings spent by candle and firelight became a way of life along with cold meals and tea from a flask. Miserable and missing Diane, I struggled through my final month of pregnancy.

Determined not to spend any more time than necessary at the hospital, I waited until my contractions were well established before checking in, but once inside the maternity ward all baby's activity ceased and I was sent home. Four days later we went through the same charade. A week later I again returned to the hospital. Now in the care of a gynaecologist and too weak to question anything, I accepted medical inducement. For some reason this baby did not want to be born. For three long days our son dithered between following nature's instinct and tenaciously clinging to the safety of the womb. When he finally emerged, he bawled his displeasure. Our lusty son Lance was strong and healthy but very unhappy.

My head ached for days. Just another migraine, I thought, when the doctor ordered bedrest. Each day, the other new mums came to my room and together we knitted and chattered the hours away. One morning no one came. Women passed my door but none came in. At midday Sister Trudy came alone with my lunch tray. Her expression kindly, she suggested my son be fed in the nursey for a few days. After she left, the door to my room remained closed. It was all very odd.

By late afternoon my entire body throbbed. Any attempt to lift myself from the pillows so painful, I dared not move. Clouds of white mist filled the room and I floated amongst them.

Bustling with importance a young nurse-aide came, popped a thermometer in my mouth and left. A few minutes later she returned to read my temperature. Her eyes flew open and pushing the thermometer back into my mouth she hurried out calling for a sister.

Of course I took a look. Squinting in my effort to focus, I saw my temperature had gone beyond 106 degrees. That's odd, I thought, with a temperature of 105, people died. Was I going to die?

Sister Trudy arrived at my bedside and after checking the reading, gently soothed my forehead. My doctor came. Lester made a brief appearance and there were whispered conversations in the hall. Fluid was drawn from my spine and sometime during the night an ambulance took me to the general hospital. I woke, with no knowledge of time, to find a man in a white coat beside the bed. He held a clipboard on his knee.

"Ahh. Welcome back," he said.

For days I lay in a room with the blinds drawn against sun. People came and went. All were strangers. White uniforms, blue uniforms. Groups of young men with stethoscopes and later, a young man I thought I should know but didn't. He came often to sit at my bedside, held my hand and encouraged me to get well.

One day as I ate the last of my lunch, the nurse handed me a pair of spectacles. "Here, you'll manage better if you wear your glasses," she said. The effect was magical. One moment blurry coloured blobs, the next objects and facial features. "Your husband will be here soon," she continued cheerfully.

I laid down my knife and fork. "I'm married?"

"Of course." Laughing, she whisked my tray from the bed.

Husband? Married? No face came to mind. To hide my tears I pulled the blanket over my head.

"Ana, are you awake?" The voice sounded familiar. I pushed back the sheet and found myself looking into a pair of clear grey eyes that stared back at me from beneath a thick fringe of dark hair. The face relaxed and smiled.

"Thank God, you're going to be all right." He heaved a sigh and sat on the bed close to me. For a moment I wanted to pull away, yet there was something comfortable about this stranger. He talked a lot but his words had little meaning and when I did not respond, he apologized for tiring me, kissed me and went away. The kiss was nice.

The nurse hurried in all smiles. "Your husband says he'll bring Clare to see you on Sunday."

That man was my husband? Not knowing seemed unnatural. Had I gone mad? And who was Clare? Unable to find answers, I slept.

Next morning a new doctor appeared, introduced himself and offered to answer questions. Through tears I told of knowing nothing prior to being in the hospital. He reassured me saying he expected my memory loss to be temporary. He also explained how a severe allergic reaction to a drug used to combat the meningitis had taken me close to death.

"You were in a coma for twelve days. I understand how bewildered you must feel but I'm sure there will be no long-term memory loss. I want you here for at least another fourteen days. You will need to take things easy for a while." He moved closer and patted my hand. "Don't worry, Ana. Try to live as calmly as possible. You're young. In a month or so you'll feel very much better."

Later the same day the nurses moved me to a four-bed ward. The other occupants, all elderly, meant well but I found keeping up with their chatter impossible.

At visiting time on Sunday I lay propped against the pillows listening to the footsteps coming down the corridor. Visitors surrounded the other beds; people who acknowledged me with kind greetings but then left me alone.

A man's slow footsteps accompanied by small feet wearing thongs that flip-flopped noisily along the hallway grew louder then stopped. My visiting man appeared in the doorway, a broad grin lighting his face as he held out a hand to encourage someone in from the hall.

Her yellow curls bobbing, a small child shot into the room. Seeing me, she stood on tiptoe, gazing through the metal rails at the foot of the bed, a pair of pink thongs clutched to her chest. "Mummy. My mummy," she kept repeating as her thongs discarded, she clambered up the bed to clasp small hands about my neck. We were all in tears before she finally slipped to the floor and stood leaning against the knee of the man I now knew to be my husband.

"Is this beautiful child Clare? I didn't recognize her," my voice came out in a whisper.

He smiled his disbelief, his lip trembling as he spoke. "Jeez, Dr. Morris was right. I didn't believe him. You didn't know me either, did you? I wondered why you never said my name."

Tears running down my face I shook my head.

Leaning over he tenderly mopped my tears with his handkerchief and Clare, holding tightly to his leg, came with him. With her on his knee and my cheek resting against his shirtfront, his arms holding us, he told me we had been friends all our lives and married for six years. He talked of his work as a salesman and of Colin, the best employer ever. "Colin and his wife are looking after Clare and Lance."

I lifted my head. "Lance?" I asked. Lester's grip tightened and he muttered a rude word.

"Lance is our baby son; a little butterball of a kid who is no doubt growing fatter as I speak. He was born five weeks ago. Don't you remember that?" I shook my head.

"Perhaps it's just as well. You had a rough time. Lance is a tough little guy; strong as an ox and roars like a bull."

"Is that all? I mean Clare and Lance. Or are there more?"

"No, only two, Ana-Banana." His look was one I had seen before, loving but sad.

After visiting hours I lay thinking about the things Lester said. He called me Ana-Banana. Then I saw him, the same man, calling me by the same name. He stood in a doorway with a policeman beside him and I trembled with nervousness as I waited. Waited for what? I had no idea. As suddenly as it appeared, the image vanished.

Allowed out of bed at last, I sat by the window in the sunshine, a magazine in my lap. Opening it, I turned the pages. The lines of black letters, they made a story. One read and understood them. To me they made no sense at all. Shock turned to horror. Had I gone crazy? Crazy people were locked away, had no clothes and slept in dirty straw. But if I pretended to read, the nursing staff might think I was getting better.

For three days I traced the lines with my finger, estimating the time it might take to read. I reasoned that if I turned the pages regularly, anyone watching me would think I was reading normally. On the fourth day the black marks began to form words and although my head ached I persevered, following my finger, sounding the words until without really noticing how or when, I understood the writing. My yelp of triumph sharp, I peered around the magazine to see if anyone noticed. Not a flicker of interest.

"You may go home."

Under caution to avoid stress and have adequate rest, I nodded to show I understood but my heart thumped. Going home meant being a mother and a wife and wives shared a bed with a husband. Panic beat its black wings about me. While Lester seemed nice, he was still a stranger in many ways. What might he expect of me? Could I accept and trust this man? With no alternative, nowhere else to go, I had no option but to do my best. In a flash of remembrance, I rode a bicycle, pushing hard against wind and shouting at the top of my voice, 'This is a test, do your best'. Determined to confront the problems before me I said goodbye to the nurses and followed Lester to the carpark.

When the engine fired I clapped my hands over my ears. The noise, so loud after living in a quiet, slow moving environment for so long petrified me. My body rigid, I grasped the edge of the seat, pulling back in terror as all the noise, colour and speed of fast moving traffic rushed headlong toward me. I wanted to crawl beneath the dashboard, close my eyes, cover my ears and hide.

We called first at Colin's home where I sank gratefully into an armchair in a quiet room. His wife, Mary, gently placed a plump child wrapped in a blue bunny rug on my lap. He was a handsome child and as we studied each other I waited for a spark of recognition, a rush of love, anything that would create a bond between me and my son. But nothing happened. I might have been holding a doll.

"I'm sorry. I will learn to love you. I promise," I whispered as I hugged him close. Shaken by my lack of emotion, I looked to Lester for help as Lance chose to demonstrate the great power of his voice. His face red, he bellowed loudly and beat the air with his fat little fists.

Colin grinned. "He's going to be a singer like his dad," he said as Mary lifted the angry infant and rocked him until his yells subsided.

"We have a suggestion," Mary looked from Lester to me as she spoke. "Colin and I are willing to have Lance here with us while Ana continues to recuperate. Caring for a baby is demanding and this one is more demanding than most." She smiled, "If it will help you, Ana, Lance is welcome to stay a while longer."

With my eyes I asked Lester to make the decision for us and he understood.

"Thank you. I think a few days to settle in would be good."

"You're both very kind. Thank you. Can I please hold him again before we go?" Mary passed my now relaxed son back to me. I held him close marvelling at the perfection of his small body. Soon we would get to know each other.

My ability to deal with the basics of housework returned quickly and easily. Clare was a blessing. A happy, carefree little girl with an incredible memory who, when asked the whereabouts of something, knew immediately where to find it. She chattered non-stop and often made me laugh out loud. When exhaustion brought tears of frustration she would scramble onto my knee, place her baby hands on my cheeks and gazing into my eyes say, 'Poor mummy' with such solemn sincerity, I had to smile and reassure her.

Lance came home to serenade us with his raucous vocals. As the days extended into weeks, my memory slowly returned. By early summer we had settled into a routine. Lester retired first and rose early, leaving me to sleep after a wakeful night with Lance. I now did my own grocery shopping and was no longer terrified of the traffic on the streets.

Lester and I lived as two old friends, comfortable in each other's company. There was no real romance. Throughout that summer he worked fifteen hours a day, six days a week, leaving the house before the children woke and returning after dark. I hoped a little enticement might persuade him to stay awake an hour or two longer and lifting a long silky nightdress from my drawer I laid it across the double bed.

That night I prepared a special dinner, his favourite fillet steak and oysters followed by apple and almond pie with whipped cream. We ate dinner together and talked. Not that I had much to offer other than the funny things children do.

"Clare coaxed Lance onto the couch beneath the cuckoo clock and showed him how to cup his hands. Then climbing up beside him, she aimed her popgun at the clock and said, "When that bird comes out, I'll shoot him. You catch him."

Lester laughed but he had more serious news. Colin, the employer in a million, planned to retire at the end of the year. With luck, Lester might be offered the manager's job. I spoke without thinking.

"That will involve a lot of organization and paper work. Can you manage that?"

"Do you think I am stupid? I'd have a secretary." He spooned the last of the dessert into his mouth, wiped his hand across his lips and announced he was going to bed. My visions of a romantic night dashed, I filled the sink with hot water and slowly washed the dishes giving Lester time to fall asleep.

When Colin retired a new manager was brought in. A tough, no nonsense man with whom Lester had little in common and whose imagined shortcomings became a constant source of dissatisfaction to my husband.

The clear cold nights of winter brought crisp frosts and still Lester rose at 5am, leaving the house before sunup. When I questioned the need to continue the long hours, his reply was abrupt.

"If you want money, I have to earn it."

A couple of days later I noticed Lester was not wearing his wedding ring. "It caught on a nail. Near tore my finger off," he said. The same day I answered a call from a bright young female who asked to speak to Les. When told he was not at home, she hung up. An hour later she rang again and when I said hello she asked who was speaking.

"Mrs Pierce." I put emphasis on the Mrs.

"Oh," she chirped, "may I speak to your son?"

I turned to where Lance sat on the kitchen floor surrounded by the clothes pegs, a mushy piece of rusk oozing from between his fingers as he aimed it at his mouth.

"You could but I don't think he'll talk to you. His vocabulary is very limited."

There was a small silence.

"I think I may have the wrong Pierce. Goodbye."

The phone continued to ring at odd hours. When I answered, no one spoke. Instinct warned me confronting Lester would be unwise. I needed to be subtle. What I did not understand was why, if he had another woman, did he continue to provide a home for us? Perhaps he felt guilty. There had been some grim and unhappy times in our relationship. If ever I referred back to those times, Lester changed the subject or encouraged me to recall happier incidents. I thought he did this to help me, as an attempt to lift the postnatal depression that clung to my mind. Nagged by a growing fear he deliberately kept the past hidden for his own benefit, I reasoned he might also hide present indiscretions. When I finally asked if he knew who the caller might be, he shrugged his shoulders and denied knowing any young girls. The calls stopped after a day or two and I did my best to forget them.

Any lingering concerns were pushed aside when Lester arrived home driving a lolly-pink Volkswagen. Full of excitement at finally owning a car again, he insisted we all go for a drive. He bought it, he said, from a young girl who worked at one of the shops he delivered to on the beachfront. Well, that could explain the phone calls.

Throughout the long summer holidays the children and I accompanied Lester to many of the special events held at the seaside. Lance now walked unaided but still preferred to crawl when in a hurry. While Lester worked nearby selling soft drink from the mobile shop, the children and I dug sandcastles and paddled in the sea. It was a summer of healing, mentally and emotionally. It also drew Lester and I back together, revitalizing our love for one another. We even talked of renewing our wedding vows.

After a morning of playing on the beach the children and I joined Lester for a picnic lunch on the loading ramp behind the kiosk. As we ate, Lance dropped an apple, chased it and tipped headlong over the edge. Lester reached out and grabbing our son by the shirt, pulled him to safety. In the effort, Lester somehow overbalanced and fell heavily to the ground below. He sat, his face twisted in pain, hugging his legs. A St John's Ambulance man arrived and deftly strapped a splint to his leg before sending him to hospital in an ambulance. With the children tucked up in the van alongside the shop, I continued selling until the firm's manager came to take over. By the time I reached the hospital Lester was in surgery having metal supports fitted to fractures in his lower leg and ankle.

While recovering in hospital, Lester struck up a friendship with a poultry farmer in the next bed and told him of his fears for the future.

"All I know is driving and selling. Now they say I can't drive. Not for six months or more. It's unlikely the boss will keep my job open."

The farmer offered Lester a proposition. "You have two strong arms and I have two good legs. Between us we could do the work required to keep the hens happy. I can offer you and your family a three-bedroom house. The yard is shaded by trees and well fenced; safe for the kiddies. My wife would be tickled pink to have children about the place. There's ten acres of oranges trees and peaches ready to be picked. What do you think, lad?"

"It sounds too good to be true. Do you have a rent in mind?"

"I assume you'll have sick pay, so if you had the house and electricity free and say fifteen pound a week, do you think between you and your wife you could put in six hours a day, three on Sundays?" Gob smacked Lester nodded.

"I'd be grateful for your help, lad. Shall we see what the ladies think when they come to visit?"

The ladies thought it a wonderful idea. Kevin's wife Alice was a small, round faced woman with fine grey hair that continually escaped from the bun on the top of her head. I'd never met a kinder pair. Friends helped me to move while Lester remained in hospital. Alice and I worked well together and in no time I became a proficient helper caring for the hens and picking fruit.

Twenty

The dull thud of the curtain weights falling back against the wall woke me. Wind whistled through the cracks and I lay listening as somewhere behind the house a loose piece of iron scraped against another. Taking care not to disturb my sleeping husband I slid from the bed and moved quietly through the house closing windows.

In the children's room I lifted strands of blonde curls from Clare's forehead and left a kiss in their place before tucking the blankets around Lance, who sprawled face down in his cot, a toy car still clutched in his hand. Not until I paused at the kitchen sink, filled a glass with water and drank, did the smell of smoke become apparent. My hasty but thorough search of the house failed to find anything burning.

The smell grew stronger and I hurried outdoors, past the passionfruit vines to the five-bar gate at the entrance to the poultry yards. The instant my fingers grasped the latch, flames shot high above the roof of the middle poultry shed. I ran. Dragged open the heavy doors. But the stupid chooks refused to move. They huddled together in the far corners away from the flames. No amount of stamping or yelling was going to shift them. Distraught, I raced back to the house screaming for Lester. He met me at the door pulling on a coat over his nightwear.

"I'll get the hose. You get Kevin."

"You can't. Your leg!"

"I'll be fine. Now get going." He swung toward the sheds, his crutches taking the weight from his recently fractured leg.

I chose the shortest path, stumbling through long grass and brambles to pound on Kevin's door. No response. Hurrying around the back I rapped repeatedly on his bedroom window. At last, a light and Kevin appeared blinking owlishly. Behind me the fire lit the night sky, the wind carrying smoke away from Kevin's house and toward our cottage.

Alice prodded her husband from behind. "Move," she ordered pushing Kevin aside.

"Right. I'll get my boots." Kevin disappeared back in the house.

"I'll ring the fire brigade. Ana, you bring your children here," Alice said.

I nodded and ran.

Lester stood silhouetted against the flames, hose in hand. The hens clacked, the sound horrid, pitiful. Panic stricken, some ran. Others lay still on the ground. The smell of burning feathers turned my stomach.

Smoke drifted through the rooms of the open cottage as I lifted the crying children. Carrying them to the double bed, I bundled them into their dressing gowns and shoes. The children settled with Alice, I hurried back to the sheds to find Lester hobbling back and forth with the hose as Kevin struggled to open the doors of the end shed.

"Ana. Can you get the hens out the other side? I have to move the petrol," Kevin shouted.

"Yes. Go. Go." I pushed with all my might to open the seldom used double doors. Prayed the tractor would start first time allowing Kevin to shift the trailer load of fuel drums stored only a short distance from where flames crept along the rafters.

Hens from the first pens fluttered out into the night. But when the tractor roared, the remaining fowls baulked. Frantic arm waving and shouting useless, I climbed into the pen and threw them one by one toward the open doorway. Intent on my effort, I missed the three men who strode past to rip sheets of iron from the wall and chase the hens out into the night.

Outside there was pandemonium; fires engines, flashing lights, men and hoses. The school master pushed his way through a crowd of onlookers carrying trays of young chicks that peeped and squeaked as he packed them in his van. Small children scurried back and forth collecting white feathers, their fists and pockets full.

Near tears, I made my way to where I had last seen Lester and found him sitting behind a fire engine. He leant against the dog kennel, his face contorted with pain as he felt his injured leg.

"Ana, there you are. You look awful."

"Thanks." I nudged him over and sat beside him. Water spilled from the dog's bowl onto my hand. So wet and cool. I cupped my hands and washed my face from the bowl, revelling in the cool wetness as the water ran down my face and neck. I felt Lester watching me and heard the suppressed laughter in his voice.

"Do you feel better now?"

"Yes." I managed a smile.

"Umm. Can you find my crutches for me? I think I have done something bad to my leg. I can't get up."

I pushed upright. Flames no longer lit the sky. Smoke was drifting away and overhead the stars shone as usual.

"Lester. Ana. Are you all right?" Kevin's hoarse voice came from the darkness. He slung an arm about my shoulders. "Well done, lass. And you, Lester, thank you, son. We saved the far shed. Alice is expecting you up at the house. Hey, what is it, lad? Are you hurt?"

Lester had been struggling to his feet but moaned and fell down. "My leg hurts like hell."

"I'll get help." Kevin spun on his heel. A moment later he was back with two firemen who swung Lester from the ground and carried him, under Alice's directions, to the spare room in her house.

Those who helped save the hens gathered in the kitchen where the harsh electric light revealed red rimmed eyes and faces smeared with grime. Most had blood streaked limbs, pecked and scratched by the terrified fowls and there was a lot of coughing, soon eased by the flow of cold beer.

With Alice's help I undressed and washed a protesting Lester who refused to go to the hospital, saying he would be fine in the morning. When persuasion failed, we left him to sleep.

In the early dawn light, white feathered shapes huddled together. Barely three hours had passed since I first woke and smelled the smoke yet it seemed I had lived an extra lifetime. From the porch step I watched Kevin's red kelpie sniff through the outer debris, stirring up small clouds of fine ash that eddied slowly back to the ground, falling soft and silent on the blackened ruins.

Weary, I returned home to shower and dress in fresh clothes. In the kitchen, oily soot covered every surface. Unable to face the chore of cleaning it all, I wiped a small space and made a cup of tea.

What lay ahead? Kevin was no longer robust. He might not want to rebuild his poultry business and without the hens, we'd be without work—without a home.

The sound of a slow grinding motor drew me to the door. A tractor and trailer driven by a neighbour led a small convoy of utility trucks. Half a dozen men walked alongside, picking up the dead fowls and tossing them into wire cates on the back of the vehicles as they drove slowly around the yard and down through the orchard.

Then it was the turn of the live birds. They would not lay after such trauma. Hens, that only yesterday had scratched happily in the barn straw and clucked gently as they settled for the night, were now being packed into crates and taken away.

Unable to watch and overwhelmed by the apparent futility of life, I ran through the garden and up the slope to where a line of conifers formed a wind break behind the house. Pushing my way in beneath the marcrocarpa branches I hid and, from a reservoir deep within, burst into convulsive sobbing.

"Mummy, where are you?" Clare's voice stemmed my tears and brushing the dead needles from my clothes, I stepped out into the sunlight. My lovely daughter came plodding up the slope on short sturdy legs, her fair curls bobbing with the effort. She looked up and waved.

I have so much to be grateful for. My arms wide I lifted Clare onto my back and with her crying, "Gee up, Neddy," began an erratic dance down the hill.

While thankful for the many blessings in my life, any uncertainty like the problem of our immediate future produced a melancholy that sapped my energy. Determined to remain strong I kept my concerns to myself.

In the following days anything salvageable was cleaned and set aside, the remaining rubbish carted away. After a few days' rest, Lester began work in the nearby packing sheds. The women loved him. His lively patter and repertoire of songs kept them entertained during the long hours they spent perched on high stools grading the last of the summer fruit. There, with a captive audience, he was happy.

At home he was again a grumpy fellow. Nothing I said or did ever pleased him. If I dared ask for an extra item when shopping, I was verbally upbraided in public and quickly learnt to be silent. Several times a week Lester joined Mick and his brother Eddie in their ramshackle hut down the road. Together they drank beer and played darts. After these visits, Lester returned home in high spirits and invited the children to romp with him on the floor. These games had a way of becoming rough. He teased the children and if they cried, or worse, attempted to turn the tables on their dad, he denied them pudding or bedtime stories and often sent them to bed early.

Instead of speaking out and telling Lester his actions were wrong, I made excuses for him and pacified my children with half lies. I foolishly thought Lester's behaviour a result of the continuing pain in his leg, resentment for what he called demeaning work and the tension of waiting for Kevin to decide his future, and ours. Could we stay or would we have to go — again?

Stories of Lester's unpredictable behaviour became local knowledge. His sudden tempers and the way he sulked when challenged made people wary. Afraid to challenge him, but wanting to understand, I waited for the right moment to speak. To my surprise the first move came from him.

We lay in bed, not quite touching in the darkness. Rain pounded the iron roof and somewhere in the distance a dog howled, his misery evident.

"Poor animal, I know how he feels." Lester's voice was barely a whisper.

"You sound unhappy yourself. Do you want to talk?"

For a long moment he seemed to withdraw. Then, "I think it would be best if I went back to the hospital."

"Is your leg so painful? I'm sorry. You've been walking so well. Why didn't you tell me?"

"No! I mean the psychiatric hospital."

"What?" I pushed up on the pillow and heard the smack of Lester's fist hitting his forehead, felt the bed jolt.

"Ana. Don't you remember anything?"

"Sorry. It seems so long ago and I try not to think about it."

"I am sorry too." Lester felt beneath the sheet for my hand and having found it, held it tight against his chest.

"You always were the strong one, Ana. I wanted to love you. Care for you but I let you down time after time. You always took me back; patched me up. When you were so ill I promised myself I'd be there for you." His voice broke. "I've tried, Ana but I can't do it. I feel there are half a dozen people in my mind. They all pull in different directions and I just want to run and hide." His body shook with soundless sobs and he buried his face between my breasts.

"SShhh. It's all right. We can sort this out together." I held him close, rocking him gently and murmuring comfort as one does for a child. When Lester fell asleep I eased his weight aside and staring into the darkness, wondered where my life was going.

The following morning, confident we could solve our problems, Lester and I lingered over breakfast discussing various possibilities.

Three days later in pouring rain, Kevin drove Lester to the bus station. Alice, the children and I, waved goodbye from beneath a brightly coloured golf umbrella and when Clare leant back against my skirt I folded my arms across her chest and held her tight.

By the end of the third wet week, my attempts to keep the children amused failed. Fretful, they quarrelled and demanded constant attention. At the first break in the weather I hustled them into raincoats and gumboots and together we set off for a walk. Our quiet stroll along the road became an adventure as Clare and Lance sloshed through puddles and with a stick, whacked overhead branches shaking loose showers of water. Their chuckles as I pretended to be caught unawares lightened my spirits. We took turns at kicking an empty can and enjoyed the satisfying clang as it rattled over the stones.

Hit from behind by a sudden squall, I looked for shelter. Mick and Eddie's hut was nearest but no way would I take the children there. If we continued to walk on, we'd have our backs to the wind. Susceptible to cold, his hands and cheeks turning blue Lance looked ready to cry.

"Shall we dance? Come on. Like this." I held out my arms and jigging about, sang *Let a Smile be Your Umbrella.* Clare laughed and followed my example. Lance gripped my hand and exhilarated by the force of the wind, we skipped and sang our way along the road.

The sharp honk of a car horn halted our parade.

"May I offer you a lift?" the driver called. The man was not much older than me and his deep blue eyes twinkled with amusement.

"Actually, we live that way, at Kevin MacAulay's." I pointed back the way he had come.

"Then you must be Ana. I'm pleased to meet you. I'm Rodney Gilmore, Alice's nephew. Won't you get in? I'll drive you home." My protests about being wet and spoiling his car brushed aside, we settled into the back seat.

At the house Rodney climbed out and opened the gate before driving us into the yard where he stood holding the door open as the children and I clambered from the car. Embarrassed by the thought that it would be nice to know more of this man with the smiling blue eyes, I hurried the children onto the porch and thanking him for the lift, followed them inside. "Keep smiling," he called as he drove away.

When Alice came the next morning I boiled the kettle for tea and we sat together on the front porch.

"I hear you met my nephew, Rodney," she said.

"Yes. He gave us a lift home. He seems very nice."

"Rodney is going to live in our house and look after the orchard while Kevin and I take a long sea cruise. Kevin is ready to retire. When we return we'll move up the coast, find a cottage and spend the rest of our days quietly fishing." Alice reached across and patted my hand. "I know you are on your own at present, dear. There is no rush for you to leave the house. Wait until Lester is well again. The place will not go on the market until we return from our trip."

Later, when I wrote to Lester, I decided not to tell him of the impending sale. I'd sent several letters and cards in the past month and received nothing in return. The one time we talked on the phone, he had been vague, perhaps even unwilling to talk with me. And when I suggested visiting him, he became adamant; the journey was too long, cost too much and there were the children to consider. The list of reasons for me to remain at home grew by the moment. He did not want me at the hospital.

Rodney worked hard showing a high level of competence as he ploughed and raked the blackened spaces where the sheds had been. He cleared brambles, mended fences and painted the exterior of Kevin's house. When I told him I really did enjoy wielding a paint brush, he accepted my assistance. I fell into the habit of making a flask of tea, fresh scones or muffins and carrying it to him at morning tea time. While Clare and Lance played nearby, Rodney and I talked about films, books, places we had been and the people we had met.

One morning the postman mistakenly delivered a letter for Rodney to my mailbox and I walked across to give it to him. He had pruned the fruit trees and planted new ones. The place looked like a park. I found him scraping something black and nasty from a pot into the rubbish. He pulled a rueful face. "I'm no cook. That was last night's diner," he said as I leaned over trying to guess what it might have been.

"Would you like to have dinner with us? If you can cope with the children's table manners you're welcome to come."

There was the tiniest of pauses as his eyes met mine. "Thank you. But only if I can help with the washing up."

"A man who washes up," I put on my most surprised look and throwing my arms wide said, "You're doubly welcome."

By the time the children settled for their afternoon nap, I had planned dinner and flipped the hangers in the wardrobe a dozen times. I wanted to look nice but not obvious. After all I was a married woman — and I wished I was not. Rodney was considerate, sincere and hardworking and had a kindly sense of humour. The children adored him. I clapped my hands over my mouth. What was I thinking? And returning a low-cut floral dress to the wardrobe, I replaced it with jeans and a check shirt.

Two weeks later as I set the dinner table for four, happily anticipating another pleasant evening with Rodney, the telephone rang.

"Hi, Ana Banana. How's my best girl?"

"Lester? Where are you?"

"Still in this crummy place but not for much longer. I'll be home Thursday."

Tightness clamped my throat. I thought I'd choke I felt so conscience-stricken. "Would you like to talk to the children for a moment? I need to check the dinner. Don't want a burnt meal."

"Yeah, put them on."

While Clare chattered I turned down the heat under the pots and returned to the phone. "How are you? Are you feeling better?"

"I was. Who the hell is Rodney?"

Sensing his anger I explained, feeling relief when I was able to change the subject then say goodbye. Why did I feel guilty? I'd done nothing wrong. It was just that Lester had a way of making me feel bad about myself.

Rodney's knock sounded at the door and the children raced to greet him. Laughing he swung Lance up onto his back and handed me a letter. "It's from Alice. I thought you might like to read it." As he passed me the letter I thought how nice it was that he always knocked and waited to be invited in.

After the dishes were put away and the children washed and ready for bed, I read the letter from Alice. Folding it back into the envelope I looked across to where Rodney knelt beside the coffee table helping Clare build a tower with playing cards. Lance sat quietly watching as each new level was carefully set in place. The scene was one of contented domesticity. Rodney looked up and smiled, the look in his eyes immediately becoming one of tender concern as he sensed my reflective mood. The card house fell, the moment gone and calling to Rodney to please make coffee, I carried my protesting children off to bed.

Seated at the kitchen table we discussed the news from Alice. Kevin was unwell. Nothing too serious but they planned an early return.

"Lester will be home the same day." I bowed my head. I'd been so happy these past two months and dreaded Lester's return, feelings I had to keep to myself. His hand cupping my chin, Rodney raised my head until our eyes were level.

"Do you want to tell me why you're so sad?" he asked.

"It's the not knowing. Lester is often moody and I'm afraid of upsetting him, making him angry."

"Listen to me, Ana." His hand trailed from my chin to my hand giving it a little shake before letting go. "Whatever the situation, we each choose how we react. Me, you, Lester, we all choose our behaviour. We can be mad or sad. We can laugh it off, ignore it. We can be understanding, forgiving or try to get even. What we do and say is our choice. We always have a choice, Ana. *You* always have a choice. No one can take that power away. Do you understand what I am saying?"

I nodded.

"Good." He stood up. "I should go. I don't expect I'll be back. Reverend Jenkins has invited me to dinner tomorrow and I need to go home for a few days."

I rose and walked with him to the door. "Rodney."

He turned.

"Thank you, thank you for being a friend." For a precious moment we hugged. His eyes moist Rodney held my hands. "If you ever need anything, call me. Goodbye Ana."

"Goodbye, Rodney. Goodbye."

Kevin and Alice sold their property to a neighbour within days of their return and I packed our belonging ready to move. Lester went to the head office of the soft drink company hoping to reclaim the position he had before breaking his leg. He phoned late at night, his voice triumphant. Not only did he have a new job as a car salesman, but a house as well. "I've hired a truck. I'll be there first thing tomorrow," he said, his enthusiasm as contagious as always.

Our latest home was old but spacious. It sprawled over a large overgrown section at a dip in the road. A long flight of steps led down from the street and along a side boundary, a line of citrus trees heavily laden with small green fruits overhung the path.

On the other side an acre of high grass and old fruit trees hung with morning glory vines separated us from the neighbours.

At Lester's suggestion and with an eye to making some extra money, we advertised for boarders to fill the spare rooms. A month later my panic over providing furniture and bedding for such a venture subsided. New curtains hung at the windows, the inherited silver cutlery shone and with cups, plates and pots counted, we were finally ready. A curate, a bank clerk and a mechanic moved in followed by young Ben. Ben was eighteen and working as a builder's labourer before going to university. Arriving home after work, he'd kick off his boots and call, "What's to eat?" then raid the kitchen cupboards demolishing a packet of cracker biscuits, half a pound of cheese and two apples before reappearing at the dinner table to eat a three course meal.

The little notebook I used to record finances showed a lot of red ink during Ben's six week stay. Once he went I managed to make a little money but it was hard work washing, ironing and making packed lunches for everyone. When my sister Fran wrote asking if I'd consider giving a home to an unwed and pregnant girl willing to help in the house, I jumped at the opportunity.

Calm capable Jill. She took care of the children and proved herself an innovative cook in whom the old gas cooker could instil no fear. Our long busy days rolled into months. The mechanic married, the bank teller transferred and we were left with the curate.

In the lull that followed their departure, I looked for my husband but he was rarely about. I caught fleeting glimpses of a man leaving the house, running up the steps to the road and driving away. On occasions I hurriedly ironed him a fresh shirt and pecked his cheek as he passed me in the hall on his way out the door into the darkness of the night. "Don't wait up," he'd call then come home late, smelling of drink and often perfume.

We arranged a Christmas holiday. Lester had the use of a station wagon from work and we planned to take the children to Waikaremoana — this visit surely better than the last. Jill was going to her boyfriend's parents.

On Christmas Eve I went into town to buy last minute items. When Lester finished work, we'd meet and collect the children's gifts from the toy shop. I hoped there'd be time to go somewhere nice where we might sit and talk, just the two of us, celebrating Christmas together. I longed to recapture our earlier closeness and had decided to flirt openly in public if necessary.

Instead of the station wagon Lester came to meet me in a huge saloon car, all fins and gleaming chrome. He'd sold every car on the lot, including the wagon. His employer opened the drinks cabinet and, in some fleeting moment of near sobriety, when he realised Lester no longer had a car to take his family on holiday, the boss loaned him his son's souped up vehicle.

"A gas guzzler if ever there was one," Lester complained as he lurched across the pavement carrying Clare's new tricycle. "The petrol for the trip will cost a fortune." Unsteady, he bumped his head on the boot lid. "Hell that hurt." Staggering back, he rubbed his forehead.

We collected the rest of the toys and when Lester declined the offer of coffee, headed home. The drive up the main street and across the river was fraught with near misses as Lester wove the enormous car through heavy traffic. The car reeked of alcohol and after the wheels mounted the gutter for the third time, I demanded he stop the car saying, "I will walk. You can kill yourself if you want."

"Suit yourself," he said and drove off leaving black marks on the road and a smell of burning rubber in the air. At each bend of the road I expected to see the car piled against a lamp post and Lester's limp body hanging out of the door but there was no sign of the car until I reached home and saw it parked outside the gate as usual.

Jill and Lester stood beneath the porch light. They seemed to be arguing. Seeing me approach, Lester pointed. "There. See. I told you she'd be all right." He turned and bumping his way along the wall to the dining room slumped onto the couch. Jill and I went to the kitchen.

"He's really drunk." Jill made no attempt to hide her disgust.

"Here. Have this." I placed a large mug of black coffee beside him. As he reached for it he slid forward and would have fallen to the floor had Jill and I not grabbed him.

"What now?" she asked as we supported the semi-conscious man between us.

"Can you help me put him to bed?" On her nod of consent, we hoisted Lester's incumbent form and tried to get him through the door. After several attempts to angle Jill's big tummy and my husband's floppy limbs we managed to line everyone up and giggling and panting dropped him onto the bed.

Refreshed with coffee and cake, Jill and I checked the children were sleeping soundly then climbed the steps to the street. The car was locked; the toys inside. We dug into Lester's pockets. No keys. We shook him. It was hopeless. All he did was snore.

We were standing beside the car armed with a screwdriver and wondering where to start, when the curate rode to our rescue, cycling down the street whistling *Come all ye Faithful*. Not only did he spot the keys hanging from the ignition but using a wire coat hanger he sprung the lock on the door and handed me the keys. The three of us carried the toys down to the house where Jill and I quickly wrapped the gifts, filled the Santa stockings and parked the shiny new tricycles beneath the Christmas tree.

Clare and Lance found the trikes before sunup. They clambered over our bed scattering books, toys and sweets across the quilt while imploring their father to look, to see what Santa had brought.

I gained a certain satisfaction watching Lester's miserable response as Lance sat astride his stomach and pushed a red jelly baby into his father's mouth. "One for Daddy," he said as he bounced with excitement and Lester turned green.

"Let's go and show Jill your new bikes," I suggested ushering them out the door as Lester swayed his way to the bathroom.

Jill's boyfriend arrived to drive her home. With the birth of her baby so close I did not expect her to return and our farewell hug was long and tearful. An hour later the curate carried his suitcase to the front door and having blessed us all, departed to spend two weeks at the beach.

A huge sigh escaped my throat. I spread a rug on the lawn beneath the trees and left Lester to watch the children. Even on Christmas day there was washing to be done. While pegging small garments to the line, I heard the phone ring and paused, waiting to see if Lester would answer it. He did. The calls were always for him.

The washing finished I returned to the kitchen to make tea. Lester's voice, low and insistent came from the hallway. "Stop crying. I said I will come. Wait there. I'll be along shortly." Hearing me, he replaced the receiver.

"Who was that?" I called.

"Problem at work. I have to go in to the office."

I poured our tea and glasses of milk for the children, added a plate of baked biscuits to the tray and called the family to come. Clare and Lance came running.

"Where's your Daddy?" I asked them.

"Gone. In the car."

I went to check. The car was gone. I tipped Lester's tea down the sink. I wanted to hurl the cup across the room. Thump the walls and slam doors. It was Christmas day damn it. The round-eyed gaze of the children forced me to calm down.

On impulse I phoned the office. A feminine voice answered. "Oh," I said pretending to be surprised. "Who am I talking to?"

"Lisa. A1 Car Sales."

"I'm sorry, Lisa. I must have dialled the wrong number." I'd met Lisa, the part-time office girl, a plump, fluffy little blonde, barely seventeen. Well, Lester Pierce, you had better have a good explanation for this.

Wild thoughts fuelled my imagination. I would call a taxi, go to the office and catch him in the act — the act of what? It might be an innocent office mix-up Lisa was trying to sort out. Besides, barging in with two children in tow wasn't really my style. I needed to be patient. I did not have long to wait. At the sound of the car arriving I went to meet Lester.

"The money," he said in reply to my questions. "There was a bag of money in an open drawer when I locked up last night. I didn't have the safe keys, so I brought it home. Now I'm going to take it over to the boss." Pushing past me he muttered, "I didn't steal it if that's what you think." He returned with the bag and I stood aside as he strode past and out the door.

"How long will you be?" I called.

He gave no answer.

Late in the afternoon he returned and pleading exhaustion and a headache went to lie down. The effects of the previous night's drinking evident, I quietly closed the door leaving him alone. He emerged after the children had gone to bed and fell into an armchair opposite me.

"Ana, I don't feel very well. Would you mind very much if we didn't go away? We have the house to ourselves; it would be like a holiday here at home, just you, me and the kids." His smile was wistful and I was immediately won over.

"I'd like that. I'll ring and cancel the booking right now."

"No. I'll do it. Be a darling and make me a strong black coffee will you?"

The following morning the 'gas guzzler' had gone. I decided not to ask questions.

Several days before the end of our holiday, Lester announced he had an interview in Auckland. The kind of sales job he dreamed of, he told me. Horrified, I protested. I did not want to live in Auckland. I was not a city person. He'd promised. Promised we would stay in this house; and a lot of other houses, I thought. Placing his hands on my shoulders Lester turned me about, compelling me to look into his eyes.

"Let me try, Ana. Anyway, the job is not in Auckland. It's based in central Waikato. You'd be back with your friends."

In the hope my silence was as meaningful as my words, I shut up. Silence, pleading, anger, it was all water off a duck's back to Lester.

Twenty-one

How Lester won the prodigious position of sales rep with a major oil company was a mystery to me. He even found us a house to buy and pays the mortgage direct from his salary. Each month I note the payments on the calendar, my sense of pride and security growing with every deposit.

The house is small but functional. Newly pruned fruit trees grow alongside camellias, magnolias and rhododendrons in a garden reminiscent of my childhood home. Across the road black and white cows graze in green fields and at a dip in the road beside a stream that marks the town's boundary, petrol pumps and a garage shop provide for travellers on the main road.

Perhaps I was inoculated with DIY at an early age as I see potential in the most rundown of houses: I overflow with nesting instinct and have an inborn drive to clean, paint and decorate. Since our marriage nine years ago rental after rental has been turned from house to home. Vegetable patches dug, seeds planted and the harvest left behind. Now, with Lester away four days a week, I am once again redecorating.

Though I miss my man and look forward to him coming home at the end of the week, I quite enjoy the days when he is not around. It is a lifestyle that suits us both.

At lunchtime on Friday the smell of baking fills the kitchen. Outdoors the wind blew. Sheets flapped and tugged at the pegs on the line and I heard the children laugh as they spread their arms in the hope a big gust might lift them — make them fly.

An hour later Lester arrived, gave me a peck on the cheek and emptied his suitcase onto the bed. "I need this shirt to wear tonight. Need you too, Ana. Get a babysitter. We'll be out to dinner, home by ten." He spoke affably but I resented his take-it-for-granted attitude. I'd rather be asked than told.

While the kettle boiled I called the children who launched themselves at their dad, both wanting a place on his lap. Lunch over Lester collected his wallet and car keys. "I'll be back for you at six, Ana. Wear something nice, we have clients to impress. And don't forget to wash my shirt."

He was beginning to sound like Eric. What makes him think I'm his personal slave? Angry, I pushed his washing into the machine. "Why do I have to do it all? Is it beneath your dignity to bath the children while I iron something to wear?" Mumbling to myself, I did as he asked.

At dinner Lester kept everyone entertained. Tired, and a little woozy from the wine, we drove home in silence. When the car stopped I asked if I might have some money to pay the babysitter.

"I've no change. You see to it," and stepping from the car, he strode through the garage.

Now what? For six months he'd been happy, eager to be home at weekends and rarely drank spirits. Tonight he had consumed more than usual. By the time I walked the sitter to the gate and prepared for bed, he was asleep. Lying awake in the darkness, I hoped he took his medication while away from home.

In the first few months of the job Lester had phoned from distant towns, sharing his day and asking after our welfare. Recently the routine changed. He seldom phoned, and pleading a reluctance to drive while tired, he often returned on Saturday or even Sunday. Occasionally he forgot to give me the housekeeping money.

This was the second week in a row I had been left without. There was little food in the cupboard and even less in the refrigerator. I tipped the money from my purse. No notes appeared, only coins. The money I spent on the house I eked from the housekeeping, working many hours to create a comfortable home — until three in the morning hanging the living room wallpaper, wanting to surprise Lester when he returned. If I'd known this would happen, I'd have saved that money.

Let's see what he has to say about it, I thought as I found his itinerary and checking it against the calendar, lifted the phone and dialled.

"I'd like to speak to Mr Pierce, please."

"There is no Mr Pierce here."

"Lester Pierce, company rep for Bishop Oil."

"Oh, *that* Mr Pierce. He doesn't stay here now. Sorry, I cannot help you."

What did she mean, *that* Mr Pierce? I tried to think of legitimate reasons why Lester might change his accommodation. There were plenty, but they did not stop me phoning three other motels on the list. Lester no longer used any of them.

For an hour I paced the garden, mistrust brewing inside me. I needed answers and returning indoors, I telephoned Pete, Lester's immediate superior at the company's head office.

"Ana, how are you? This is a nice surprise. Is there something I can do for you?" Pete's voice sounded so unperturbed, so ordinary, I felt badly about the lie I was going to tell.

"I'd like to be in touch with Lester but I can't find his itinerary. Can you tell me where he's staying tonight?"

"Nothing wrong is there?"

"No, nothing serious, but I would like to talk to him."

"Hold on a moment."

I could hear his voice on the intercom. A door opened and closed again. Why was I holding my breath?

"You there, Ana? He's at the Crest Motel in Paeroa tonight, The View at Matamata tomorrow. Would you like the phone numbers?"

"Yes please." I pretended to write. "Thank you."

Pete's information was the same as mine. We'd both been duped. Would Lester stay in cheaper accommodation and pocket the difference? If so, why was I receiving less money than before? Having no answers I fell back on old habits, throwing myself into a frenzy of gardening. If the worst came, we would live on vegetables. For three days I worked like a crazy woman, cleaning and gardening, hoping I would sleep at night. Exhausted, I immediately fell asleep but woke an hour later to toss and turn until day break.

On Friday I poured the last of the cereal into the children's breakfast bowls and watered down the milk. They ate in silence, no doubt sensing my black mood. The dog lay beneath the table, her chin on her silken paws, but watching my every move. Unable to withstand her pleading looks, I broke a slice of bread, mixed it with water and gave it to her.

"Be grateful Sapphire. The cat had to find his own food this week." Bending down, I patted her to show I was sorry.

Five year-old Clare packed and unpacked her new school case, pushing her small fingers into the lunchbox compartments while reciting, 'sandwiches, cake, fruit'. Then looking up, asked, "Mummy, will I have a proper lunch when I go to school?"

"Yes, of course. Everything will be fine when Daddy comes home." My words, hollow as they were, cheered us and with a picnic lunch of butterless marmite sandwiches and carrots, we set of for a walk to the park.

On our return down the hill I saw Lester's car in the driveway. Relieved, I handed the two remaining pennies in my purse to Clare and Lance. "Come on. Let's buy Eskimo babies at the garage shop."

Surprised to see Mrs Bailey arranging stock near the front counter, I stopped to say hello. We had bought our home from the Bailey's. "It's nice to see you again. Are you here for a holiday?" Without speaking she turned her back and walked away. A moment later, Mr Bailey appeared

"What can I get you?" he asked his tone abrupt.

Puzzled by the reception I explained the children wanted Eskimo babies. I babbled on saying how much I loved the house, how rich the soil was and told him of my plans for the garden. He merely grunted. "Mr Bailey, is something wrong?"

"I should think there is. When are you going to pay us some money?" He spat the words at me.

"What! What money?"

"The money we agreed on. We've not seen a penny."

Bewildered I stared at him. "But the money goes into the bank every month. Lester pays it into the bank."

He stared back. "We've received no money. I'm here to get it sorted." The man looked so fierce Lance left his sweets on the counter and backed out the door. Clare picked them up and leaving the two pennies, joined her brother outside.

"Mr Bailey, I'm sorry. I'm sure there's an explanation. I'm certain the money has been paid. I'll come back as soon as I've spoken to Lester."

He leaned across the counter, his chin jutting into my face, "See that you do," he hissed.

Lester's suitcase and shoes, the laces still tied, lay beside his chair in the living room. I found him sprawled across the bed in his underwear and shook him by the shoulder. "Lester, wake up." His inert body stank of alcohol. After a moment of helplessness, I wanted to hit him, hard—very hard. My fists clenched, I went out kicking the door as I passed.

The children looked up from where they sat nibbling their sweets.

"Look Mummy, I've eaten off his head," Lance held out his lolly.

There's a bigger head I'd like to knock off, I thought and dropping my coat over a chair, sat with my head in my hands.

Waiting for Lester to return to his senses and account for his part in this stupefying state of affairs tested my patience to the limit. In the darkness of night, lying curled on the couch I alternately damned and defended my husband, my reasoning becoming blurred as the long wakeful hours dragged by.

At dawn I peered into the bedroom. Lester had not moved. The children came to the breakfast table full of chatter, ate and went out to play. Vexation brought tears that dripped into the washing-up water. A plate, slippery with soap, fell and chipped. My jaw tightened and so fierce was my wringing of the dishcloth, my knuckles hurt.

How could he *not* pay? He promised. Past experience told me this was not a mistake. Exasperated, I flung the cloth at the wall and returned to the couch.

Lester finally emerged at lunchtime, pale and bleary-eyed to droop over a large black coffee. From across the table, I saw a different man. Not the suave salesman I identified as my life partner but an unwashed, unshaven wreck and the sight gave me strength.

Erect on my chair, hands clasped in my lap, I explained my meeting with Mr Bailey and how he had accused us of failing to pay the mortgage. "Not a penny he said."

"So?" Lester stared me down, his eyes narrow and hard.

"So I want to know. Did you pay the money or not?"

His eyes dropped first and as he lifted the coffee cup to his lips, I fought to control my rage. "How could you?" The words burst from my throat in an animal scream. "How could you do this to us? You're away all week swanning about the country in the best hotels, eating out every night. You wear expensive clothes and drink yourself silly while the children and I live on bread and potatoes because you don't leave me any housekeeping." My fist slammed the table and I wished it was his face. "I need regular money, Lester. Do you hear me?" Again, my fist thumped and coffee spilled into his lap.

He stood and stepped toward me, hand raised. Afraid, I pulled back. "You can have your money," he snarled and to my relief, turned away.

Shaken, I rose and made a cup of tea.

Down the passage, the toilet flushed, followed by the sounds of the bedroom drawers opening and closing. Then the catch on his suitcase snapped. Lester carried the case to the front door and leaving it there, returned to lean against the kitchen doorframe.

"Little Ana," he mocked. "Where have you kept that temper hidden all these years?" He pulled notes from his wallet and held them out to me. But as my fingers touched the money, he snatched it away, holding it above his head. "Oh dear, where are your manners? Say please."

I glared at him.

"Come now, say pretty please for the man with the money," he wheedled.

I stood unmoving. Beg. Not likely.

Lester finally lowered his arm and threw the money onto the floor. Then digging into his pocket, he scattered coins around the room.

"Go on. Pick it up." He gripped my shoulder forcing me to kneel. "Good girl. Find it all now." As my hair swept the floor, his cruel fingers released their hold. Collecting his case he strode down the steps to the car.

I gripped the sink for support. My head spun. I reached the front door in a staggering run. Heard the children call goodbye from the tree house as Lester drove out onto the roadway. The sound of the car faded. A deep silence settled over the house. My legs gave way and racked by uncontrollable sobs I sank to the floor.

On my return visit, the Bailey's listened politely. I told them Lester and I had argued, offered them one month's payment from the money he gave me and promised the rest very soon. My offer accepted I went home to fret over an obligation impossible to fulfil. On Monday the bank confirmed my fears. Not one penny had been paid off the mortgage.

I expected Lester to return at the end of the week, breezing in as if nothing had happened. My trust shattered, I felt I'd been pushed through a shedder and when a second week passed without word from Lester, my anxiety increased. I searched for work, but in a small town jobs are few. At the Welfare office a softly spoken lady offered only sympathy, saying if I was unsure about being a deserted wife, she was unable to help me. By the end of the third week a lack of food and sleep had weakened my body and dulled my mind.

Lance pushed a hash brown around his plate.
"I'm sorry you don't like it. That's all there is today," I told him.
"No!" He put down his spoon.
"Lance, you sit there and eat." His bottom lip protruding, he folded his arms. Any other time I would have laughed, defused the situation, but not today. I raised my hand.
"Hello, anyone at home?" a voice called from the front porch.
"Eat," I said, shaking a finger at Lance before going to the door.
Joy, whose husband had worked with Lester at the soft drink company, stood on the door mat holding a large carton. When welcomed in, she carried the box to the kitchen. Lance's plate was empty. The dog licked crumbs from the floor.
"Can I go now?" Lance paused halfway off his chair.
"Yes, you little imp."
Joy was small and dark haired. Her brown eyes reminded me of my school-friend, Ming.
"We work for Trent's now and get lots of free stuff. I've brought you biscuits and some cordial," she said putting the carton on the table.
"Thank you. Won't you sit down and I'll make you a cup of tea"
"Sorry, Ana, I can't stop. I came to see you were all right and to bring you this. I have to get back." We walked together to the street where Joy stood looking across the roof of her smart red van, her eyes serious. "Bye, Ana. Call me if you need help."

With a cheerful toot of the horn she was gone. What made her think I might need help? Perhaps Lester asked her to come.

The carton was a treasure chest. It contained biscuits of every description; plain and fancy, chocolate coated and the children's favourite, pink iced wafers. Over the weekend, we, and the cat and dog, feasted on biscuits. Plain ones for breakfast and the crème filled for lunch. At dinner time, dressed in our best clothes and wearing brown paper crowns, we partied on chocolate biscuits and drank lemon squash from stemmed glasses.

On another day our dog, Sapphire came trotting up the drive with a large meaty bone in her mouth. When coaxed, she loosened her grip and let me have it. Washed and boiled with grated vegetables it became a tasty soup; the bone then returned to the dog, who gnawed on it for days.

Clare began school. With Lance in the pushchair and Sapphire trotting alongside, we walked to the primary school, returning at two in the afternoon to collect her. One rotten, wet and windy day as we battled up the hill on our way to the school, a car pulled in alongside us.

"Hello, I'm Marie. Your Clare and my Susan are friends. Can I take Clare to school for you?"

"My daddy's gone away," Lance piped loud and clear.

Marie understood at once. "I'm sorry. I'll bring Clare home for you if you like. I should be at your place by a quarter past two." Grateful, I helped Clare into the car and calling my thanks, waved them goodbye.

Marie brought Clare home as promised and over a cup of tea, offered a sympathetic ear. Her calm presence encouraged me to share my shame of being a deserted wife; my fears about unpaid accounts, the sleepless nights and concerns for the children. She sat quietly beside me throughout and as I mopped the last of my tears, Marie suggested her husband could help.

Her husband, Drew, appeared at my door early the next morning. He arranged help from a community service. Coal was delivered and a weekly credit arranged at a local shop enabling me to buy food. He drove me to the welfare office and arranged a benefit. Then to an accountant, who refusing payment, took over the accounts and told me not to worry. Once my benefit came I was to pay him a set amount each week and he would take care of the rest.

Relieved of the financial worries I expected to feel better, but tears often flowed and a good night's sleep was rare. Marie insisted I see a doctor who prescribed both anti-depressant and sleeping tablets. After three weeks, having regained the confidence I needed to manage alone, I stopped taking them but continued to collect the free medication in case I needed it later.

Ever hopeful I looked for Lester each time I went to town and on my way home, hurried to the point where I could see our driveway, expecting his car to be there. The slightest sound in the night woke me. Tense and anxious, I waited for him to return.

On the Saturday before Lance's third birthday a parcel and a large letter arrived. "Look, it's for Lance," Clare called excitedly as she carried the packages into the kitchen.

'Me? For my birthday?" Lance tore off the brown paper and found two brightly wrapped gifts. Again he tore the paper. "It's a Barbie doll." His disgust obvious he pushed it aside.

"Let me see. Did you look at the card? It says to Clare with love from Daddy."

Lance passed the doll to Clare and while I turned the brown paper searching for a post mark, he unwrapped the second gift.

"A paddle boat. Can I put it in the bath? Please?"

"Yes, but only with cold water. Watch him please, Clare."

I scanned every inch of the papers hoping for a note. There was nothing for me but Lester had remembered the children and sent a gift and his love to each of them. Hope swelled and bobbed like a balloon but was quickly deflated by the contents of the second packet. Unopened envelopes marked by the Post Office spilled onto the table. Inside them were bills, for petrol, tyres and accommodation, meals and drinks. There was an account for paint and wallpaper, long overdue. I had given Lester the money for these things when I asked him to collect them from a large store in the next town. A small hand written note requested payment for three bouquets delivered to an address in Hamilton. Who received the flowers? Not me.

A splash and a loud wail sent me running to the bath room where Lance floundered in the tub. Stripping off his overalls and jersey I wrapped him in a towel. His teeth chattered. Rubbing firmly until his skin turned pink once more, I helped him into warm clothes and sent him to run in the winter sunshine. The sound of the children's voices and the occasional bark from Sapphire came from the garden as all three chased a ball across the lawn.

I stood watching from the window, the bills scattered over the table beside me. My thoughts far away, back in golden fairy-tale days of plans, promises and eternal optimism. I ached for the return of such happiness. Lester! Where are you? I want you. I need you.

Shamefaced, I took the bundle of bills to the accountant who promised to write to creditors.

"Most will wait rather than go to court for such small amounts," he told me. The amounts might have seemed small to him to me they were insurmountable and a sick giddy feeling washed through me each time I thought of the consequences of not being able to pay.

Spring arrived accompanied by cloudy skies and frequent showers. When the rain finally cleared canopies of pink and white blossom appeared. The fruit trees, magnolias and the tall flowering cherries at the gate provided nectar for the bees and the air filled with their sedulous singing. The lawns grew and needed cutting but the old Morrison lawnmower was difficult to start. I finally got it going but was unable to reset the height of the blades. Confronted with inadequacy, I blamed Lester and throwing down the pliers stomped off to find a spanner.

From inside the shed I heard Lance laugh and the sound of the heavy mower as it chugged sedately down the drive, headed for the roadway. In my haste to chase it I tripped and fell flat on my face. Winded, I watched aghast as the mower crossed the road before upending itself in the deep water ditch on the other side. Heavy footsteps broke the silence and a neighbour from up the hill appeared beside the now silent machine. I climbed to my feet and ignoring my grazed hands and knees hobbled to join him.

"Howdy." He leered up at me from where he crouched beside the drain. His small bright eyes flickering greedily over my shorts and halter top. "How did ya manage this?"

"I don't know. It just rolled off by itself."

He snorted. "Well if you can find a length of 4 × 2, I'll help you get it back on the road."

Between us we managed to lever and drag the heavy machine out of the ditch and back to the shed. There he took over. I watched him work, taking in his unusual appearance as he stripped the engine and laid the pieces on the path beside him. His hair was black, his skin swarthy. His bright wet lips had a permanent pout. Taking his time he flushed the engine with petrol and eventually started it. He stood beside the mower, a short stubby man wiping his grease covered fingers on the old towel I found for him. "There, that ought to be worth something," he said.

Something? What kind of something? Did he want me to make him a cup of tea? As I opened my mouth to ask he reached out, grabbed a handful of buttock and pulling me toward him, pressed his fat soft belly against me. "Just a kiss. Come on. Give us a kiss."

Squirming out of his grip I stood back flushed and angry. "Don't be silly."

"Aw, come on. You've been alone a long time now. You must miss it." Again he grabbed.

"Get away," my voice low and intense, I twisted my wrists from his grasp and taking Lance by the hand, pulled him toward the house. From the safety of the porch I looked back. "Please go away."

"All right, I'm going. You know where I am if you fancy a bit of fun." His vile laugh followed me into the house. Tears rolled down my cheeks as I bathed blood and grit from my injured knees. Please, Lester, please come home. I cannot do this on my own. I cannot.

That evening the phone rang. "Hello, Ana. It's Laurie, remember me. You bought a doll's house from us some time ago."

"Yes?" The Gifford's were nice people and Laurie kindly delivered the doll's house for Clare.

"Well, I hear you're on your own down there and I wondered if you needed any help — someone to talk to perhaps?" The whispered intensity of his words made me wary.

"No. Thank you for your concern . . ."

He cut in. "The kids are back. Have to go. I'll call later."

Laurie was the first of the faithless and oh-so-misunderstood small town men. Men who came from behind shop counters and office desks, down from telegraph poles and out from under cars, wanting not to give, but to take advantage of a lonely young woman desperate for comfort.

One or two were genuine. They came accompanied by their wife or child. The rotten planks on the front porch were replaced. The locks changed and swollen window frames planed so they fitted snugly. The unwanted attention of the would-be Casanovas made me nervous and I was grateful for the increased security. Anyone attempting to enter my home after dark would have to break a window, which I was certain to hear.

The best locks in the world could not allay my fear of possible intruders. In the dark of night, alone and afraid, my body froze in an intensity of listening if a twig snapped or a fish flopped in the pond next-door.

Four months passed without a word from Lester. At times my thoughts turned inward. The children found it hard to gain my attention and resorted to noisy and sometimes bad behaviour. Preoccupied and distant, I reacted angrily to their intrusion, my anger immediately followed by contrition. There were moments of quiet when I saw reflected in my moodiness the temperament I previously found so unnerving in Lester. Appalled by the parallels between us, I resolved to instigate a more balanced approach to my problems and did my best to reassure Clare and Lance.

Bright yellow sunlight shone through chinks in the curtains. I rubbed the sleep from my eyes and looked around the room. The day felt different, highly charged and zingy, a day when something wonderful might happen.

Marie took Claire to school and I sorted last summer's clothing. Lance needed new clothes. I counted the money in my purse. There was enough for shoes and shorts and after lunch, Lance and I set off up the hill to the shops. It was a long walk for little legs and on our way back we stopped halfway to rest on a bench outside the fish and chip shop. I was musing about this and that, waiting until Lance was ready to continue walking, when I sensed his attention focus on something across the road. As I turned to look, he slipped from the seat and stumbling down the gutter ran out into the roadway.

A massive logging truck topped the rise, my son directly in its path. The blare of horns drowned my scream. A man sprinted from the garage. Swept Lance into his arms and pulled back as the great bulk of a fully laden logger thundered between us.

Across the vacuum left by the truck, Lester and I stared at each other. Around us cars slowed. People gathered in little knots, their voices inaudible so distant were we from their world. Lester stood in the centre of the road, his son in his arms, his tie flung across the boy as if to bind them even closer. The magnetism between us so strong, not even a second logging truck could have prevented our headlong rush to hug and exclaim our amazement. We clung together, lost to the world, until his boss, Pete, came and guided us off the road.

"Get in and I'll drive you home." He held open the car door. Halfway there I remembered Clare. Pete offered to take Lance with him and collect her from school. "You two need time to talk," he said. "Okay if I take the children for an ice-cream?" Still shaken, I nodded my agreement.

Lester and I sat at opposite ends of the dining table. Neither of us spoke. After the heady emotion of our meeting, I felt drained. A dozen questions formed and faded before I could speak and when I did, Lester spoke at the same time. There was another hesitation.

"Did the kids get the gifts I sent?" he asked.

"Yes"

"Did Lance like the boat?"

"Yes." I did not want to talk about children or boats. I wanted to talk about *us*.

"Lester . . . ?"

"Don't ask, Ana. I have a different life now." He sat back staring out the window. "Just leave it will you."

"Lester, please look at me. I need an explanation." He pulled out his cigarettes and tapped one on the table top. I rose, took an ashtray from the cupboard and placed it before him. It was like watching a play, waiting for the actors to speak, waiting to see what would happen. I reached out and took hold of his hand, turning it to feel its smoothness, its strength and longed for a touch, a caress, a kind word. For a brief moment his fingers gripped mine. Both pain and need filled his eyes. Still not meeting my gaze he withdrew his hand and lit the cigarette.

"I still love you." I spoke quietly, afraid of his response but needing to say the words.

He twisted in his chair and sighed before looking into my face. 'I am no good to you, Ana. I continually let you down. You are better on your own."

"Surely that is for me to decide," I countered as Lester stood up.

His reply came through gritted teeth. "Leave it, Ana. Just leave it." He turned away and walking into the children's room, stood looking out the window. A tired dejected figure, his shoulders slumped. I wanted to hold him, to offer comfort but feared rejection.

"What am I supposed to tell the children, Lester?"

"I don't know. I don't know what to say to them." He sighed again. 'I would like to come and see them sometimes." His eyes were bright with unshed tears and I latched, limpet-like to this glimpse of his vulnerability.

"Of course you can. They're your children."

"Thanks. Do you think I might have a cup of coffee?"

I nodded and rose from the table as the sound of excited voices and young feet pounding up the front steps preceded an onslaught of small bodies. I opened cupboards revealing empty shelves and saw Pete's eyes widen. "I'm sorry. There is no sugar," I apologised as I set the steaming cups on the table. Clare and Lance took over, pulling out their toys and showing off their achievements.

Pete went to fetch his cigarettes from the car and I asked Lester when he might spend time with the children. He looked up from where he crouched on the floor; Lance balanced on his knee, the pair of them surrounded by the bubbles Clare was blowing. His hair had fallen over his eyes and I thought my heart would break as he tossed it back with the well-remembered action.

"I could come the last weekend of the month. Is that okay with you little man," he addressed Lance who squirmed with delight as Lester tickled him.

"Tickle me. Tickle me," Clare shrieked launching herself at her dad. He fell to the floor with the children on top of him.

Pete left the doorway where he had been watching us and went out to smoke his cigarette. Still laughing, the others scrambled up from the floor as he returned.

"We should get going, Les. Thank you for the coffee Ana. I'll wait in the car."

"A man of few words. Nice though," I said to Lester.

"He's a good boss. I owe him a lot. Come on young man. Let me see if I have any chocolate in the car." He swung Lance onto his shoulders and led the way out of the house. Our goodbyes over, I guided the children back into the house. Happy with their chocolate they showed no sign of missing their dad.

During the last week of September I scrubbed and polished the entire house. The place gleamed. I wanted Lester to see how much better off he would be living at home. In the evenings after the children went to bed, I sewed myself a new dress. I too would be looking my best.

On the morning of Lester's visit I rose early to light the coal range and make a batch of his favourite sultana biscuits. While the cookies cooled I soaked in the bathtub and then rubbed myself with fragrant oil. Shortly after breakfast the phone rang.

"Les here. I'm just leaving. I have to make a couple of calls on the way. Thought I'd take the kids to the beach. They would like that."

I digested this idea then enquired playfully, "Am I invited too?"

"Yeah. If you want to. I'll be there by ten."

While I put a lunch together the excited children collected the paraphernalia needed for a day of sun and surf. I added a rug and sun umbrella to the pile on the porch.

Ten o'clock, eleven, at midday Lester's car rolled into the driveway. With the engine still running he leaned out calling, "Good day, kids. Jump in and we're off." The children tugged open the doors and piling into the back seat, bounced with excitement. I stood on the porch beside the lunch basket, sand buckets and towels. "What about this stuff," I called.

"Throw it in the boot. Here's the key." He dangled it out the window. The gear stowed, I climbed in beside Lester ready to exchange a smile, and hopefully, some hint of intimacy. But he was turned away, looking behind, as he reversed the car out onto the road.

When Lester spoke it was to the children. I was just a hanger-on along for the ride. At the beach I was ignored and while the others splashed in the shallows I retreated beneath the sun umbrella to nurse the acid pain of rejection. The drive over the hills had shaken the sultana biscuits to crumbs and I scattered them to the seagulls.

On the way home the children fell asleep. There was so much I wanted to ask. Where did he live, was he coping and the one I dreaded but most wanted to know, do you have a girl friend? Unwilling to confront him, I clung to the idea that if I remained calm and agreeable he would eventually open up as he had in the past. So the real issues were set aside, overridden by meaningless small talk and long silences.

When we arrived back, I asked him in for tea.

"No thanks." His brusque refusal sealed my sense of failure. "You see to the kids. I'll put your things on the porch."

I shook Clare awake and urging her up the steps ahead of me, carried the still sleeping Lance to his bed. I heard the horn pip but by the time I reached the front door, the car was gone. No good bye. No thank you. Nothing.

In the days that followed I stumbled numbly through the hours of daylight fighting to hold my reason. I loved him. I hated him. I hated him and still wanted him. In my mind I planned all manner of pleadings and sometimes, plotted revenge.

Another month of lonely nights passed with the ever hopeful and wayward husbands still telephoning my house at all hours. Usually they called from a public phone box and at the sound of dropping coins I hung up rather than battle wits with the caller.

"Get lost whoever you are!" I hissed into the receiver after once again hearing the distinctive clink of pennies. It was late and this was the fourth call in thirty minutes.

"Ana, talk to me."

"Lester!?"

"What's going on? I've been trying to phone all evening and just when I get through, the line goes dead."

"I'm sorry. I hang up when other men call."

"What other men?" Lester's voice exploded down the line.

'I don't know half of them. Silly men who think I need male company."

"Bastards. Bloody bastards." When he spoke again it was with probing concern. "Did any of them touch you? Did anyone hurt you, Ana?"

"No. I told you. I hang up when they ring." This was not entirely true. I had talked with some. They poured out their woes and I listened.

"Jeez, Ana. I'd break their bleeding necks if I thought—bastards."

Time to change the subject I thought and asked why he had called.

"I wanted to come and see you but thought a knock at the door might frighten you. So I tried to telephone. I've been in this phone box forever. The glass is all steamed up."

"Where are you?"

"Across the road at the garage."

"Give me five minutes. I'll put the outside light on."

No one breaks speed limits like a woman preparing for the man she loves. I was a washed, dressed and scented package in three and a half minutes. The bed was straightened, the pillows plumped and clutter swept behind a cushion before I heard his knock. Wearing my best Mona Lisa smile, I opened the door.

Lester appeared from behind a huge bunch of red roses. My likeness to Mona Lisa faded to that of a gaping fish as I took in the immense size of the bouquet and Lester's changed appearance. His hair had been cut very short. He wore silver rimmed spectacles and was dressed in soft tweeds instead of the usual dark suit and tie. He settled in an armchair while I put the roses in water. Placing them on the coffee table, I sat opposite him.

We talked; about the children, the animals and the garden. He admired the redecorated living room, perhaps seeing the changes for the first time. When I offered to make coffee he followed me to the kitchen and lent against the cupboards as he had so many times before. As I reached for the coffee jar he took my arm and ever so gently turned me to face him.

"I've missed you, Ana Banana, missed you very much." His lips brushed my forehead, a brief butterfly touch that turned my knees to jelly.

For a moment I held back. Then as his warm arms enfolded me, his hand soothing my neck and shoulders, I leaned into the embrace with a rush of relief.

We fell asleep fully dressed on the bed having talked for hours. I woke in the early dawn feeling cold and edging across the bed, lay back to back with Lester, comforted by the warmth of his body and the rhythm of his breathing.

The children found us there. The dog came in with them and licked a surprised Lester into full alertness. He retaliated with a pillow and we all joined in, tumbling and laughing until the feathers flew. Then calling a halt, I sent the children to dress for breakfast.

From his seat on the edge of the bed Lester pulled me down to sit beside him. Silent, his eyes searching mine, he took my hands in his, caressing and turning them, lowering his gaze as he did so.

"Ana, will you have me back? I am truly sorry I was such a rotten person."

Then looking into my eyes, he waited for my reply.

Twenty-two

Lester's return brought renewed happiness. He drove away on Monday mornings, phoned home throughout the week then returned amiable and bearing gifts for his family on Friday afternoons. Out of habit, I watched for signs of change. After six weeks I relaxed. With the cupboards restocked and the children happy I thought Lester had at last settled into the role of husband and father.

Fool me. Two weeks later he again failed to come home at the expected time. By midnight I was distraught. After working through the fears of accidents and disasters I became incensed at my own stupidity. I'd been a fool to take him back. An idiot to think he would fulfil my expectations and an even bigger idiot for having any expectations at all. I was living a miserable martyrdom and longed to be free.

The stars paled and I shrugged my shawl closer. Cool morning mist drifted into my hair and settled lightly on my arms as leaving my vigil at the gate, I walked back across the lawn to the house. There I lit the coal range and made a cup of tea. I sipped slowly; the hot liquid chasing the chill from my body. A longing for comfort brought my mother to mind; a foolish thought as I would find neither comfort nor sympathy there.

Lester returned the following weekend. "Catch," he called to the children tossing a bag of sweets to each of them. "And for my lovely wife, her favourite Granny Mints." I had no idea what Granny Mints were (they proved to be delicious chocolate-coated morsels) but I could not help wondering who else might expect a sweet surprise from Lester.

'Do you have a second lovely wife hidden away somewhere? One who likes Granny Mints?" I asked my voice light and teasing.

"Don't be so damn daft." He scowled and avoiding my gaze, tipped the contents of his case on the bed. "Can you wash this stuff now? I can't stay long. You kids want to go to the playground while your mother does the washing?" He turned to Clare and Lance who waited in the doorway behind me. Clare took my hand.

"I want mummy to come."

"I told you; your mother is going to do the washing. Forget about the playground. We don't have to go. You kids can play in your room." Two little faces dropped. I sighed. Lester's mood changes took some keeping up with.

"It's all right Clare. You and Lance go with Daddy and I'll make a sponge pudding for tea, the one with meringue on top." The children scampered off to collect shoes and jackets.

On their return from the park, Lester settled in his armchair with his work books spread on the small table beside him. Clare brought her doll to the kitchen and while I peeled potatoes at the sink, we chattered. I saw Lance pull a Sooty glove puppet onto his hand then creep toward his father's chair, no doubt about to give his dad a surprise by tickling him with the puppet. I listened, waiting for an amused response from Lester. Lance made little snuffling sounds, suppressing his laughter and delighting in the game he was playing. Curious, I went to see the fun. Lance stood on tiptoe, pinching his father's ears with the puppet.

"I told you, if that bear does that again, I'll rip its head off." Lester spoke quietly. Then as puppet continued to ruffle his hair and nuzzle his neck his hand flashed up, wrenching Lance's arm and lifting him off the floor. Lance screamed in pain and I moved forward as Lester calmly twisted the bear's head from the glove and tossed the pieces across the room.

Crouching down I held out my arms to Lance.

"Don't touch that boy. He has to learn."

"Come here, Lance. Let me look at your arm."

"Do none of you listen? I said not to touch him. He can't stay a baby forever." Lester strode over and grasping his son's shirt, clumsily propelled him to his bedroom. "You can stay there until dinner is ready," and dismissing Lance's tearful pleas, closed the bedroom door.

"And you," he leaned toward me, poking a finger at my face. "You'd better listen to me. When I say don't, I mean don't. Do you understand?" His hand gripped my shoulder, his fingers digging into my flesh. I nodded. "Good. Now let's eat. I'm hungry." Rubbing my shoulder, I began laying the table. Clare had disappeared.

"Clare, tea time." When she did not come I searched, eventually finding her in the coal shed. She sat in the far corner; her knees beneath her chin, her little face pinched with inner pain. Choking back tears I held her close.

"Ana! Where the hell are you? The dinner's burning." Lester yelled from the back step. Coaxing Clare to her feet I took her hand. "Another cry baby. What bunch of milk sops you are," Lester sneered as we climbed the steps. "Hurry up. Let's eat. I have to be going soon."

"But I've not ironed your clothes. Some are quite damp. Can't you wait until morning?"

He made no reply but sat at the table, drumming his fingers and glaring at the children.

Dinner was a silent meal. No one wanted seconds of the burned meringue dessert. Finally Lester set down his coffee cup, stood up and stretched.

"Well, I'm off now."

"What about your washing?"

"Just shove it in a bag."

Okay, suit yourself, I thought fitting the bag into his suitcase. At the front door we each waited for the other to say goodbye.

"May I have some housekeeping money before you go," I asked.

"Yeah. Even milk sops need to eat." He took out his wallet and pulled off a number of notes. "Don't spend it all at once," and picking up his bag, he stepped out into the night, my goodbye unanswered.

Hours after going to bed images of Lester's brief homecoming rose to taunt me. Lance's tear-streaked face, the way he flinched when touched. Bright, ever-loving Clare had shut me out. Climbed into bed without saying goodnight and ignoring the kiss I placed on her smooth brow, turned her face to the wall.

Because I was weak the children had been hurt. I should have stood up to Lester. Told him . . . No, demanded he . . . What was the use of pretending? I'd always chosen the way of least resistance. Wanting peace and prepared to pay the price. I always soothed things over, not wanting the neighbours to hear us arguing. My mother's words echoed inside my head, her indoctrination still controlling my life. What will the neighbours say? What will they think?

I struggled, trapped, helpless and useless within my own pride, unable to admit I should have listened to my mother. She tried to warn me about Lester and suggested I find someone else. She must have known he was mentally unstable. Why did she not speak out? Because I would not have listened. Sixteen and full of the idealistic belief, I'd taken the teachings of the church at the most basic level and been convinced one had only to love enough to turn suffering to joy, illness to health and evil to good. How could I have been so stupid?

Sometime later a sound woke me. I heard Sapphire leave her blanket in the kitchen, her claws clicking across the linoleum to the front door. Someone or something was out there.

Fully alert, I slid from my bed and standing beside her, grasped her collar. The hair on her neck was stiff, her ears pricked and her eyes never left the glass panel in the door. Calling the police seemed the most prudent move. Poised to dial, my hand froze as a voice began a slurred rendition of *I belong to Glasgow*. Lester! I unlocked the door and Sapphire bounded out to greet the inebriated man lying on the front steps.

"Hello, darlin'. I'm home." Lester raised a limp hand.

Something in me snapped. "Get up, you fool. Get up." His arms and legs moved feebly.

"Can't, I can't get up."

"Of course you can."

He twitched again. 'No. I'll stay here." He began to laugh and raising his head, tried to look at me. "Come, sleep under the stars with me."

"No thank you. Now get up."

"Can't."

A light appeared next-door. I leaned over Lester. "Listen to me, you get up! Now! Rollover and grab the rail." Obediently he rolled and gripped the rail. I hauled with all my strength. Lester rose shakily to his feet. By shifting my support, I managed to steer him up the steps, away from the prying eyes next-door. Indoors he clapped a hand to his mouth and looked wildly about. Damn, he was going to be sick and shoving him into the bathroom, I left him there.

Relieved to see the children undisturbed, I gently closed their door. In our room, Lester lay on top of the blankets, his eyes closed. My head in my hands I lent over the kitchen table. An overwhelming weariness took hold of me. I wanted to lie down, to sleep and never wake up. Never again have to deal with a situation like this.

Sometime later, not wanting to disturb Lester, I slid carefully between the sheets. At least the blankets put a barrier between us but no sooner had I settled than a heavy arm fell across my body and a hand groped the blankets covering my chest.

"Hey, Chick-a-biddy. Where are you? I can't find you. Come on Chicky. I got something nice for you." Lester pressed against me breathing beer and vomit into my face. I clutched the bed clothes to my chin. Chicky? There was a name I'd not heard before.

"Come on itty-bitty hen, be nice to me." His weight pressed down on me and I struggled to hold the blankets.

"Get off. I'm not Chicky. I'm Ana. Leave me alone."

"Ana, eh? I don't mind. All cats are grey in the dark. Give me kiss." His wet mouth slobbered over my face as he searched for my lips.

"Get off. You disgust me." I sat up and pushed him. Caught off balance Lester toppled off the bed, smacking into the wall as he fell. The bedside lamp crashed to the floor. I leaned across the bed. There was a gaping hole in the wall. Lester moaned and rubbed his elbow.

"Bugger me," he said. His head rolled to the side and he lay with his mouth open. A cold chill gripped me and my fingers trembled on his pulse. His heart beat felt strong. A snore, then another. He was sound asleep.

I too slept and woke late. Lester slept on, sprawled on the floor beside the bed. Gathering my clothes, I washed and dressed in the bathroom. The children lay on their tummies on the front porch, colouring books open before them. Sitting down with them I studied their faces. "Are you all right?"

"My arm hurts." Pulling open his shirt Lance showed me the bruises on his upper arm and shoulder.

"I'm so sorry you were hurt." I hugged him close then turning to Clare put an arm about her shoulders. Her small body tensed.

"Where's Daddy?" She looked toward his car parked across the street.

"He's asleep. Shall we go in and have breakfast?"

"I don't want any breakfast." Clare opened a new page in her book.

"What if we have a picnic breakfast out here in the sunshine? Would you like that?"

She nodded but did not move.

Lance and I prepared a tray. After breakfast the children went onto the lawn where they sat brushing Sapphire's long coat, concern showing in their small unsmiling faces. I needed to face Lester, to tell him in plain terms of the adverse effect his behaviour was having on his family. I called my friend, Marie. Minutes later she arrived to collect the children.

"They can stay the night if you wish. Call me. Let me know how things go," she said.

The sound of water filling the bath and his razor being rinsed in the basin told me Lester was on the move. While he bathed I stripped the bed, put the linen in the wash and the blankets to air on the clothes line. Then having flung open the windows to let in fresh air, I threw the broken lamp in the rubbish.

As I dried the last of the breakfast dishes, Lester came to sit at the kitchen table.

"Would you like breakfast?"

"Just coffee."

I felt his eyes following me as I set out cups and boiled the jug. Neither of us spoke. I poured the coffee and sat opposite him. Straight backed I steadied my chin. Held my hands clasped in my lap. I was about to say, Well. What do you have to say for yourself? when I realized I was mimicking my mother and closed my mouth. I tried again.

"Lester, I do not like the man you have become." There. I'd said it. When he did not respond, I continued. "You really hurt Lance last night and Clare is frightened of you. You were so drunk you thought I was someone else." I took a deep breath and plunged on. "I think it would be best if you went back to that other person. I . . ." my voice was breaking, tears close. I took a large gulp of coffee, the cup rattling against the saucer as I set it down. "I can't live like this. I can't do it anymore."

"I tried to tell you that. Remember? But you wouldn't let go." His calm and sad acceptance made me feel unworthy, guilty. If he'd been angry I could have been angry too. Instead I sat limp and empty, unable to respond.

"Well, I'll be going then," he pushed back his chair.

I trailed him to the bedroom, first watching from the doorway then sitting on the bed as he packed his case. He came to stand before me and drawing me up, cupped a hand beneath my chin. With a finger he lightly traced my lips.

"Take care, Ana Banana," he said softy. Then picking up his case, he ran down the steps and onto the drive. At the gate he turned as he used to all those years ago in our home town and walking backward for a few steps, saluted.

Days turned into weeks. Christmas decorations brightened the shop windows once again and my loneliness increased. I did my best to find work but no one needed me. Without their father, Clare and Lance grew boisterous, their exuberance unbearable and at times I was unnecessarily sharp with them.

Santa set up camp at the toy shop two weeks before Christmas and as we stood in line waiting to see him, his elves offered us sweets from a basket.

"What would you like for Christmas?" one asked Lance.

"My daddy is going to buy me a scooter."

I looked down at him. "Your daddy is going to buy you a scooter?"

"Yes." Lance nodded his face serious.

"How do you know that?"

"I prayed Jesus. I'm going to have a scooter—like that one." He pointed to a large red and blue model with fat rubber tyres.

"Oh," was all I could say. But I thought about the red scooter and Lance's conviction that come Christmas morning he would be the proud owner of an expensive toy I could not afford.

That evening after the children went to bed, I wrote to Lester telling him of Lance's wish. My letter, addressed care-of the head office, would find him wherever he was.

Within forty-eight hours, caught in the tension of waiting for the postman, a phone call or the sound of a car in the driveway, I felt my entire nervous system had transferred itself to the outside of my body. Every sound was amplified, changes in the light hurt my eyes and the lightest of touches felt like a heavy blow. Sleep was only a word and all food unpalatable.

On the fourth day while perched high on the ladder, in the thick of the plum tree, I heard the phone and passing the bucket to Lance, climbed down and made my way to the house. Clare appeared on the porch.

"It's Daddy. He wants to talk to you. Hurry, Mummy." Excited, she hopped from one foot to the other as she urged me through the house to where the phone dangled on its cord. Lance, his mouth and fingers stained red with plum juice, followed.

"Hi, Ana. How are you? I got your letter." Lester's warm and friendly voice continued. 'I'll buy the scooter for Lance, but don't tell him. Let it be a surprise. Is there something Clare would like?"

"I'm not sure. Would you like to ask her?"

Lester agreed and I passed the phone to Clare. I could see she was thinking hard, shaking her head as she listened, the receiver clapped against her ear. Then, "Can you visit us at Christmas, Daddy?"

Oh, Clare.

"He says I have to ask you. Can he Mummy? Can he come?"

I took the phone from her. "Lester . . ."

"I know. It's a surprise to me too. What do you think?" Without waiting for a reply he carried on. "If I get clear, I could drive down on the 23rd, be at your place midmorning Christmas Eve. Will that suit you?"

"Yes." I searched desperately for something to say, wanting to keep hearing his voice but it seemed he was in a hurry and I was dismissed without further conversation.

How quickly children forget. The school holidays began. Christmas loomed and the children's anticipation grew.

"Father Christmas is coming tonight," Clare told Lance as she poured milk onto his cornflakes. Lance spooned the cereal into his mouth then paused.

"Will daddy be coming?" I saw the wariness in his eyes as he waited for my reply. Milk dripped from his spoon and ran down his sleeve.

"Careful." I passed him a hand towel and forcing an unfelt lightness into my voice, told him his daddy was busy but would come if he could. Hope had worn thin. I'd spent a lifetime waiting for this man. Tears of self-pity prickled my eyelids and I gripped the edge of the bench.

"Mum, can I have more milk?" I turned to Clare and with sudden anger, snatched the empty jug from her hand.

"You naughty girl, you've taken it all. There's none left for my cup of tea." Clare cringed as I reached across and shook her roughly by the arm.

"Mummy, you're hurting me.'"

"Oh God, whatever's wrong with me? I'm sorry, love. Pulling her into my arms I held her as we both cried.

The day progressed fitfully. I did my best to involve the children and myself in festive activities. We added strings of tiny coloured lights to the Christmas tree and Lance stood gazing in awe at the beautiful sight while Clare bounced on the sofa.

"Daddy will be so surprised at what we have done," she cried standing on tiptoe in her excitement.

Lance stirred the jellies, Clare whipped the cream and I prayed Lester would arrive sober. Morbid thoughts filled my mind. Where was he? Why was he not here? He said mid-morning and it was now one o'clock. The children ran back and forth to the gate hoping to see their father's car. Could there have been an accident? It was unlikely. He was late as usual. But he would come. He *had* to come.

By mid-afternoon the children were tired and fractious. I too was tired as each night for the past week I had followed kitset instructions and built them a playhouse table and chairs. Now my head ached and tension curled my hands, the nails digging into my palms. I made an effort to speak calmly and suggested we go for a walk. Perhaps when we left the house Lester would come. It was like making a magic spell and I laughed at the thought, the shrill unnatural sound startling us all. I recovered first and held out my hands. "Come on, let's go."

Our cat Minty greeted us on our return from the park. I lifted him up and hugging him, buried my face in his soft fur, treasuring for a moment the close loving contact he offered.

Late afternoon had blended into evening before the front door opened. Lance squealed with delight as Lester swung him up onto his shoulders and carried him into the kitchen.

"Daddy come and see our Christmas tree. Can I put the lights on, Mum?" Clare skipped toward the living room with Lance close behind her. Lester and I looked at each other. He looked clean and tidy but smelled of alcohol. As I opened my mouth to speak a loud bang startled us. Acrid green smoke billowed from the living room and Lester moved quickly, turning off the switch and removing the plug attached to the Christmas lights.

"Bloody metal tinsel caught behind the plug," he growled looking at the melted plug and blackened wall. "You kids should not touch these things. Anyway, it is late. Off you go to bed."

Yes, I thought, with the children asleep there'd be time to talk. With my arms about their shoulders I guided them into their bedroom, soothing them as we walked. Full of excitement they placed empty Santa stockings at the foot of their beds. With a promise to return, I left them to change into their nightwear.

I found Lester searching the kitchen cupboards. "Don't we have anything to drink in this place," he demanded, opening another cupboard and pulling the contents onto the floor. A bottle of oil threatened to spill and as I reached to rescue it, Lester straightened, knocking me and the bottle over. The cork rolled free and oil poured onto the floor.

"Watch what you're doing, you stupid cow. Can't you do anything right?"

I sat on the floor amid the mess, a thick isolating wall forming about me. Like a serpent it twisted, tighter and tighter, squeezing my chest. In their room the children giggled and scuffled.

"Those kids are supposed to be asleep." Lester strode to the bedroom. I heard his angry and threatening voice. The window opened and closed. "And there is no Father Christmas!"

His face livid, Lester strode to the front door and flung it open.

"Where are you going?"

"To get a bloody drink." The door slammed. The car engine roared and tyres squealed on the driveway. The sound of the speeding car continued up the hill toward town.

I remained on the floor, my arms wrapped tight across my chest. My body rocked. Rocked and rocked. I could not stop. Across the hall the children sobbed. Alone in my misery I blamed myself. I was a worthless mother, unable to protect her children. Useless, stupid — the children would be better off without me. My corrosive thoughts spiralled deeper. I had always chased the rainbow, believing tomorrow would be better. There was no rainbow. I might as well be dead.

When I finally pulled myself up and went to check the children, they were asleep, worn out with crying. But where were their stockings? Lester must have thrown them out of the window. I went outside and found them on the driveway. Further along I saw another dark shape. With dread in every step I walked toward it; knelt and touched the lifeless Minty. Anguished beyond words, I cradled the cat's limp body in my lap; heard again the sound of Lester's car and the squealing tyres. A deep numbness spread through mind and body. Beyond grief, beyond pain, I felt powerless. Life had no value.

Later, much later, unemotional and strangely serene, I filled a large mug with warm milk. With steady hands I lifted bottles of tablets from the top cupboard and calmly emptied the antidepressants and sleeping pills into a bowl. Slowly, methodically, I sipped and swallowed, swallowed and sipped until the mug and the bowl were empty.

Beneath a canopy of stars I buried our beloved Minty in the vegetable garden. With great care I carried the little table and chairs into the children's bedroom and set out the new tea-set. Stockings crammed with brightly wrapped presents lay at the foot of each bed. Tenderly I kissed the children, smoothing their hair, my fingers lingering, tears falling.

'Goodbye,' I whispered.

Lying on my bed in the dark I waited for death; waited for the door of my self-made prison to open. Thoughts glided by. They were distant, no longer a part of me. The children would have a new mother, a calm, sensible and loving mother. Lester would do whatever it was Lester did. I thought I saw my father. He looked sad as he gazed down at me. I was lost, adrift, sliding away in the darkness.

Slowly I opened my eyes and looked around me, at first uncomprehending, then as the events of previous night flooded back, with horror. I was awake! I was still here! My pale reflection in the dresser mirror stared back with contempt, mocking me in my failure.

A sound made me turn my head. Lester lay on the bed beside me. He had not bothered to undress. His toothless mouth hung slack, his dentures on the pillow beside him, the stale odour of his whisky breath filling the room.

Hell could be no worse.

Stumbling and gripping the wall for support I made my way to the bathroom and slid the bolt on the door. My body might be behaving strangely but my mind was clear. I still wanted to die.

I took a packet of new razor blades from the cupboard and laid them open beside the hand basin. Slowly, I drew the blade across my wrist. Deep red blood welled from the cut. I cut again, deeper. There was no pain. Blood flowed down the white porcelain. Curving, swirling as paint from an artist's brush. The blade cut deeper still.

I could hear the children's excited chatter. They were opening their Christmas presents. They must not see me like this. I turned on the tap. Red paled to pink. How long would it take?

A fist banged on the door. "Hurry up, Ana. I need the bathroom." Lester. I could hear him in the kitchen talking with the children.

Again I cut, gripping a new blade with blood stained fingers. The blade became slippery. Red mist blurred my vision.

Lester was pounding on the door. "Ana, open the door. Ana! Don't be so stupid!"

Vague images of empty pill bottles left on the kitchen bench drifted by. As if from a distance I heard Lester's voice.

"Please Clare, go to your room and stay there."

I sat on the edge of the bath. Blood soaked my nightgown and dripped on my feet. I felt nothing. A loud thudding went on and on. Suddenly, the door burst open and was wrenched aside, the frame splintered.

Lester stood staring at me. "Jesus. Look at you." He reached for a towel.

"Don't touch me. You killed my cat." I tried to move away from him.

"How could you be so stupid?" His hands gripped my shoulders. He was shaking me and I was falling. There was a sickening sound and pain shot through the back of my head. From somewhere far above, filtering through a smothering blackness, came a voice.

"Jesus. What have I done," it said.

*   *   *

My neighbour, Rhonda, was about to walk her dog that Christmas morning when she saw Lester run from the house followed by Lance, who called to his father. Lester ignored him, reversed out of the driveway and swinging the car around the corner on the wrong side, drove south on the main road. Lance ran onto the road, crying.

Rhonda had seen Lester come and go at all hours and at times, heard raised voices. Not wanting to interfere, she had kept our neighbourly conversations light. Today was different. It was Christmas and seeing Lance running down the road in his pyjamas, crying and calling for his daddy, spurred her to act. She caught up with him and turning him around, asked why he was crying. With patient listening, Rhonda learned Lance had been promised a red scooter but he could not find it. He thought it must be in his father's car.

Taking him firmly by the hand Rhonda led him home. Clare met her at the door and when she asked to see me, Clare had skipped off, calling for me to come.

The child's screams, Rhonda later said, were a sound she would carry to her grave.

She hurried to where Clare stood in the bathroom doorway. Easing her aside, Rhonda took in the scene. Empty pill bottles lay on the carpet outside the door and bloodied razor blades in the washbasin. The door hung drunkenly from a broken frame and blood covered the floor.

Gingerly Rhonda eased herself in beside me and kneeling, placed her ear to my mouth. Then having reassured Clare I was alive, she called an ambulance. Her husband, Jock came and taking the children by the hand led them into the garden. With tears in her eyes Rhonda watched from the window as her husband drew the children close, soothing them with quiet words. She then returned to where I lay unconscious on the bathroom floor, knelt down and taking my bloodstained hands between her own, bowed her head.

Twenty-three

I woke sometime during the night. An icy chill ate into my bones and I shivered uncontrollably. From behind the curtains that surrounded my bed came the muted sounds of nurses checking their patients. A torch beam flicked across my face then focused on the inverted bottle hooked to the stand beside my bed. A soft warm hand closed over mine.

"Go back to sleep. You are safe now," someone whispered.

Isolated in the corner of the ward, I lay compliant. The sun rose and the bustle of hospital life increased before fading at sunset. Night and day ebbed and flowed like a great ocean and I floated on the swell. The past could not touch me; the future was of no concern. For some reason I was alive. Now, in this moment I wanted to live. Not for Lester, not even for the children, but for my own sake.

Marie came to see me. Filled with gratitude and relief we held each other close. Clare and Lance were in good health and enjoying their holiday at her home.

"They have helped prepare a room for you. You must come to us when you leave here. Let us help you. I cannot bear to think of you being on your own," Marie's voice was husky and her eyes pleaded for me to say yes.

"Yes. Thank you."

Doctor Morgan came later in the day. He pulled up a chair beside me, his expression serious. "Ana, how are you? How do you feel?"

"I am all right, thank you."

"No. How do you feel? What are your thoughts?" He waited, his gaze unwavering.

"I feel empty. But it's a peaceful emptiness. I feel I've been given a second chance." He nodded.

"You know that suicide is an offence, Ana. An attempt to take one's life carries a jail sentence and you made a very serious attempt. I'm supposed to notify the police." He raised a hand. "I will not do that. Instead I want you to go to a psychiatric hospital as a volunteer patient."

I had guessed my sanity would be questioned and had tried to prepare myself. The notion of being an inmate of a psychiatric ward terrified me. I remembered the young mother locked in the concrete cell and her heartbreaking pleas to see her baby and husband. Saw again the paillasse on the floor and the food served in an enamel bowl without cutlery. Thankfully, as a volunteer patient, I could sign myself out. Leave whenever I wished.

"How long will I be there?"

"Three weeks should be enough. Look on it as a kind of holiday; time to give your mind and body a much needed rest." He stood up and with his hands thrust into his pockets, gazed down at me. "I'd like you to go tomorrow. Do you have someone to drive you or shall I arrange an ambulance?"

"I'll ask my friend Marie to take me."

"Very well, I'll leave a letter at the desk for you to take with you. Come and see me when you get back." His hand rested on my shoulder and his face softened. "You'll be fine, Ana, just be gentle with yourself."

Marie was happy to help and the following morning we embarked on the two hour drive north. On our arrival we stood together in the hospital waiting room and Marie drew me into her arms. "Now remember," she whispered. "This is voluntary. If it is too much for you, call me. I will come immediately. And eat. You're much too thin. Goodbye Ana."

"Marie — please hug the children for me. Tell them I love them."

"Every day, I promise." With a final wave she left and I made my way down the corridor to the cubicle that was to be my home for next three weeks.

With the help of a counsellor I rediscovered the blessings in my life; the love of my children and friends, the beauty of nature and my enjoyment of art and music. These pleasures had been pushed aside as I struggled to maintain childhood beliefs about being a good and worthy person. I'd made excuses for others and blamed myself.

Each day I gained self-confidence and felt a growing need to nourish myself. I needed no medication, only insight. I had continued to push against situations which, when viewed objectively, were unlikely to change. My major lesson — learning to let go. Lester would no longer be a part of my life.

Marie arrived to collect me and voiced amazement at my good health. At the end of our journey, as we drove up the tree-lined drive toward her gabled cedar-wood house, she tooted the horn. Clare and Lance burst from the front door. Marie's husband, Drew, and daughter Susan followed. Clare pulled the car door open and stood looking at me, her eyes searching my face. She seemed uncertain as she reached out, her fingertips touching my arm. Then to my amazement she pinched me. A smile lit her face as I reacted.

"Lance. Come and see. Mummy has come back." When at last our need for hugs, kisses and exclamations had been fulfilled, our tears mopped and noses blown, I held Clare and Lance close, one on either side, as we walked slowly toward the house.

After several days at Marie's home the children and I returned to the cottage. My cottage now, after all I was paying for it. Lester's belongings were packed and moved out to the shed. If he wanted them they would be there for him. Cupboards and drawers were emptied and scrubbed. Ceilings, walls, curtains and cushions washed. The hole in the bedroom wall was repaired with newspaper and plaster of paris, the walls given a fresh coat of paint and the broken lamp replaced. My home sparkled, the place filled with a buoyant vitality that increased my optimism.

I looked for work. In a small town jobs are rarely advertised, vacant positions being snapped up by the sons and daughters of family or friends. Unfortunately I had no such network to assist me. Lance began kindergarten and my hours at home alone seemed long and empty. As the weeks passed my optimism and motivation faded and I waited, hoping some magic would bring me wealth, love and happiness. Anything.

Summer slid into autumn and one evening as I laid the table for tea, I heard a car in the driveway. A moment later, Marie's husband called to me from the front door.

"Good news, Ana, I have a job for you."

Because of his recommendation I became the manager of a new craft shop, a job I loved. Full and satisfying days stretched on through the autumn and now one of the coldest winters on record was coming to an end. In the small office at the rear of the shop I sat as close to the heater as I dared. The ledger open on the desk before me, I tallied the month's sales. At the street doorway, in a patch of bright morning sun, James, the shop-assistant conversed with a customer. A young girl entered and I heard him direct her to my office.

"Mrs Pierce? I have a telegram for you."

Surprised, I reached out and took the yellow envelope, turning it over in my hand. The girl moved away then paused, the little half-moon leather bag on her shoulder swinging in an arc as she turned.

"I'm sorry. It's bad news," she said.

My involuntary cry brought the assistant running.

Sorry to tell you. Lester died this morning.
Car accident. Phone me. Ken.

The slip of yellow paper fell to the desk. I stared down, unable to touch it. After so many years of anticipation, I should have been prepared for this; but I was not. Facing the end of my hopes and dreams was hard and during the ensuing week

I cried a great deal. Throughout my marriage I had prayed for a miracle, hoped for the perfect outcome. God, it seemed had other plans.

He was only thirty-two, my first and only love.

One evening, three months later, I sat before the open fire thinking about Lester. As I gazed into the flames a beautiful calm flowed through me. It began at my chest, my heart perhaps, and spread to the tips of my fingers and toes. I must have dozed for when I opened my eyes and looked around, the room and the objects in it were the same but I saw them from a new perspective. The cottage had become a home; free to be enjoyed for as long as I wished. More, I realised with gratitude and sadness, Lester left me and the children to help us. He truly loved us but chose to go rather than inflict further hurt with behaviour he could not control.

The decision to pay his debts came easily. Not out of any great sense of honour but to be free of any lingering sense of obligation.

Between us Lester and I had inflicted deep scars on our children. There must be no more. For their sake I had to pull myself together, put all shame behind me and make a better life for the three of us. Until recently I'd held onto so many problems there had been no space in my life for anything new, no room for a solution. By discarding the old, I was opening the way for something better. Happiness was not to be found in yesterday. Nor did it lie in wait in distant tomorrows. Life, in all its fullness was to be enjoyed moment by moment.

Twenty-four

My long night of reminiscence over, I wake with a jump. Morning light edges the yellow blind in my mother's living room. I switch off the standard lamp, rise and stretch my cramped limbs. Then teetering a little on unsteady legs I make my way to the kitchen to rinse my mug. At the sink I cup my hands and splash my face with water. It takes a lot of cold water to erase the shadows of my past.

Remembering my promise to collect the cards from the wreaths on Mum's grave, and thinking fresh air will help to clear my head I pull on my jacket and set off. The cemetery is behind the native park at the bottom of the street. Not far away.

Most folk are still sleeping, the street quiet. As I approach a ginger cat jumps from a letterbox and runs up a driveway. Beneath the trees at the dip in the road I pause to inhale the earthy odour of decaying leaves. Soft brown curls of bracken grow through the wire fence. Gently, I unroll a furry bud. This is where Lester and I stopped to kiss; my very first kiss. Lester — one minute outgoing, loving and funny, the next brooding or angry; I never knew what to expect. Not really. I just hoped for the best. Yet I loved him dearly and remembering that first kiss gives me a warm and tender feeling. Released, the bracken curl springs back into shape.

Tall reeds grow to the creek's edge; the bordering bare-earth tracks beaten hard by the running feet of small children are gone. For a moment I feel a deep sense of loss; for Lester, for childhood, and wasted opportunities.

Things change, I tell myself. There was a time when I resented change, when I felt forced to move forward before

I was ready. I now understand it is not moving forward but holding back that causes the pain.

In a moment of daring I stand on the bottom wire of the fence and gripping the top, bounce. The ear-grating twang so loved by children horrifies me and jumping down, I run. At the top of the rise I look back. This, the last street of the borough, once opened onto the fields where my father grazed cows and the visiting circus raised it tents. Twenty years ago only a scattering of houses lined the road. Now there were many, all surrounded by smooth lawns and concrete-edged flower beds.

The gravel path alongside the park is the same. Through gaps in the greenery I see everything here is as I remember. Moss and tiny ferns still grow in the shade of the trees and daisies flourish in the sunlight. Ducks preen on the grassy banks and in the shallows a white swan beats her wings before gliding out over the still water. Beyond the tall orange-stemmed bamboo that shelters the pond I climb the driveway to the cemetery. People, their silhouettes dark against the low, early morning sun, move quietly about disposing of dead flowers and filling jars at the tap.

Collecting the cards from the many wreathes on Mum's grave takes a while as I read them all hoping to find the identity of my mystery man. The cards give no clues. The photograph in her handkerchief drawer remains an enigma.

Drawn by the peaceful surroundings and warmed by the sun, I linger beside her grave. Love for my mother wells inside me. Like bubbles rising from a spring it comes, until overflowing with remorse, I whisper apologies for past wrongs and thank her for the good times we shared. Tears roll down my cheeks and in the cool sweet balm that sweeps over me, I feel her forgiveness.

There is a new lightness in my step as I search and find Ming's resting place. A simple wooden cross bears her name *Margaret Olive Thomas aged 13 years.* My knees sink into the soft grass and leaning forward to trace the lettering with my finger, I see again the smiling face of my childhood friend at the wicker gate, her arms filled with cherry blossom.

An unexpected snuffling and wetness in my ear causes me to turn sharply. The dog, a red setter, his weight pressed against my shoulder, is very friendly. I look about for his owner and see him some distance away, walking briskly toward me. As he draws closer, I recognise Ming's older brother, Ian.

"Hello, Ana. How are you? I see you've already met Ruben."

"Yes. He's lovely." I fondle the dog's silky ears while taking in Ian's dark clothing and back-to-front collar.

"I know. It must be a bit of a shock. It's all quite new. I'm still getting used to it." He slid a finger inside the collar easing its stiffness.

"When I last saw you, you were going to college to study horticulture."

"And I did. I recently sold my nursery to Rodney Gilmore. I think you know him, and his aunt, Alice. It is strange meeting you here. I planned to call on you this afternoon. I have a letter for you from Rodney. Nice guy. Said he'd lost touch and would like to hear from you."

I feel warmth in my cheeks and know I am blushing as I recall the first evening Rodney came to dinner and I wished . . . I wished . . . "Yes, I do know him. His aunt and uncle had a poultry farm. Lester and I worked there. Rodney was kind to the children, and to me."

"Ana, I heard about Lester. I am sorry." Ian's hand on my arm is light but comforting. "Now your mother. Are you managing? Are you all right?"

"Yes, thank you, I am."

He stooped to place a single pink rose at the base of the cross. Watching him, I regret not having brought flowers for Ming. On the way to the gate I chat to Ian about my home and the craft shop. We find a bench beneath a pepper tree and sit down to talk. Rather it is me who talks; telling Ian of events that have been bottled up for year, my pain, withheld for so long, breaks free. Ian is so relaxed, his legs stretched out before him, one arm along the back of the seat and although I do not know him well, I feel at ease in his company. When at last I stop talking, he asks, with hint of a smile, how I feel.

"Happy. Free. I feel like me — I feel I know who I am." I lean back against the tree, not knowing whether to laugh or cry at the enormity of my discovery. As if on cue, a meadow lark bursts into song. Far above it hovers, the glorious sound cascading around us. Was there ever a more uplifting sound?

We walk together to Ian's car. Ruben takes immediate possession of the front passenger seat, sitting upright and looking through the windscreen, eager to be going. Ian hands me Rodney's letter.

"Are you sure I can't give you a lift back to the house?" I smile my refusal and Ian opens his arms. "May I hug you?" His hug is warm, brotherly and I have to wipe away a tear. "May you wake each day with a light heart, Ana."

When Ian's car has disappeared over the hill, I open Rodney's letter. His broad sloping script fills two pages. He has only recently heard of Lester's death and apologizes for offering his condolences so late. His uncle Kevin has also died.

Alice is a great help to him, he tells me, as he has not yet learned to cook. He and Alice share a home near the nursey. Extensions are planned and he needs more staff. *I think of you often,* he ends, *and hope you are well. Give my love to Clare and Lance and please, write soon. Yours, Rodney.*

I feel so alive; tingly with anticipation. Over the years I often thought of Rodney, and it seems, he of me. Folding the letter into my pocket with the cards, I hurry back past the park and over the hill.

At the house I find Fran and her eldest daughter, Kate laying the table for lunch. Apologizing for my long absence, I put the cards with the others. Fran hands me an apron. "Can you finish the salads, Ana? And slice the cold lamb. I'll go and pick some mint."

"How many people are we expecting?" I ask Kate.

"Ten, if Uncle Doug comes home."

Fran's younger children run in complaining of hunger and wanting to know when lunch will be ready. "Soon," I tell them flapping my apron at them, chasing them away outdoors. Then realizing I have acted exactly as my mother did when I was a child eager for food, I shake my head and laugh. Perhaps when Clare is older, she will copy me and I see how important it is to set a good example.

Aunt Libby arrives with Lawrence. Her open arms enfold me and with his arms encircling us both, Lawrence rests his chin on the top of my head. Love takes the place of words as for a long moment we stand still and silent.

Aunt May comes alone bringing homemade cake and biscuits. She bustles about laying the table and we make polite conversation but she does not look at me when she speaks.

After a quiet start, the talk at the lunch table grows first loud then uproarious, as hilarious tales involving mother are told by our aunts and Lawrence, who was in her class at school.

"Dear, oh dearie me, I've not laughed so much in a long time." Aunt Libby dabs her eyes with the corner of a lace handkerchief. '

One by one we leave the table. Lawrence and the younger children take some bread and go to the park to feed the ducks. Fran and Aunt May take over the washing up. Aunt Libby slips her arm through mine drawing me out to the garden. We sit on the bench behind the shed. A large Callistemon, its fiery vermillion bottle brushes alive with honey bees, casts feathery shadows over the lawn. Libby takes my hands in hers, and turning my wrists to expose the scars, soothes them lightly with her finger tips. "How are you, Ana?"

"Better, thank you, Aunt Libby."

"That's good. Now please, tell me about your children and your home. Do you have a garden? Are you able to work?"

I do my best and Aunt Libby nods and smiles as I chatter on.

"The past ten years must have been difficult for you, Ana. Yet you have come through with the same optimism and determination you showed as a child. I am happy to see you recovering so well. Will you and the children come and stay with us soon? Lawrence and I would like you to come."

"Yes. I'd love to." She gathers me close and pressed against her soft angora jumper I can smell the apple shampoo in her hair.

Fran and Aunt May are deep in a serious conversation that ceases as Libby and I approach. I think they must have been talking about me as my aunt, her frostiness forgotten, smiles and asks if I am ready to sort Mum's personal belongings. Then standing aside she allows me to precede her up the passage to Mum's room. Kate joins us and we bunch together in the doorway.

"Shall we begin with the wardrobe?" We jostle about so Fran can open the wardrobe doors and while the aunts discuss style and quality of fabric, selecting garments and laying them on the bed, I join Kate at the window. Christmas lilies still grow against the wall, a wall that has surely shrunk.

Kate saw me looking and said, "I can jump off that wall. It's good fun."

"Really? Your Uncle Doug and I used to jump from there," and I tell her of the day when, inspired by the Milly-Molly-Mandy stories, I settled atop the wall and lowered a basket hoping someone would put something nice to eat in it. Instead of biscuits, my big brother, Ray put his pet rat, Oggie in the basket. Finding Oggie wrapped in a handkerchief had given me such a fright, I fell from the wall into a bed of smelly African marigolds. Smiling, Kate wrinkles her nose. "Pooh!"

An explosion of merriment behind us makes us turn. Aunt Libby is fanning herself and laughing as May parades before the mirror wearing one Mum's hats, a fox fur about her shoulders and dangling a fancy handbag from her wrist. "Oh my, you do look a sight," gasps Libby,

"Twenty-five years ago we all wore clothes like this. Don't you remember, dear?" Aunt May waggles a finger at her younger sister.

Kate tugs at my sleeve and standing on tiptoe whispers in my ear. "Auntie Ana. Grandma had a pretty brooch, a spray of pink and white flowers. Do you think I might please have it?"

"Let's see if it is still here." I open the dresser drawer and am immediately aware of the subtle scent of lavender. I pick up the photograph and am closing the jewellery box after giving the brooch to Kate, when the photograph is plucked from my hand.

"Sneaky old Rose. She had this all along." May is looking at my mystery man.

"That's mine!" Aunt Libby grabs at the photo but May holds it close to her bosom.

"No it isn't. It's mine." Fran and I exchange looks, surprised at the petulant, childlike tone in our aunt's voice.

"It's mine. Give it to me."

"Will not." To our amazement, May stuffs the photograph down the front of her dress. She and Libby face each other, their chests puffed, chins tucked and smack at one another's hands.

"Please, what is this all about? You look like a pair of turkey gobblers setting up for a fight. What's so special about the photo?" I ask.

They both sit heavily on the bed. Libby leans forward. "You know it's mine," she whispers to her sister.

I fold my arms. "Now, please, tell me. Who is the man?"

"Leslie Howard."

I'm puzzled. "Do you mean the Howard who did funny skits on the wireless?"

"No, Leslie Howard was a film star." Fran offers.

"He played in *Gone with the Wind*. He was gorgeous," Libby sighs.

"He was the Scarlet Pimpernel." Aunt May beats time on her knees as she recites "They seek him here, they seek him there, they seek him everywhere." Triumphant and hugging the photo close, she leans towards Libby. "And now he's mine." Libby pushes her.

"'Enough!" Fran holds up her hands. "I don't understand what this fuss is about. Where did the photo come from?"

"Our brother Bill sent it from France during the war. He met Howard and they became friends. Knowing how we girls idolized him, Bill sent us the photograph. We fought over it of course and Father ordered us to draw straws to settle ownership. Rose won."

Libby takes up the story. "But Rose was walking out with Percy Gibbon and Percy did not like her giving so much attention to a film star."

"So clever Rose put Leslie's picture on the mantle shelf and told us whoever did the most work for her during the next week could have it to keep. And I won." May pokes a pink tongue at her sister.

"The fairies will come with scissors and cut it off if you do that. Anyway I won. You did not wash Rose's smelly stockings."

"I darned them though, and cleaned her shoes."

"I brushed her hair for hours and made her bed every day."

"I went to the library in pouring rain to get her silly books."

"You should hear yourselves! Two old ladies behaving like children." I could not help laughing.

"Enough of the old," Aunt Libby tells me. "Anyway, on the sixth day the photograph disappeared. Mother said she did more work than any one, so she deserved to have it. Father was fed up with the nonsense and we assumed one of them had taken it to put an end to the squabbling."

May takes out the picture. "Fancy Rose hiding you away for thirty years," she said.

"All my life he has been my mystery man. As a child I concocted fanciful stories about him." I tell them how I thought the vicar's assistant, the short pudgy Mr Haycock, might have been Mum's lover.

"He was invited to afternoon tea and I imagined a fabulously romantic reunion. I hid behind the curtains in the hall, hardly daring to breathe, waiting for my mystery man to arrive. Instead, the rotund and effusive little Mr. Haycock appeared."

How my Aunts laugh, Fran and Kate too. When we are finally able to speak, May said, "I think Ana deserves to have her mystery man, don't you?"

"Yes, put him in your scrapbook, Ana and tell the story to your grandchildren," says Libby.

Harmony prevails as we continue to sort Mum's belongings. When Lawrence returns with the children we all troop to the kitchen to drink tea, eat cake and talk. The barriers are gone. I am reunited with the family.

Later, as we ferry cartons and bags to the cars on the street, we see the dark clouds on the horizon. Fran takes me aside. "I think I might leave now. Get away before the storm." She indicates the approaching storm. She pulls me to her. "Look after yourself, Ana. Above all, be kind to yourself. Perhaps I could come and visit you in the school holidays?"

"Please do. I've a large garden. We could put up a tent, let the children sleep out. They'd love that." We stand close, our arms linked. Kate comes to thank me for the brooch she wears pinned to her dress.

Doug arrives to find his relatives bunched together in big hug on the front lawn. Tears and smiles mingling, we break apart and amid a flurry of waving hands and calls of farewell, the family leaves my mother's house.

The storm broke during the night, waking me from a dream in which I rode a magnificent white horse, galloping across open plains beneath endless blue skies.

Outside in the night, lightning is followed almost immediately by loud thunder. As a small child I had slipped from my bed in this same room and run down the passage to stand at the foot of my parent's bed begging to be held warm and safe until the storm passed. They protected me. Now it's my turn to take on the role of parent. I am the mother now.

I also own half of Mum's house, which Doug is going to buy from me. There will be enough money to freehold my place up north. The children will have a real home at last.

Heavy rain hammers the windows as Doug and I sip tea at the breakfast table next morning. We are both subdued knowing we are at the end of something that lingers, uncertain, here in the house. Our links with the past are fading by the moment, disappearing as we attune ourselves to the present and connect with the issues of the day. There is a reluctance to say goodbye.

My bags are packed ready to leave. "I'll take a taxi to the bus station. There's no need for you to wait, Doug. Go to work."

"Okay, if you're sure."

We say goodbye at the kitchen door, my face pressed to the chest of my little brother who now towers over me.

"Take care, Sis. See you at the wedding." Umbrella aloft, he strides out then stops to wave one last time before turning the corner of the house.

By the time I carry my bags to the front porch the rain has eased and small ragged patches of blue have appeared in the cloud. I walk slowly through the house, room by room. The place is hushed, still and I move quietly, not wanting to disturb the peace. Soon a new generation of children will live here and the rooms fill with love and laughter. With a final whispered goodbye I close the door on my childhood home.

The cheerful beep-beep of the taxi sounds at the gate. The driver steps out. "I'll carry those, love. You hop in out of the wet."

The glowing colours of a rainbow arch across the sky, directly over the house. Together the driver and I watch a second softer rainbow form beneath the first.

"Have you ever thought," he asked as the car moved slowly forward, "it takes rain to make a rainbow?"

Acknowledgements

*My sincere gratitude to my writing companions Aaron Blomeley, Jenny McLaughlin, Christine Liddle and Jeanne Squires. Your encouragement, insightful comments and unlimited enthusiasm helped bring this story to life.
Thank you.*

www.ingramcontent.com/pod-product-compliance
Lightning Source LLC
Chambersburg PA
CBHW020056020526
44112CB00031B/190